Miracles

Jean Hellé [pseud]

MIRACLES

by
Morvan Lebesque

Translated by
LANCELOT C. SHEPPARD

LONDON
BURNS OATES

231.73
L49m

MADE AND PRINTED IN GREAT BRITAIN BY
LOWE AND BRYDONE (PRINTERS) LIMITED, LONDON, N.W.10
FOR BURNS OATES AND WASHBOURNE LTD
28 ASHLEY PLACE, LONDON, S.W.1

First published 1953

Contents

Miracles

Introduction

THE interest of this book would be nullified if extravagant claims were made for it. It has no pretensions to being a complete history of Christian miracles—a sort of *Summa miraculorum*—nor yet is it an essay in the dogmatics of the subject. In the first place hundreds of volumes would hardly suffice, and in the second, an article in the *Dictionnaire des Connaissances Religieuses*, or a page or two from the pen of Father de Tonquédec, S.J.,[1] would supply all that was needed and with an authority that I do not possess. It has been my desire merely to furnish the general reader with a summary of the question based on carefully chosen examples. Nor do I conceal my further desire to arouse the reader's interest in an enthralling subject which is unfortunately very frequently misrepresented for sectarian reasons and, more frequently still, completely submerged beneath the weight of the indigestible books about it.

It is a fact that neither believers, including those who are slow to accept miracles, nor unbelievers will deny that at the present time miracles are important and, from the journalistic point of view, topical. Miracles indeed make news. It might almost be said that they form an element of daily life, a kind of surrealist counterpart to our ordinary human actions. Modern times seem particularly fertile in miracles. At the very moment that these lines are being written, Lourdes, Fatima, and many another holy place continue to present their enduring problem to faith and science. Newspapers that in general are devoid of any spiritual preoccupations inform us of the "supernatural" cure of a certain Marie-Thérèse Canin; the statue of Our Lady of Assisi draws great

[1] For the English-speaking reader the equivalent of these would be *The Catholic Encyclopedia* or the writings of Father Herbert Thurston, S.J.—*Translator*.

crowds before ecclesiastical authority has given any decision about the phenomena connected with it; in an Italian friary a priest is asserted to have received the stigmata; finally, in a lowly village of the Vendée there is talk of a mysterious crown of white roses appearing on the brow of a dying child. Then, too, might be mentioned the various investigations now taking place, and the evidence, offered from motives of devotion or gratitude, in favor of certain persons more or less recently deceased. Skeptics may proclaim to their hearts' content that our troubled times provoke a need for supernatural phenomena, and their opponents may continue to reply that God makes choice of these days to remind men who have despised His law that it still exists.

It is not my purpose to take sides here, save in the last part of the book when I deal with facts about which there is general agreement: the fake miracles, frauds and impostures which have been exposed by scientists and priests. For the rest, I wanted to write a book which would turn no believer from his faith and which, by the same token, would provoke no atheist to protest or in any way constrain him to a hasty and superficial conversion. I have no hidden purpose.

A few fundamental ideas on the subject of miracles will not be out of place at the beginning of this book.

What Is a Miracle?

The word itself has given rise to long controversies and there has not always been complete agreement about its meaning.

All ages of humanity have witnessed, or have claimed to witness, marvelous occurrences. All religions necessarily give them a certain prominence, for they are the primary and most obvious manifestation of Divinity, the bridge between God and man. Since it is only Christian miracles which concern us in the following pages it is relevant to trace them back to the very beginnings of Christianity. The first miracles in point of time are, indeed, those worked by Christ, and they alone are entirely binding on the faith of a Christian. Historically Christ appears in the world as a wonder-worker. His teaching is accompanied by an upsetting of the natural order resulting from His divine essence. He religious authorities. In fact, the obligation to believe in them is extremely restricted and, save for the miracles of Christ, the Christian has the right to refuse belief in all others. In some sort it is a matter between him and his cast of mind.

This refers, of course, to miracles accepted by the Church. Others which have been rejected by her after serious scrutiny raise no question in the minds of the faithful. As long as the case is "pending" there is complete freedom to come to a personal decision on the subject. And thus we may frequently witness clergy and laity making ardent propaganda, orally and in print, in favor of the authenticity of some dubious apparition. After all there is no reason why a believer any more than others should be preserved from error. Lectures are given, pamphlets, newspaper and review articles pile up. But when the Church speaks rejecting this miracle, with one accord the whole thing at once comes to an end. Indeed the Christian who, acknowledging his mistake, thus places filial obedience to the Church above all else finds in the decision motive for joy. He incurs no penalty unless he had adopted an attitude harmful to the faith; it is now an increasingly rare occurrence but was the cause formerly of more than one distressing apostasy. Until the truth is proclaimed allowance is made for natural enthusiasm and zeal. Any other attitude would be harsh and inhuman. Public acknowledgment of error cannot fail to be a noble gesture and, in my opinion, extremely edifying for the faithful.

Great saints have often given an example of extreme skepticism. Most of them, and especially the mystics, reveal themselves to those who study them as men or women of great common sense who have their two feet firmly planted on the ground and are not easily hoaxed. St. John of the Cross was such a one; he was so very cautious in these matters that he even refused to visit religious who were reputed to be miracle workers or the recipients of exceptional graces. When in 1585 he was in Lisbon for the Chapter of the Discalced Carmelites, he was told of a Dominican nun, prioress of the convent of the Annonciade, who bore the stigmata; *la monja de las llagas* ("the nun with the wounds") on her bed of suffering received visits from all the most important ecclesiastical personages of the time. The author of the *Mystical Poems* refused to follow the crowd; he shrugged his shoulders and, we are told, took the opportunity to go off to meditate by the seashore and praise God for the wonderful harmony and colors of nature. The immediate future showed him to be right. The "stigmatic" did not withstand the first test, that of hot water and soft soap. It might be deduced that St. John of the Cross relied on his intuition or that he was in possession of more accurate information about the pseudo-stigmatic than the Portuguese clergy; to do so would be to leave out of account his general attitude to miracles and the numerous passages where he explains it.

These passages deal particularly with phenomena of visions, stigmatization, and ecstasy. But they could be applied to all miracles. Contrary to what an atheist might well suppose, they sum up the ordinary view of a Christian about visible supernatural phenomena. Since the Christian believes in the supernatural and is, so to say, familiar with it, he is not concerned over an upsetting of the natural order. When it occurs he sees in it not so much a proof of the existence of God as a message; and he treats the message as of greater importance than the phenomenon itself. In addition, the Church, as was pointed out above, leaves the faithful complete freedom to believe or not in the authenticity of supernatural phenomena about which sermons are preached. Lourdes is an example in point; the miracles of Lourdes have been *certified as true* and made public by the Sovereign Pontiff; nevertheless the Pope does not forbid the faithful to doubt them. He confines himself to the statement that a believer in the miracles of the Grotto has "a nine to one chance of not being mistaken." [2] But a Christian can save his soul and remain all his life an obedient son of the Church while refusing to admit that on February 11, 1858, Our Lady appeared to a little fourteen-year-old shepherd girl named Bernadette Soubirous. The reality of the apparitions of Fatima seems to have been generally accepted in the Church, and in a series of lectures the bishop of my diocese has proclaimed his belief in them; yet among those I consulted on the subject of this book, a venerable religious, dependent on the same bishop, rejects

[2] *Dictionnaire des Connaissances Religieuses.*

the Portuguese miracle entirely and makes no mystery of his skepticism about it.

Anyone with common sense must recognize that the Church does not seek to derive any utilitarian advantage from miraculous phenomena. Faith is a spiritual matter, entirely independent of some more or less spectacular phenomenon. During my researches for the purpose of this book I noticed continually that those believers who were most eager to accord primary importance to visible supernatural phenomena were in nearly all cases lay folk. Does that mean that miracles are not intended as proofs of the supernatural? It would be most improper to say so when certain visionaries indeed demand this *proof,* and it is granted to them, and granted, as we shall see, with exceeding liberality. Recent miracles incontestably exhibit this probative quality. But the immense majority of Catholics admit the reality of miracles like those of Lourdes, Pontmain or Fatima; indeed it would be surprising if they did not. From the viewpoint of the materialists no point in the discussion is conceded, and their assertions are apparently far more categorical in nature.

Their position is, of course, based purely and simply on the denial of all miracles. There is no question of discussing their origin or authenticity. The signs and wonders of the Gospel are the first to be rejected in the name of reason. Nature forms the only guide. Nature is unchangeable; in it occur no sudden advances, no prodigies. *And only what is natural is scientific* (Renan).

Renan is quoted again at the first stage of the controversy concerning miracles of past times, those, that is, of which the witnesses are dead. We have no other proof of these miracles, it is said, than history, and to them is applied the axiom that in a conflict between history and science, it is always science which prevails. Consequently, for the materialist the scientist's negative conclusion takes precedence over the affirmative assertion of a contemporary witness. And it can be asserted in all good faith—provided of course that the materialist view is upheld—that such a principle seems sound enough; supposing the contrary were held to be true and were applied to all fields of knowledge (for the materialist the religious field is no different to others), we should quickly be faced with the abject failure of all explanations of natural phenomena. Miracles occurring at the present time, which may in consequence be witnessed by a scientist, are held to be capable of a scientific explanation or tainted with error.

Now science itself is not unchangeable. It is continually developing—we shall see that the fact that miracles also develop to a certain extent forms one of the more disturbing elements of the whole question—and almost every day widens the bounds of our knowledge. This fact is a source of joy to the materialists, for at first sight it appears to furnish a satisfactory explanation of supernatural phenomena. Sooner or later, they claim, science will reveal every mystery to them. In this way after the experiments of Charcot at La Salpêtrière and of Freud in Vienna they feel themselves on firmer ground to refute the divine origin of many visions, ecstasies, and even *charismata*. At a lower level the freethinker at Lourdes is merely waiting for it to be discovered that the waters of the Grotto possess properties which are both extraordinary and natural, and continues to hope for a world wherein the most marvelous event will be no more wonderful than an eclipse of the sun. But scientists themselves realize that a halt must be called to reasoning of this kind. Science, in fact, analyzes; it creates nothing. Psychoanalysis can throw light on the mental processes of a visionary and predict the precise moment at which she will declare herself to be in communication with the supernatural; but it is manifestly powerless to collect in a few seconds a calcareous deposit that will knit a bone together, rectify a club foot, or heal a fracture instantaneously. Science remains identified with the natural order, and its limits are known in advance. To bestow excessive powers on it amounts to a denial of it. The essential barrier, the prison within which it is held, is this: it cannot reach up to God.

This point requires emphasizing. When a scientist like Pasteur declares that "a little science estranges men from God, much science leads them back to Him," he is giving utterance to a merely moral assertion, originating in his reasoning. The harmony of creation suggests to him the existence of a Demiurge, but furnishes no proof of it beneath the field glass, the scalpel, or the microscope. He does not discover the divine element, and for a very good reason. In fact the day when science reaches up to God will be the cause of the greatest revolution of all time; that will be a day, it can be imagined, of such tremendous joy that the mere thought of it makes imagination boggle. But there is no sign that that day is near, no scientist has yet discovered God at the end of his laboratory experiments, save as the result of an inner light. Nevertheless, several have prided themselves on doing so. The most recent is John Dunne, the author of *An Experiment with Time,* who incidentally was an atheist at the beginning of his researches; he claimed to have discovered a material proof of the existence of God in conjunction with a new dimension of time. It is still premature to discuss this "discovery" which has, moreover, little interest for the Christian. It has always been admitted that faith penetrates where science refuses to go.

The materialist prison was alluded to above; the term is by no means disparaging. The materialist, seeing the world as finite, of his own free will encloses himself within it and recognizes its limits. He is a voluntary prisoner. It is only the philosopher who can venture the further step and claim, on a last analysis, that miracles do not really exist since all phenomena outside nature are incorporated in it by the very fact of their occurrence. In answer to a recent questionnaire a materialist thinker furnished an example of this method of reasoning: if, he said, the Blessed Virgin were to appear to a hundred thousand persons at high noon in the Place de la Concorde in Paris, the occurrence would clearly belong to the natural order. For it is the natural order and not the supernatural which classifies, regulates, and in a word presides over all things in due order. That theory forms, no doubt, a satisfying intellectual scheme, but our thinker would surely agree good-humoredly enough that such a miracle would not leave him completely undisturbed.

This survey would be incomplete without mention of the large numbers of human beings whose position is midway between atheism and belief. It is not to be supposed, in fact, that theirs is a permanent, well-established and enduring state. Many of our contemporaries, perhaps the majority of them, adopt an attitude equidistant between belief in religion and belief in materialism. But rarely is the balance an even one; it leans sometimes to one side, sometimes to the other; in most cases it is actuated by an emotional bias. Consequently, it is easy enough to conceive the importance of a miracle which, acting like a magnet, tips the scale to one extreme or the other. For it would be wrong to claim that a miracle operates always in the one direction of religious conversion. Even when it is very largely accepted, a miracle encounters opposition in the agnostic's mind because, for example, it requires of him a certain rule of thought and conduct. And yet miracles are expected and hoped for by many. They may be treated as either the small change of the supernatural, or as the supreme point reached by charlatanism and fraud. At the risk of falling a prey to sentimentality, I must confess my feelings of great pity for all these poor creatures athirst for supernatural manifestations, treated with indifference by believers and atheists alike. Ridiculous as they are in their own way, they give expression to the immense anxiety of humanity. Not everyone has the happiness of possessing a staunch faith, a secure belief; not everyone feels calmly resigned to the idea of extinction after death. To many the possibility of miracles is a tremendous comfort, for they see them as heaven visiting the earth. They mean that God has not confined His message to men to one single utterance, that He cannot leave the world to its own devices without intervening, an intervention that is the result of His love. Miracles mean that the signs and works spoken of in the Gospel continue and are enduring. Miracles are the heart beats of the Divinity.

SCOPE AND PLAN OF THIS BOOK

The preceding sections are intended as an introduction to the subject, and I have no doubt that anyone, with the aid of his reason and his memory, could have written them. I have merely propounded the problem in outline, reserving the detailed treatment for a later stage; as this study proceeds the ideas of this introduction will be developed at length as they require.

The main lines of this book must now be sketched. As I entered on this immense subject I was compelled to make a choice. There could be no question, as I have said, of relating the thousands of miracles that stand out in the course of the history of Christianity —it would have been an impossible undertaking in any case since there could be no way of including hidden miracles in the list. The size of the book obliged me to a very limited selection, but fortunately the subject itself was a very considerable help as to a certain extent it required to be treated in one particular way.

Although miracles are numerous and apparently very varied, they fall naturally into certain categories and can be divided, for example, into those in which the beneficiary was preserved from some danger or sin by an effective intervention, or those in which he enjoyed a supernatural vision or some other supra-normal communication. It seemed to me that an account of a restricted number of phenomena, related and explained at length, would be of greater interest than a larger number necessarily summarized to an excessive degree. Moreover this method allowed me to compare with great economy of effort several similar cases as illustrations of a typical case in the same category. On the other hand, I have deliberately left out of account all miracles in which the human intermediary does not hold an important place, is not, to put it plainly, an essential character in the story. A Christian certainly can hardly fail to be greatly moved by miracles worked by relics of Our Lord, but I hope I shall be forgiven for not mentioning these favors granted to souls and bodies. In the same way I have omitted to deal with Blessed Nicolazic whose "presence" at Sainte-Anne-d'Auray exerts less attraction on— shall I say?—the outsider than that of Bernadette at Lourdes. There was an additional reason for this choice.

It is obvious that contemporary events, or at least those of more recent occurrence, influence the mind more than those buried in the past. It seems almost absurd to mention time when one is venturing into the field of mysteries which specifically by-pass it. But no one, I believe, will regret my preference for the present, nor find fault with me for providing a modern basis for future discussions on the subject founded, among other things, on the

latest scientific discoveries. I have therefore boldly given preference to miralcles of this century or the last, though again it should
be clearly understood that they frequently form the pretext for
extended mention of those of more ancient times. This is perhaps
a very personal way of treating the subject and indeed somewhat
revolutionary. Thus, Bernadette Soubirous, the visionary, shines
with an exceeding brightness in the firmament of saints, but it
would be to diminish her earthly role very considerably if it were
confined to the events of Lourdes. In reality the characteristics
of this case are typical of many others, and study of it discloses
how valuable it is for our purpose. The children of Pontmain,
of La Salette, and of Fatima especially are heroes of a miraculous
adventure with its roots in the past. Also, I have no hesitation in
grouping the phenomena of visions and stigmata round the case
of Therese Neumann in spite of the fact that it is not recognized
by the Church, because an observer can rapidly discern in it all
the elements of such cases; but that does not prevent my mentioning the stigmata of St. Francis of Assisi, the ecstasies of St.
Teresa, the *charismata* of St. Francis Xavier. The miracles of
Beauraing are instructive in many ways. In the last place, as I
said above, this study is completed by several cases of undoubted
fraud and imposture, among which are those of Madeleine of the
Cross, Ramona of Ezkioga, Nicole Tavernier, and Rose Tamisier. This last chapter forms an indispensable element in the
structure of the book. My purpose is to construct a synthesis or,
more modestly perhaps, an attempt at a synthesis. Rightly or
wrongly I have formed the conviction that a work of this kind is
required, in the shape, at least, in which it is now offered to the
public. There is indeed no lack of books and pamphlets providing detailed accounts of this or that miraculous event, from the
pen of some ecclesiastic, some illustrious Catholic writer, or no
less illustrious freethinker. By itself a bibliography of miracles
would form a stout volume and that indeed is one of the reasons
why none has been added to this book. The books in that bibliography would each be relevant to but one chapter of this study,
and in addition they would relate only a one-sided version of the
events. Other works which are conceived on similar lines to this

one are either impossible to obtain (except in private libraries to which the public is not admitted) or are composed exclusively for the use of specialists. In this book I have carefully avoided the use of philosophical or metaphysical terms as likely to disconcert the reader—except, of course, for those which have no equivalent in ordinary speech. At a period when the technical language of philosophy is gaining increasing acceptance in literary works, I preferred for my own part to avoid every kind of verbal complication and was inspired by my subject to speak in all simplicity of the marvels which were witnessed by those who were themselves very simple people.

I sincerely trust that unwittingly I have shocked no one. I trust, too, that I have aroused some curiosity so that to a certain degree perhaps because of what I have written many readers will become passionately interested in the question raised, however imperfectly, in this book. Beyond the venture into the domain of the miraculous lies the Divine Presence. A man may believe in God or deny Him; in both camps honorable, upright, sincere men are to be found. But one who has never asked himself the question, who has never interrogated heaven with fervor or anxiety, such a one, whatever the length or the fame of his earthly span, is a nonentity, less than a nonentity, a more or less foolhardy nonentity clinging to the walls or the floor of his prison.

J. H.

· 1 ·

Ars and Lourdes
Miracles of Humility

Behold the ignorant arise and
snatch heaven beneath our eyes!
—St. Augustine.

THE case of Jean-Marie Vianney, the Curé d'Ars, is unique perhaps in the annals of the miraculous. All the saints who were privileged with supernatural powers during life were, at the outset, greatly astonished if not dismayed; they threw themselves at the foot of the Cross protesting their own complete unworthiness. But they were all well aware of this extraordinary sign which distinguished them from their fellows. It was the lot of the Curé d'Ars to experience crowds athirst for marvels thronging round him; to cure tumors, see cripples rise and walk; for years to be the recipient of the wild gratitude of the crowds. And yet he died believing that he had accomplished nothing out of the way and convinced of the dullness and perhaps the uselessness of his "poor life."

This "poor life" of the parish priest of Ars can be divided into two periods. The first consists entirely of striving and failure. This young peasant of the Jura had dedicated himself to the priesthood. His faith was strong. He dreamed of serving God until death as priest of a country parish. There was no opposition to his vocation, rather the contrary; his father's land was not fertile enough to support the whole family, and, besides, his parents thought it was not a bad thing to have a priest among one's children. Unfortunately Jean-Marie had not the necessary education;

16

indeed he was dull-witted, a confirmed dunce, the bottom of the class and, as he said himself, the "fool of the family."

With the greatest of difficulty, and by dint of many a blow from a ruler, his teachers managed to drum into his head the elements of arithmetic and grammar (throughout his life his mistakes in spelling and syntax were those of a child of ten). He could pass no ordinary or competitive examination, and now he must learn Latin and theology. At the seminary at Lyons the professors recoiled from the task, and after six months the rector encouraged him to leave. Jean-Marie clung to his vocation. He sat for an examination. He failed almost ignominiously. He still persisted. Further failure. At last, on the recommendation of a priest of some standing in the diocese, and especially because in 1815 there was a considerable shortage of vocations, this hopeless dunce was admitted to ordination—at thirty-two. After he had spent some time as an assistant priest, the authorities managed to get rid of him by sending him, to all intents and purposes, into exile. He was given the poorest, the wildest, the most remote parish of the diocese: Ars, in the Dombes, a village of two hundred souls. That was about all he was fit for, it was thought, and pretty much what Ars deserved. He would have been forgotten there had he not occasionally written to the bishop one of those letters that he alone could write, scribbled on the cheapest of note paper, without punctuation, needing frequent re-reading to puzzle out the sense, and a source of amusement to the secretaries. He spelled *camail* (cape) with two *l*s and an *e* at the end!

The second period begins, then, in 1818 when Father Jean-Marie Vianney took possession of his parish; his first task was to take the furniture out of the rectory, give back tables and armchairs to the gentry who had loaned them, distribute the rest to the poor of the village, and retire for the night to the attic where he lay down on the bare boards with a bundle of wood for his pillow. This period was to last forty-one years; it came to an end one stormy day in August, 1859, as the thunder growled and blinding flashes of lightning lit the sky, with the death of Vianney the parish priest, with the death of a saint, and an apotheosis that is glorious in the annals of the Catholic Church.

I am concerned here only with the miracles attributed to Father Vianney; the detailed story of his life has been told by more competent and more talented authors and is of interest here only so far as it furnishes evidence for the record and provides answers to the fundamental questions raised at the outset by supernatural phenomena. These questions are the following: (1) Can the person to whom the miracle has occurred—the wonder-worker or the intercessor—be accused of deception? (2) Is he in a questionable physical condition? (3) Does he derive any material benefit from his miracles? (4) Does he gain any moral or personal advantage from them?

The whole life of the parish priest of Ars furnishes, I believe, a definitive answer to the first question. He had many enemies, and they were not solely from the ranks of unbelievers but were often to be found among believers and sometimes among priests. He was frequently slandered, particularly during the first ten years of his priesthood (the word *slander* is used specifically only, of course, when the charges made were acknowledged to be untrue and were subsequently withdrawn by the authors of the slander). He was accused of all kinds of crime, including for instance, seduction of girls or, on religious grounds, with having dealings with the devil. At one time an ecclesiastical commission of inquiry was demanded. Finally, a campaign was conducted against him in all sorts of ways by speeches, public meetings and newspaper articles, but no proof whatever could be found for any allegation of fraud, and even the Grand Masonic Lodge definitely ruled it out (1868).

The life of the Curé d'Ars was lived, as we shall see, in a regular glass house and, toward the end of his life, in the midst of a great crowd which encircled him even when he slept. It should be added, in the last place, that he himself was never privileged with a personal miracle, and received no alleviation of his numerous physical ills.

An accusation of *fraud* cannot be upheld, in my opinion, in view of Father Vianney's supreme disinterestedness, his continual anxiety to save his soul and, in addition, the absolute impossibility owing to the simplicity of his nature, of his ever faking anything. He would have been found out on the spot. Another reason, and by no means the least, is that he never expected, never "provoked" miracles. In his early days as a priest the thought can scarcely have entered his head. Later on, when the first supernatural phenomena occurred, he denied quite spontaneously that they emanated from him. He always refused to attribute them to himself. Refused is not strong enough—rather, never for a moment did he dream of attributing them to his own power. He went further than that: he rejected them and asked God to heal souls and not bodies, or to heal bodies elsewhere than in the district—"elsewhere, not at Ars, anywhere else, and no one will be any the wiser."

An allegation of fraud may be maintained on two grounds. The perpetrator of bogus miracles can practice deception for his own benefit or for the greater glory of the Church. What has been said above invalidates this twofold supposition in Father Vianney's case. He evinced no astonishment whatever at the miraculous occurrences and thought them entirely in the natural order of things. It would never have occurred to him to use them as a *means*—a means which, I repeat, he distrusted and considered absolutely useless as proof of the existence of God.

His physical condition. It is quite clear that Father Vianney's physical condition was no common one, if he is judged by the standards of ordinary mortals, but from the ascetic point of view his was a very usual case. For it was due entirely to asceticism. He was a sturdy peasant who of set purpose entirely ignored his body and his health. He had habitual recourse to severe mortification and fasting. He practiced terrible corporal penances on himself. Gradually he contrived almost to forego sleep and food. He neglected himself in illness and got rid of severe toothache by having the tooth taken out by the blacksmith with a pair of pincers. Medicines he disregarded and eased his headaches with an ordinary damp cloth. He continually overestimated his strength and died of exhaustion, though, before that occurred, on two or three occasions, his organism rebelled and he attempted, though in vain, to escape from his village, his flock and his work which were combining to kill him.

c

At the outset, therefore, there was no organic disease but only extreme asceticism. The consequence of this condition, in the supernatural order, is common knowledge; St. Anthony furnishes the most remarkable, the classic example.

Like Father Vianney, St. Anthony began as a working man, an energetic countryman of great strength. One Sunday morning, shortly after his twentieth birthday, he heard the priest in the pulpit reading that passage from St. Matthew's Gospel in which Jesus tells the rich young man: "If thou wilt be perfect, go, sell what thou hast, and give to the poor, and thou shalt have treasure in heaven." St. Anthony obeyed this command to the letter. He gave up all his goods and took refuge in the desert, living there in solitude, first in a cave and then in a tomb; he was a hundred years old when he died and for upward of eighty years was in direct contact with the supernatural, and experiencing ecstasies, temptations, visions of all sorts and shapes, converse with angels and with devils. A materialist might say that these phenomena were the penalty of asceticism and the same materialist would quite logically expect the Curé d'Ars to experience them to the full.

Nothing of the kind. Vianney saw no visions, was favored with no apparitions of Our Lady and the saints. Apart from the miracles which are attributed to him, the only intervention of the supernatural in his life is to be found in the contest which the devil —the *"grappin"* as he called him—more or less visibly engaged with him. And he was the last to admit this intervention. One morning his bed was found mysteriously out in the middle of the room; Father Vianney when he woke up was amazed, asserting that he had noticed nothing during the night. The whole village at once thought that it was the work of the devil. But the parish priest did not believe it. It is a fact that he was always talking of the devil, and discerned his presence every day in men's evil actions; but that was merely an expression of his religious outlook. He can scarcely be said to have set great store by supernatural phenomena because, for example, when his rectory was burned down he jokingly exclaimed, "So the *grappin,* unable to catch the bird, has burned the cage."

We are concerned, then, with a man who was entirely unsophisticated and who enjoyed the excellent physical and mental balance of simple folk which the severest asceticism could not damage or cause him to hanker after supernatural phenomena. There is abundant testimony to show that it was not for want of continual provocation. Every day, toward the end of his life, people asked him whether he had not really *seen* God, Christ, or the Blessed Virgin; they were idle, stupid questions which the old priest did not even answer. He had no need to *see* God in this life. He believed in Him with the same simplicity that he believed in the stones of the village, the furrows in the fields or that birds could fly.

What about material advantages? Jean-Marie Vianney, in the last fifteen years of his life, handled considerable sums of money. It is estimated that on some days the "takings" were upward of ten thousand francs.[1] This money was handed over directly to him and went straight into his pocket but never stayed there any longer than two hours. At the height of the "prosperity" of Ars, Father Vianney was seen darting from door to door begging for vegetables or bread for his hospital. He never spent a penny on himself; his clothes and his food came from charity, and he distributed to the poor even the money that had been given him to provide his own doctor's fees—he told the physician not to call as he could not pay for the visit. But there is one incident which is extremely enlightening in this connection: it is the well-known difference which arose between Father Vianney and his assistant, Father Raymond, on the subject of the Ars pilgrimage.

Father Raymond occupies an important place in Father Vianney's life. A great deal has been written about him and assertions made which, all said and done, are extremely offensive. There is, of course, no comparison between the assistant and the parish priest. Father Raymond was no saint; he was just a country priest, no better and no worse than many others, somewhat narrow-minded and inclined to be selfish; in an ordinary parish he would have been found to be quite up to his work. But God—or Destiny—decreed that he was not to be nominated to an ordinary parish.

[1] Worth in those days about $2,000.

Ars with its marvels, its crowds, and the fervor of its thousands of pilgrims went to his head. Evil triumphed over good in his soul.[2] He came to the conclusion that the Ars pilgrimage was a paying proposition; he wanted to put it on its feet as a business. He decided to organize processions and, to some extent, to regulate the charities and the church collections. Almost at once he fell out with his parish priest. Their disagreement was so obvious that it induced Father Raymond to forward his complaints to the bishop, denouncing Father Vianney and calling for his resignation. Unsuccessful in this he did not scruple to take his place, deputizing for him at the reception of the smarter and more important pilgrims and openly signing his letters, "Raymond, pastor of Ars." What was this priest's principal complaint against his superior? Precisely that Jean-Marie Vianney understood nothing about financial matters—in short was no business man. After that, it cannot be denied that Jean-Marie Vianney cared little for material advantages.

Not only did he refuse riches, he rejected honors as well. There are abundant instances of this: his refusal of a more important parish (Salles), of the Legion of Honor, of a canon's mozetta. In each of these three cases, refusal is hardly the word. He implored the bishop not to give him the parish, believing himself unworthy of even the meanest in the whole region; he had no idea of the significance of the Legion of Honor, and ingenuously gave it to his assistant "because it will give him greater pleasure than it will me," as if it were an ordinary present that could be given away to someone else; the mozetta had to be put on him by force, and thus "rigged out" he dared not show his face in public for the rest of the day. In the evening he disposed of it to one of the women of the parish for fifty francs, the price of the cloth, to enable him to help a poor man. Father Vianney gave way to extravagance only in decorating his church. He would manage to get a little money together, rush off to Lyons and come back with some dreadful little wooden cherubs for the high altar or some fearful pictures in the purest Rue Saint-Sulpice style, in gilded frames,

---

[2] It should be pointed out that biographies of Father Raymond speak of his last years and his death as "very edifying."

absolutely valueless. He suffered from a really terrifying lack of taste. And it was, it should be added, art of the Rue Saint-Sulpice at the time of Louis Philippe.

Moral or personal advantages. What has been said above is a sufficient answer to this question.

The first "miracle" of the Curé d'Ars could not be admitted by the ecclesiastical commission of inquiry, or, still less, by opponents of the supernatural, for it consists in the influence of Jean-Marie Vianney and the undeniable genius of his sermons together with his extraordinary power of provoking confessions and confidences.

Appointed parish priest of Ars, he was faced, he considered, with a gigantic task. He could manage all right to say Mass and mumble over those bits of Latin that he remembered; but he had also to catechize and preach on Sunday mornings. And this man of little learning, "the fool of the family," was fearfully muddled by the questions and answers of the simple diocesan catechism and, as for preaching, he might as well have been asked to write one of the classics. But after all, he reassured himself, the catechism is for children and he would manage somehow or other to explain to them original sin or the doctrine of the Trinity. As for the sermons it would be easy enough; he would write them out as well as he could and learn them by heart. And that is what he did. Unfortunately on the very first Sunday he was seized with fright in the pulpit. Right in the middle of a sentence, bathed in sweat and feeling that what he was saying had little meaning, he lost the thread, tried in vain to recapture it, stammered, muttered an apology, and fled distractedly from the pulpit, his face betraying his shame.

On the following Sundays he tried again. The Curé d'Ars recited his artless sermon to a congregation of two or three dozen, more than half of them old women of varying degrees of deafness, steeped in a dry-as-dust piety. Few in Ars went to church. Father Vianney gave this sparse congregation elementary teaching; as well as he could for their benefit he repeated what he himself had heard from other preachers; he told them they must go to Mass

and vespers, that drink is harmful for men, dances for girls. Down
with the tavern, and the fair, and church for all every Sunday.
They listened to him, blew their noses, scraped their chairs and
a week later the same old women in black were handing each
other holy water while the same peasants clinked glasses at the
inn and the same youths and girls danced in the public square
before they went off, at dusk, in pairs to the dark lanes. He had
failed completely. The new priest had turned out no better than
his predecessor; he was by no means as clever, and in addition
was ugly, dowdy, and ludicrous. People laughed at him behind
his back as he walked along the only street in the village.

Father Vianney was greatly upset by his failure. He came abruptly to the conclusion that his obstinacy in being ordained was
an infamy, a crime. He had obtained for himself a mission that
he could not fulfill—a mission of importance, the bringing of
God to man. He had the cure of souls, two hundred of them, and
the burden was too heavy for him. He would have done better,
he thought, to have chosen the Trappists, for as one of them he
need only humble himself and pray. And then he found himself
with, so to say, a knife at his throat. One Sunday when he got up
in the pulpit with his sermon in his head—his usual sermon, common, ineffective, rambling—he was completely overcome by the
feeling of his own unworthiness. He trembled and stuttered, and
then entirely lost the thread. Yet say something he must. So the
Curé d'Ars, forgetting all he had prepared, improvised. He spoke
and went on speaking, gesturing towards the tabernacle, pointing
up to heaven; he talked of sinners, the wounds of Christ, the tears
of the Virgin Mother; he wept, he sobbed out his words. He no
longer knew what he said. And then, opening his eyes on a sudden, he was dismayed to see the copious tears in the congregation's eyes.

In church as a child and at the seminary, Father Vianney had
listened to famous preachers, Dominicans more often than not,
bespoken for a First Communion or to give a retreat. They were
born orators, with a command of language, real masters of their
craft. He admired them without understanding all the learned
words that from time to time issued from their lips. And now he

began to be in demand himself: first in a neighboring village, next in another, then in an important parish of the diocese. "You want *me* to preach?" exclaimed Father Vianney. "But I can't utter a word!" For a little more than two years he had been unable to "utter a word" every Sunday morning in his own church; for two years he had spoken just as the fancy took him, "just anyhow, and it seems to be all right." And that church which no one ever went to, that dilapidated, silent church was full: the men came from the tavern, the youths and girls from their dancing; people from the neighboring hamlets and villages walked or drove there in wagons, and filled the church to capacity; they stood in the aisles, they clung to the pillars, they crowded round the pulpit, they were crammed against the doors, and overflowed on to the public square outside. Laborers when asked to work on a Sunday to hasten a job would refuse "because they were going to the sermon by the priest of Ars." The local gentry, persons of importance, people from the towns and, lastly—"No one let me know, they've played a joke on me"—priests from the cathedral town, professors of theology, "people of importance" as he called them, real pulpit orators, came and were amazed at his preaching.

What did he say? He spoke only of extremely simple things, in the language of a homely unpretentious man; his sentences were often upside down, his terms not always the right ones, his French sometimes faulty. Awkward and clumsy, he was entirely absorbed in the divine work he had to do. He made no plan, he no longer prepared at all and spoke of one subject only, God, the love of God. "Brethren, I am going to talk to you about the love of God." And he plunged right into his sermon. There was no premeditated oratorical effect. But he suffered visibly in mentioning the Passion, was roused to indignation by sinners and called on them to let their hearts be touched, to come and kneel with him; he spoke to the little children, the old folks, the birds, the flowers; he praised all creation, he wept with Our Lady and Mary Magdalen, he quarreled with the devil; he would pass abruptly to the things of this earth; he extolled humility and poverty, and spying suddenly a beggar among the congregation, fetched him and placed him near him; at length his fire seemed to burn out, he made a vague gesture and finding no more to say recited the Our Father; he left the pulpit and went back to the altar as if it were all a mere nothing while behind him could be heard the shuffling and murmur of the great crowd.

This gift, obviously, was not exactly that of eloquence. The fervor of the crowds was aroused by all the actions of this funny little man in a cassock green with age, and by the more than human religious spirit that emanated from him. In short it was not only his sermons which were the attraction for those who came to him from afar. Sundays were not the only day of the week that Father Vianney touched men's hearts and minds; gradually it was rumored that he heard confessions differently from ordinary priests and that penitents came from his confessional completely changed by a combination of hope, joy, and repentance; that he could read men's souls like an open book, could understand and move them—intuitively and without the aid of any gift of psychology. People crowded even to his Thursday catechism lessons, for when he spoke to children—he was still quite unable to keep exactly to the lesson in the little book—in reality he was addressing humanity at large, for he realized, again as always, by intuition, that this humanity was composed of adults who were indeed all children and that the well-known "Suffer the little children" applied to people of all ages. The catechism lessons after a time were attended regularly, were followed like his sermons (people took time off from their work to listen to them), and gradually every moment of his whole life was *followed* in the same way. The first to arrive informed the newcomers, and thus those who were astonished to discover that Father Vianney was so unprepossessing in appearance (he described his own face a figure of fun) learned the details of his daily life which he could not hide for long. They heard that this comical-looking little man rose at two in the morning and made his way to the church with a lantern, in all seasons and weathers, to pray until dawn for the salvation of sinners; and he prayed "in his own way"; he did not drone out prayers, but conversed with God, imploring him, bowing down before him, weeping and beating his breast. They discovered that it was he who with his own hands built the hospital—fancy a hospital at Ars!—in which he would welcome all in need, asking nothing of them, from aged cripples to destitute unmarried mothers, hounded from the parental roof. They were told how he made his supper off a bowl of soup—and then someone had to bring it to him between two confessions and stand over him while he drank it—that there were never two shirts in his cupboard because he always gave away the second one to the poor, and sometimes even the only one in his possession.

Maxence Van der Meersch, better informed on the life of the Curé d'Ars than on the latest advances in medicine, has produced the definitive work about him. "This man," he says, "believed in God and loved God as we can no longer believe and love. This man lived by the word of God . . . and it was that which drew the crowds; they came to see in material human form what we so often assert to be an impossible dream: a man who realized in himself the teaching of the Gospel."

Father Vianney's power was due, primarily, to his faith, perhaps, indeed, to nothing else besides. But we know that faith can move mountains. "If you had faith like to a grain of mustard seed, you might say to this mulberry-tree, Be thou rooted up, and be thou transplanted into the sea: and it would obey you." Van der Meersch draws a striking parallel: perhaps between God and man there is only a thin paper partition; but no one dares tear through this partition save, occasionally, men like Francis of Assisi, Vincent de Paul, and Jean-Marie Vianney. As for the crowds, their function is to flock round. And at Ars they did not stint themselves. The duffer, the "fool of the family," the priest who had been ordained out of charity, to whom another priest [3] had the face to write, "In your place, knowing so little theology, I should never dare even to enter a confessional," became in a very few years a famous person, an important figure in a century that could show several in every sphere. There is sufficient proof of it in the fact that at the Lyon-Perrache station a special window in the booking office was reserved for Ars, and eight-day return tickets between Lyons and Ars were issued because it took at least as long as that to wait a turn for confession, even though Father Vianney was in the con-

[3] Father Barjon.

fessional for fifteen hours a day. The lowly village of Ars, "the poorest of the poor," was now a place where the Holy Spirit breathed. People crowded into the inns, many spent the night under the stars for want of a room. At church, in the street, they thronged around the parish priest and nearly suffocated him—a bodyguard had to be appointed, three determined lusty fellows who with fist and elbow could cleave a passage—they pestered him with questions, overwhelmed him with their secrets, waited eagerly on his every word. They implored his blessing. Children and the sick were brought to him. There remained but one thing more: soon his handkerchiefs were filched, his breviaries and his devotional pictures went the same way; pieces of his cassock were chopped off with scissors or pocket knives as he passed by, portraits of him were made and sent all over France and Europe. Very shortly—a few years only sufficed—men no longer spoke merely of the Curé d'Ars but of St. Jean-Marie Baptiste Vianney, a saint who worked miracles.

As I have already said the miracles did not catch Father Vianney napping. When suddenly one day a deaf man could hear, a lame one stretch his leg or shouts went up "He sees!" "He walks!" the priest of Ars merely put it down to divine intervention. To him such supernatural occurrences were entirely natural for they had an explanation. Only one thing surprised him: that these miracles should take place in his parish. His faith compelled him to believe, then, in the presence of an intercessor. The church at Ars contained relics of St. Philomena, and St. Philomena, he had been told, had already worked miracles at Naples and elsewhere. It was obvious: St. Philomena was still working miracles; Father Vianney fell on his knees and thanked her.

Never for a moment did he dream of ascribing to himself the supernatural phenomena which were making all the stir in his village, any more than he imagined that he possessed any special oratorical gift. And of course his assistant was hardly the one to contradict him. Father Raymond looked on Father Vianney as poor, ignorant and stupid; and just when the assistant was beginning to wonder what could make these crowds gather so hectically, the cult of St. Philomena made it clear to him: "Come to Ars and

pray to St. Philomena, and she will hear your petition." And just
at first the crowds granted the truth of it. Men came to Ars to
pray to St. Philomena, virgin and martyr, before whose statue
Father Raymond had placed an alms box, whose picture he had
distributed round the shops. But gradually the truth compelled
recognition; for, in fact, miraculous phenomena occurred only
when Father Vianney was there—or when the person favored with
a miracle had addressed a silent prayer to Father Vianney. And
when he went to Dardilly to visit his brother the miracles at Ars
stopped. They cropped up elsewhere, at Dardilly. It looked as if
they dogged his footsteps, and of course the crowds soon fell into
step behind. In a day or two the hapless St. Philomena was left
all alone, the humble protectress of a deserted parish and no
longer the patroness of a pilgrimage quite in the latest fashion.
In heaven, a Christian may well imagine, St. Philomena smiled to
herself. At length his parishioners went in a body to the poor
priest to beseech him to return, Father Raymond at their head. He
came back again, and no sooner reappeared accompanying the
devout procession that had gone to fetch him than it was seen
that he brought back the miracles as well.

These miracles are of two kinds. For the purpose of this study
we omit those miracles which materialists would contest on *a priori*
grounds, all those, that is, which concern the healing of souls. Of
course, it may seem extraordinary that an atheist should be converted by the parish priest of Ars (even at Ars, indeed, everyone
was not converted; in opposition to the crowds of faithful who
were rushing to Ars movements were started, though they were
certainly of less consequence, to oppose the "idolatry" of the crowds
regarding this "old sorcerer of the countryside"). No less amazing
is the fact that an entire section of the population or a whole
social class hitherto resolutely agnostic—the quarry workers of
the district—should quite abruptly begin to be concerned about
the existence of God. The Church, obviously, must take such
miracles into account: for outstanding figures, guided by their
faith, impart it in the same way to a large number of men. They
act primarily as magnets. But among miracles it is the healing of
bodies which ranks first, and Ars arouses our interest to the degree

in which this healing was, or was not, realized. That is the first category of miracles. The second is peculiar to the case in hand, and concerns the gift of second sight and prophecy that Father Vianney is reputed to have possessed in connection with his parishioners, visitors, and especially his penitents in the confessional.

We can begin with these phenomena, for Father Vianney was particularly puzzled by them and only with difficulty could he attribute them to St. Philomena. The first occurrence of this kind took place in March, 1831. Father Vianney went into his church, elbowing his way through the crowd of faithful, when he noticed a woman kneeling in the third row of benches to his left. He had never seen her before, but an irresistible force seemed to impel him towards her, and, thinking that he recognized her, asked her severely, "Have you thought seriously? Have you made up your mind now to have your husband back from the hospital?" The woman jumped to her feet. "How do you know that?" she demanded. "I've only been an hour in Ars!" "Didn't you tell me about it?" stammered Father Vianney.

"*I* tell you of it, this is the first time I've seen you!" Father Vianney pushed on toward his confessional and arrived there, paused a moment. To the crowds all around it he exclaimed artlessly, "Well, I've been properly caught!"

This gift of second sight was never to leave him, but remained a moral torture until his death. Examples of it are innumerable even if all instances reported by the beneficiaries are explicitly set aside (an elementary precaution to obviate fraud which may be caused by vanity, the desire to play a part, or a thoughtless endeavor to aid religious propaganda). Sometimes Father Vianney alluded to a secret hidden in the more or less recent past, at others he told one of his visitors straight out the very private reason for his coming to implore a favor. In every case the occurrence was before witnesses (the people crowding round, Catherine Lassagne, Father Raymond, or Father Toccanier) and without a moment's warning. It might be asserted with real truth that Father Vianney completely reveals himself, except that, in point of fact, he was quite unaware of the lack of tact he was about to show.

In every case, too, notice how flustered he was, in a hurry to be off just as if he had "dropped a brick," and endeavoring to hide his embarrassment with the first excuse that occurred. "There now," he exclaimed on one occasion, "I prophesied without knowing it, like Caiphas," or, "What a bit of luck, I hit it on the first round," or again, "Just like those almanacs, it happened to be right by a fluke." Sometimes he would say, "It was a foolish idea I had," or "It just happened to occur to me."

Needless to say these "explanations" explain nothing at all. The law of coincidence does not apply to so many instances. Indeed it has been carefully studied from this standpoint in connection with the predictions of almanacs and the revelations of fakirs and fortunetellers. The number that turn out correct is scarcely two per cent. So well-known a clairvoyant as Madame de Thebes when she revealed the past was right in only five or six cases: and even among these we do not know what proportion can be accounted for by mere generalization or trickery. Any *bona fide* observer will agree that one successful result is enough to make a *fakir* famous. Now, the "successful results" obtained by the Curé d'Ars are past counting, and in the weighty file of favorable and contrary evidence which was collected to elucidate his case not a single error is reported. Furthermore, the point under discussion is not the existence of error or fraud but whether certain men and women can possess this gift of clairvoyance.

In its present state science can give no valid answer to this question. Yet everyone, at least once during a lifetime, has had an intuition of this kind—but these incidents are isolated. If the person in question is especially well equipped psychologically he will have some clue to the shape of the past by the exercise of character study, since human situations are resolved in the same way as those of the theater. But at the very first meeting he could never guess that a woman had forsaken her sick husband in a hospital.

Morpho-psychology—an entirely new science with a great future —also enables character to be read and, to a great extent, the past and the future to be deduced, by means of a simple glance at the face. But morpho-psychology had not been invented in the days of Louis Philippe. All the phenomena of clairvoyance attributed to the Curé d'Ars transcend any possibility of a special understanding of humanity, and even of such an understanding rendered exceptionally keen by long hours in the confessional. On a last analysis, indeed, John Dunne in *An Experiment with Time,* which has already been quoted in our Introduction, seems to be on the verge of a possible explanation, "is getting warm," as children say in their games. John Dunne discovered "serial time" and even tried out his hypothesis on himself and seven young men at Oxford. We need not concern ourselves with the extremely complicated explanation that he gives; even an incomplete summary would require some twenty pages and several diagrams. It will be sufficient for our purpose that "serial time" has to do with the possibility of everyone foreseeing the future by means of dreams. Obviously, it is a serious matter which will completely nullify the various "keys" to dreams offered to the public in penny pamphlets. "Go to sleep," Mr. Dunne tells us, "and on waking note down your dreams and you will presently find that some of them come true." Time no longer follows a course, time is static. There is, therefore, no present, past, or future, but one single instant without effective length into which all possible instants are merged.

Mr. Dunne's experiments, of course, were based on his own observations and those of his friends. He had to neglect all predictions of the future or disclosures of the past which did not affect them or him but which, if his theory is correct, are not necessarily wasted material since they may concern strangers and unknown people. It is possible, too, that dreams are a field of experience which may perhaps be continued in a waking state. (Mr. Dunne includes in his book an additional section on predictions in this state.) It remains to be seen how this explanation can be applied to the phenomena of clairvoyance observed at Ars. It remains to be seen especially to what extent Mr. Dunne's discovery will be acknowledged to be true—and this, whether he likes it or not, is a question of time. Mr. Dunne is a well-known serious-minded physicist, whose opinions merit our respect. For the present we must await further developments, though it must be emphasized that *An Experiment with Time* leads to the inference of the existence of God and that this "explanation," therefore, is on the side of the advocates of the supernatural—at Ars and elsewhere.

With regard to the healing of bodies, the discussion, as is to be expected, assumes far greater importance. I should devote a long chapter to it at this point if Ars could be considered the typical case, in the nineteenth century at least, for the present study. But this chapter is naturally incorporated in the study of the following case which includes all these miraculous phenomena as they actually occurred.

In the middle of last century Ars aroused the enthusiasm of crowds from all over the world. It seemed that this period "rich in wonders" had now proffered the most remarkable of all. On August 4, 1859, Jean-Marie Baptiste Vianney, parish priest of Ars, at length received from heaven the final approbation of every human life: his "poor end," which relieved him of all his earthly tortures and, principally, of the crowds pressing round him. On a stormy night, at four in the morning, very suddenly, in the presence of his heart-broken, weeping parishioners kneeling there, that humble emaciated face was raised from the pillow and then fell back again as the last breath issued from his lips. The torch race of the classics was no mere inconsequential myth. A year and a half before the death of the parish priest of Ars, another village in France, equally unpretentious and unknown, little more than just a dot on the map, had been the scene, and the witness, of the greatest miracle of modern times.

I

On Thursday, February 11, 1858, at half-past nine in the morning, three little girls of the village of Lourdes, the two sisters Toinette and Bernadette Soubirous and their playmate Jeanette Abadie, set out to pick up firewood to provide heating for the Soubirous family's home—we shall see later what sort of a place it was—and to cook their midday meal. They had to look for it beyond the houses of the village, on the other side of the old bridge at a spot called Massabielle or Massabieille (from *Massa-viel,* meaning old rock). One of the Soubirous children, Bernadette, accompanied the others somewhat against the will of her mother who, mindful of her daughter's distressing bouts of asthma, at first bade her stay at home; but the child had implored her to be allowed out for a little play and in the end a neighbor's appeal, coupled with the loan of a white hood to keep out the cold, caused the mother to give way. Laughing and chattering the three little girls set out, and the neighbors who saw them go by—Nicolau, a miller, and a woman, Samaran—testified afterward that they seemed particularly playful and gay. Sometimes Bernadette's companions ran on ahead and then let her catch them up, only to run off and leave her behind again. It was all part of their fun.

Even nowadays, in a Lourdes which bears very little resemblance to the village of that period, it is possible to trace the route taken by the three little girls. First, going down through the village, they came to a path bordered by a quickset hedge leading out to the country; later it was to become a street with narrow pavements, traffic lights and pedestrian crossings: the Rue de la Grotte. At that period it was only a track worn by the pigs. Thence, in 1858, it reached the Gave at the point where it was joined by a branch canal whose waters were swollen by a little stream, the Merlasse, which worked the Saci mill. Massabielle was at the end, on the other side of a small island joined to the bank by the mill bridge. On that day, February 11th, the canal was almost dry for the mill was undergoing repair and the sluice gates were closed, but it still contained sufficient water to prevent its being crossed dry-shod. Thus it was that two of the little girls paused on the bank to take off shoes and stockings and called out to the third, Bernadette, to do the same. But she was reluctant to do so. She was afraid of catching cold in this little tongue of icy cold water (even for February the temperature that morning was very low). She would have preferred her companions to have taken her arm to help her across. But the only response to this proposal was an expression of derision from Toinette. She watched them both make their way over the ford poking fun at her as they went for being afraid of the cold, and imagining that she would very soon follow them. From farther off, on the other side, they shouted to her, "Now then, lazy bones, come and get some wood with us!"

Bernadette, who had stayed on the island, squatted down and began to take off her shoes. Quite suddenly she was aware that something extraordinary was taking place. She felt a sharp gust of wind abruptly whipping against her cheeks and hair, lashing her body and whistling in her ears, but at the same moment she noticed with amazement that no ripples formed on the water and that the branches of the trees opposite her were quite still.

The whole thing lasted but a moment. We can pause here, and try to imagine the scene: the child, Bernadette Soubirous, standing in front of the grotto of Massabielle, bewildered, harassed by the wind all round her, and all round her, too, the immense silence and the motionlessness of nature.

When the two other children returned to the opposite bank they saw Bernadette kneeling, her hands joined; they were not in the least astonished. "Just look at her," exclaimed Jeanette Abadie. "Still praying! That's all she can do!" Once more they called to her and this time Bernadette rejoined them and crossed over the ford. "But the water's warm," she cried, "the water's warm just like the dish water." Peals of laughter met her remarks.

Then they rained questions on her and chaffed her thoroughly, "Why didn't you come with us. What were you doing?" Bernadette related what had happened to her. And as her playmates looked at her with astonishment she went over her story again and again, punctuating it with questions in her turn. "What about you? Didn't you see anything?"

What happened to Bernadette was beyond all laws of the visible world. As she gazed at the grotto of Massabielle she had suddenly seen a bright light flash in the natural recess situated to the left of the overhanging rock. Just at that spot was a wild rose bush, but bared of flowers and foliage by the winter. The bright light lit up the wild rose and the recess, and then there appeared an overwhelmingly beautiful figure. "A young girl in white," explained Bernadette, "a young girl of about seventeen." She had blue eyes, wore a white dress with a blue sash, coming down to her feet; a white veil covered her head and shoulders; in her hand

she held a rosary made of a golden chain and beads which sparkled
as if they had been cut from pieces of light. The girl's feet rested
on a golden rose. She smiled at Bernadette and signed to her to
come nearer. Instinctively the child fell to her knees. Once again
the girl bade her come a few paces forward. Bernadette complied.
Almost at once the apparition began to vanish. At first it seemed
gradually to lose color and become blurred; at length it vanished
completely and nothing remained save the rock and the bare
branches of the wild rose in the grey shadows of the February
day.

"Silly idiot!" exclaimed Toinette. "Fool! you'll make everybody
laugh at you!"

"Well then," replied Bernadette, "you must say nothing about
it."

Who but a child would venture to request the silence of other
children about so stupendous a secret? Hardly were they back in
the village than Jeanette Abadie began gossiping about it; Toinette
had already forestalled her at the Soubirous home. In a few hours
Bernadette's "secret" was known to about fifty persons. By the
evening of this same day (February 11th) most of the villagers of
Lourdes had heard about it. It must be said at once that the incident provoked merely a few smiles, and some shrugging of shoulders. "Just the sort of thing that would happen to the Soubirous!
That's the last straw!" Even Bernadette's parents were not greatly
worried; after all, they thought, it was not unusual for children
to embroider the truth to make themselves interesting. The general opinion was that Bernadette had wanted to make herself
interesting, and she was told straight out that she would have done
better to bring back some firewood like her companions or even
to have looked over her catechism after last evening when she was
questioned by the parish priest and had been found unable to
expound the mystery of the Trinity, and extremely backward for
her age. Her age, in fact, was fourteen, the very time when imagination and vanity often begin to play tricks on girls. That night,
as they went to bed, Bernadette's mother finished off her reproofs
by saying, "At least you might have chosen a better time than
Lent for your little carnival. You deserve a box on the ears."

Bernadette very nearly received that box on the ears from her mother quite shortly afterward. It was Sunday, February 14th, in front of the grotto. The child had gone again to Massabielle and once more the "girl" had appeared to her.

This second apparition was in every way similar to the first; the same silent vision, the same telling of rosary beads. But Bernadette now added this new feature to her account: she asserted that an irresistible and indescribable force impelled her to the grotto. It was, so to say, a summons, yet she did not hear it with her ears; "right inside her" someone abruptly gave her the order to go to Massabielle; it was peremptory though beyond, outside expression, and as she hesitated to carry it out she felt extremely unhappy; then as she made up her mind to do so and took the first few steps in that direction, her heart was filled with the greatest joy. This time, moreover, there were more people with her: the little girls from the school, her playmates, and a few villagers. And she had not brought merely her rosary. She had provided herself with a small bottle of holy water and right at the beginning of the apparition had uncorked it and, awkwardly enough, tried to sprinkle the "girl." A few incidents occurred. Jeanette Abadie was heard to swear; she gesticulated rudely and threw a stone at the grotto. The miller Nicolau, a great strapping fellow of twenty-eight, made an exhibition of himself by sniggering and gesturing. Then Bernadette's mother came on the scene and threatened to cuff her daughter: "When you've quite finished," she cried, "I'll give you something to remember, you great silly, with all these pious goings on!"

In short, the people of Lourdes looked on the whole affair as a kind of free entertainment provided for their benefit. Though not quite all of them; an exception must be made for the usual little group of pious, superstitious women, greedy for manifestations of the supernatural and inclined to discern their presence everywhere. It was the beginning of the second half of the nineteenth century: devotion to Our Lady was held in particular esteem and, one may venture to say, was very topical (the dogma of the Immaculate Conception had been defined three years before); the whole of France was divided into two parties on the question of the apparitions at La Salette. The day after Bernadette's second apparition people from the neighboring countryside started arriving in Lourdes, inquiring what had happened and asking to be shown "the visionary."

The third apparition took place on Thursday, February 18th, at dawn. On this occasion Bernadette was joined by two Lourdes women who were convinced that the apparition was one of their departed relatives. One of these women took with her a sheet of paper, pen and ink; she hoped, no doubt, that the "ghost" would express and set down its wishes. And for the first time, indeed, the "girl" spoke to Bernadette. She told her, "It is not necessary to write down what I have to say to you," and then, "Will you be good enough to come here for a fortnight?" She concluded with these words, "I do not promise you happiness in this life, but in the next."

It need hardly be said that when Bernadette repeated these announcements they aroused very various reactions. No one, save Bernadette, heard them: indeed, no one had heard Bernadette herself speak although her lips were observed to move. At one point the others present gained the impression that the apparition had vanished. They broke silence and no longer stayed still, they gathered round the little Soubirous girl. The child was kneeling, her arms stretched out crosswise and her face bore all the marks of ecstasy. It was the face of a corpse, not merely colorless, but pinched and gaunt like a mask. They thought that she was going to faint, or even worse. They stood round her, raised her up and supported her. But suddenly the color came back to her cheeks, she smiled and began to speak naturally, almost gaily. She repeated simply all she had heard, and that, by itself, was quite enough to lessen very considerably the respect they had for her. So the "girl" spoke the local dialect, did she? She spoke to Bernadette as *vous*, and not with the familiar *tu*. She asked her to be good enough to come to Massabielle. It all seemed very baffling and rather odd. Bernadette was taken home and given a bowl of milk.

From that day, until March 4th, Bernadette went to the grotto every morning. It only remains to set down the apparitions as they occurred, day by day, without comment for the time being.

On February 19th, Bernadette was at the grotto in company of her mother and aunt and with the crowd at her heels. Directly the vision appeared a great din of shouts and yells broke out (inaudible to all save Bernadette, of course) all round her. There were cries and curses: "Be off with you, go away, right away from here!" Bernadette clearly saw the "girl"—from this 'day onward she called her the *Lady* or the *Young Lady*—frowning; at once the uproar ceased. Then the rosary was said. Bernadette's mother was greatly upset by the sight of her daughter's face in ecstasy; she no longer recognized her daughter and thought she was at the point of death. "My God, don't take her from me," she shrieked.

On February 20th, the Lady spoke again. She taught the child a prayer not to be found in the catechism, making her promise to say it every day, but to reveal the words to no one. It was to be a secret between the Lady and the visionary. Bernadette made the promise and kept it. She revealed not one word of this secret prayer even to the priests who tried to make her mention it.

On February 21st, those who were present received an impression of some new occurrence. They left their places and surrounded Bernadette in ecstasy; it was then that they perceived that she was weeping. They waited, nevertheless, until she came to herself and then began to question her at once. Bernadette answered that the Lady had looked into the distance with an expression of intense sorrow on her face and had said, "Pray for sinners!" On that day there was a crowd of about a thousand people from Lourdes and the district round. As usual, no priest from Lourdes was present; the parish priest had called his assistants together and forbidden them to take part in these manifestations. He confessed his own incredulity. "Obviously the girl's mad or ill," he asserted, and added, "and in any case God will enlighten us."

Between the apparition on February 21st and that on the following day the civil authorities took a hand. On their return from the grotto Bernadette and her parents were summoned by the Imperial Procurator; he received them in uniform, standing beneath the portrait of Napoleon III, and with the local captain of police at his side. He began by outlining what had so far occurred, laying great emphasis on the discredit that the "alleged apparitions" would bring on the district, resulting in nothing less than misfortunes of all kinds. He gave an instance: Lourdes had applied to be served by a projected railroad; but the line would not now go through the village because the place had made itself ridiculous and was suspected of starting a "stunt" to attract money; in any case, there was one reason, the most important of all—the public peace had been disturbed.

In consequence it was absolutely essential that the "miraculous phenomena at the grotto" should cease forthwith; if they did not, severe steps would have to be taken. The Imperial Procurator left no doubt as to what he intended these to be if the culprit repeated her offense: she would be sent to prison or an asylum. With these words he threw over to Bernadette's father clippings from the newspaper circulating in and around Tarbes, the nearest town; all treated the affair humorously and illustrated their paragraphs with cartoons; they made fun of the visionary, the peasants, and the authorities. The Procurator did not stop there. He interrogated Bernadette and, in collusion with his clerk who took down the answers, contrived to make it appear that the child contradicted herself. When the clerk read over her deposition Bernadette corrected the mistakes as they occurred. No, the Lady was not wearing a white sash; her dress was not blue, it was white. This interrogation lasted three hours, and Bernadette underwent it standing there beside her mother who also was not allowed a chair. At the end of three hours the Procurator's wife came into the room and, seized with pity, brought forward two chairs. Bernadette, in a fit of temper, declined hers. "What an idea" she retorted, "I should make it dirty." Twenty years later she was to weep at the memory of those words. "Dear me," she exclaimed, "how naughty I was!"

Bernadette left the Procurator's office almost certain that she would be unable to go back to the grotto. Besides, her father had openly sided with the official. "All I ask," he declared, "is that my daughter should be prevented from doing wrong." And that very evening the Soubirous parents made up their minds to prohibit definitely any further visits to Massabielle. The child deferred to this decision and on the next day endeavored to revert to her usual mode of life: she went to school. But in the afternoon, as she made her way along the road known as the Chemin de l'Hospice, her mysterious interior voice bade her once more go down to the Gave. At first she refused to comply. The villagers, who were watching her from behind their window curtains, saw her stop right in the middle of the street, as if rooted to the spot, unable to go backwards or forwards. Then, she seemed to come to herself and walk on again. And she went to Massabielle. Some discussion ensued among the villagers and then they followed her, keeping an eye open for the police. Bernadette stopped before the grotto and knelt down. Shortly afterward she got up again and went home without a word. The Lady had not appeared.

On February 23rd Bernadette was at the grotto followed by an increasingly dense and excited crowd; the police, in default of clearer directions, shepherded it into place and confined their efforts in the meantime to maintaining order. Bernadette knelt down and almost at once fell into ecstasy. It was an ecstasy which on this occasion lasted longer than usual and at the end of it, when the child had regained consciousness and her habitual complexion, she disclosed to those who were by her that the Lady had entrusted her with three secrets. She did not explain further. That evening she seemed very excited and visitors who asked for her noticed her fresh complexion; on the other hand those who were well acquainted with her stated that her demeanor had changed, that she had become very quiet and earnest and that she said her rosary with great concentration.

On February 24th Bernadette once again fell into ecstasy at the grotto. But on this occasion there was still another phenomenon. So far the visionary had merely prayed and told her beads; abruptly now she began to speak very quickly, and in a despairing tone. She sank to the ground, burst into sobs and cried out, "Penance, penance!" The incident caused the greater astonishment among the crowd because up to that moment her face had been beaming with joy.[4] As if by instinct all present followed her actions and imitated her posture. All fell on their knees. This apparition came to an end in uproar; two policemen forced their

---

[4] Bernadette claimed afterward that the Lady also had at first appeared very joyful and then extremely grieved.

way through the people round Bernadette and shook her roughly by the shoulder shouting, "Stop it, you little play actor!" One of them faced round to the crowd and began to harangue them, "And to think that nonsense like this can happen right in the middle of this nineteenth century!"

That night a regular council of war was held at Lourdes. The interest aroused by Bernadette was at its height. It was maintained that twenty thousand pilgrims were getting ready to be present at next day's visions. On the one hand skeptics, unbelievers, and some few Catholics who were determined to regard all these occurrences as nothing but a scandal put their heads together to force the authorities to act and oblige them to carry out their threats. And indeed an atmosphere of scandal prevailed in Lourdes. Several of the villagers at that time became mentally unbalanced, a peasant swore that on his way home in the evening he had heard voices by the calvary at a crossroads; children of the same age as the visionary had hysterical attacks at the grotto, convinced that they had seen the Virgin on the rock; and, in the last place, a tavern maid from Tarbes made her way to Massabielle and feigned an ecstasy in order to poke fun at the visionary. Moreover, all those who had no desire to doubt the supernatural origin of the apparitions besought Bernadette to furnish them with some proof. People were seething with excitement; it might almost have been said that miracles were in the air. There was little sleep in Lourdes that night and when February 25th dawned it brought with it the hope that a definitive conclusion, one way or the other, would be reached on that day. Directly it was light, a large crowd beset Bernadette's home, waiting for her to set out. She came out and went straight to the grotto. The crowd was so considerable that the police thought it necessary to protect the child; they made a ring round her and with drawn swords conducted her to Massabielle.

Bernadette prayed, said her rosary, and then quite suddenly there came a long drawn-out "Ah" from the crowd as she got to her feet but not, so it seemed, to go home; her face showed more clearly than ever that she was in ecstasy. She looked in the direction of the Gave, took a step towards it and then went back again; she fell on her knees once more as if panic-stricken "like a child who had lost the way and was imploring an invisible passer-by for help." Then with her fingernails she began to scratch at the ground quickly, with feverish intensity. A puddle of muddy water appeared. Bernadette bent over it, put her lips to it and then daubed it over her face. She tore up some blades of grass and ate them. She filled her mouth with mud and chewed it up. She ate this dirty, muddy earth by the mouthful, the handful, and then, abruptly, retched and vomited. At once came a shout from all parts of the crowd: "That's enough! That's enough! Down with the lunatic. Shut her up!" Some rushed at Bernadette, jerked her to her feet and carried her off. People were shouting and others were sobbing; the majority expressed their feelings in derisive laughter. Silence reigned at last—the silence of a tremendous disappointment. Slowly they all returned the way they had come.

At home again, Bernadette explained what had happened. The Lady had said to her, "Go and drink and wash yourself at the spring and eat the grass that you will find there." At first she had made a mistake and gone towards the Gave. But the Lady had called her back, and showed her another place which was apparently dry. Bernadette was bewildered at first and then instinctively understood that she must scratch at the ground. She had obeyed the orders to the full and eaten both grass and earth "because the Lady asked her to." Bernadette gave this account toward the end of the morning. At the beginning of the afternoon a few pilgrims who had lingered at the grotto noticed a trickle of water running over the ground, springing from the spot indicated by Bernadette. At five in the evening it was rumored in the village that a spring had appeared. In a few hours this spring was seen to have made a considerable output; already a channel had to be made for the water and a hollow tree trunk used as a pipe.

This spring gushing up at tremendous pressure seemed inexhaustible. On the second day it was giving eighty-five liters (approximately eighteen and a half gallons) a day. In a few hours it had formed a pool. This was the spring, the miraculous spring, whence came the holy waters of Lourdes, the waters of healing, which have today found their way all over the world.

The events of that day caused such excitement among the whole population that afterward no one was able to say for certain whether an apparition occurred at the grotto on February 26th. Father Cros thinks that there was one, Fathers Duboë and Sempé maintain the contrary. But on the following Sunday, February 28th, occurred a further apparition, which was explained at length by Bernadette; there was also another secret conversation. On March 1st, Bernadette went to Massabielle holding a rosary that one of her friends had passed to her. She was observed to hold up this rosary level with her head and the crowd fancied that she did so as a signal, or in consequence of an order given to her; they imitated her, rattling their beads and praying with increased fervor. A few moments later Bernadette, who had come to herself again, explained that there had been a misunderstanding. The Lady had asked her, "Where is your own rosary? That one is not yours," and then added in a tone of command, "Use your own." Bernadette obediently changed back to her own.

On March 2nd, the Lady at last uttered the first words which, properly speaking, enlightened Bernadette as to her identity. She gave orders: "Go and tell the priests to build a chapel here. I desire people to come here in procession."

Once again Bernadette complied. Immediately on leaving the grotto she went straight to the rectory to find the parish priest of Lourdes, Father Peyremale. He was in his garden, with clogs on his feet and a hoe in his hand. He saw the child coming and behind her the crowd, but was not in the least surprised; he had been expecting this visit for the last ten days, and merely maintained the attitude which he had adopted from the beginning so that when Bernadette pushed open the gate—somewhat uncertainly, for this stout and rather surly priest frightened her [5]—he asked her gruffly what she wanted; might she, he suggested, have come for confession? Bernadette began to repeat the Lady's words; the priest cut her short and, opening the door of his house, told her to go in. There in the half-light of his living room he began to upbraid her. "A procession? Now?" he stormed. "Are you quite

[5] She afterward affirmed that he frightened her much more than the Procurator and the police.

out of your mind?" Bernadette, terrified as she was, managed to keep calm. She allowed him to get his breath back and then slipped in the words that the priest had misheard or in his anger had no time to hear. There was no question of a procession on that day, but of future processions and also a chapel. Renewed anger on Father Peyremale's part; at the mention of the Lady he shrugged his shoulders and told Bernadette straight out, "All right then, if it's really Our Lady, let her work a miracle." The gushing spring was not enough for him. He wanted his own miracle and indicated his choice: the Lady, in the presence of the crowd, was to make the wild rose flower of its own accord. Bernadette promised to present this request and, considering that she had accomplished her errand and with no particular desire to prolong this alarming interview, dropped a hasty curtsey and quickly made her exit. Father Peyremale acknowledged afterward that at that moment he made as if to snatch up the broom in the waiting room to strike a blow at the child as she went out.

On March 3rd, there was no apparition. On the next day a posse of police and a detachment of soldiers from the garrison at Tarbes shepherded the crowd on their way to the grotto. On this occasion Bernadette was surrounded by soldiers. The village authorities with Mayor Lacade [6] at their head were also present; the secretary from the prefecture was there to represent his superior, Baron Massy. Bernadette made her way to the grotto along her usual route, passing down a lane between the crowds, massed on either side, made up of the avidly curious, the devout, skeptics and scoffers. On arrival she knelt down and fell into ecstasy. With tears of sorrow alternating with tears of joy, this ecstasy was far longer than any of the preceding ones. It seemed indeed like a continuous, rather moving conversation which though inaudible was mimed throughout. It appeared as if it were unending. Nevertheless the Lady did not say her name and no visible miracle occurred.

The same evening Baron Massy sent an account of the day's

---

[6] Lacade had already considered how to turn the spring to his own advantage: he had sketched out in his head a leaflet advertising *Eau Lacade* (Lacade Water) and plans for a spa.

events to the Minister of Education and Public Worship, M. Rouland. So the "Lourdes affair" had reached as far as Paris; and Lourdes itself began to seethe with tremendous excitement. A blind quarryman, named Bourriette, had rubbed his eyes with water taken from the spring in a flask. At once his sight was restored. Dr. Dozous, to whom he had gone posthaste, shouting "A miracle! a miracle!" wrote a few words on a scrap of paper and put it before him. Unhesitatingly Bourriette read it out: "This patient is suffering from incurable amaurosis." "A miracle! a miracle!" shouted the crowd and Bernadette's house had again to be guarded lest it be carried by storm in the excitement. From that day onward visitors without number began offering money to the Soubirous; very meritoriously they refused it all.

Everyone though was waiting for the Lady to name herself; there had been no want of suggestions. She was a saint, but which saint? Our Lady herself as at La Salette? The Annunciation occurred on March 25th. It was hoped that the apparition would not allow that day to pass without disclosing her secret, although the fortnight required of Bernadette was over. In the morning the crowd besought Bernadette to ask her. The child answered that it would be as the Lady desired but, always obliging, she promised to question her. She went to the grotto also with the hope, perhaps, of receiving an important message. And this message was granted to her.

When Bernadette got up from her knees, as all sign of the ecstasy left her face and she was questioned as usual, she seemed at first in a maze and almost listless; finally she allowed it to be understood that the Lady had given her name at the third request,[7] but in an odd way. She had uttered a complete sentence which was hard to remember. "What sentence?" they asked her. Bernadette repeated it as she had heard it: *"Que soyer Immaculada Concepcioun—*I am the Immaculate Conception." Bernadette then went home without further remark. On the next day Baron Massy summoned a conference of mental specialists and arranged

[7] The first and second time Bernadette said that she had merely *asked;* the third time she added, "Please Madame, although I am unworthy." The Lady, who so far had only smiled, then answered.

for Bernadette to be confined in an asylum. Monseigneur Laurence, bishop of Tarbes, was advised by official quarters in Paris to declare the apparitions a fraud. The bishop refused. The grotto by this time was filled with candles and there was even money thrown on the ground; local stonemasons had cut out steps in the rock to enable the crowd to reach it without accident.

Bernadette was not sent to an asylum. She continued to go to the grotto. On April 7th, during a further ecstasy, she inadvertently held her left hand over a candle flame; the owner of the candle was about to step aside to keep the flame off Bernadette, but at a sign from Dr. Dozous remained where he was. Twenty minutes later, when the ecstasy came abruptly to an end, Bernadette's hand was examined; there was no trace of burning. The fact was vouched for by all present; the flame had been flickering between her fingers which partially obscured it.

On July 16th, when Bernadette, impelled once more by her "interior voice," went down to the grotto, orders had come from Paris to forbid the "demonstrations at Lourdes." Workmen had cleared out the grotto and erected a wooden fence around it. Thus the child was unable to get in; she stopped on the other side of the barrier but went as near as she could to the "holy place" and stood on tiptoe to catch a glimpse of the miraculous niche in the rock. Suddenly she fell into ecstasy. A shout went up from the crowd: "She's there!" Those present noticed that this time Bernadette's face depicted joy alone. She seemed mad with joy. She smiled, she looked happy, and everyone expected a cheering message. The "interview" was somewhat shorter than usual. When it was over Bernadette told the crowd that the Lady had said farewell to her. Our Lady came no more to the grotto, and the child was not to see her again in this world. The era of the visions of Lourdes was over.

Those are the facts, set down as succinctly but also as completely as possible. I have drawn on all the authors who, in the course of the last ninety years, have related the story of Bernadette Soubirous; I have made a special study of the evidence of contemporary witnesses, among others particularly of Estrade's evidence. On the evening of July 16th, then, Bernadette returned

to her home, her face showing her happiness. Her task was over, or
at least so she thought.

And in Paris and the county-town it was thought that the
"Lourdes affair," too, was over. In reality, it was just beginning.
At this point we must go back a little, to set the stage, as it were,
and describe the actors in this amazing adventure—all the actors,
and first of all Bernadette Soubirous, the little girl of Lourdes
to whom Our Lady declared herself and gave orders to eat earth
despite the laughter and insults of the crowd.

II

Bernadette Soubirous was born at Lourdes on January 7, 1844,
on the first floor of the house called the *Moulin de Boly* (Boly's
Mill); the narrow, wretched little room, which can still be visited
by anyone who wishes to, contains a bed protected by a metal
grating to prevent the public from cutting off pieces for relics. The
room is decorated with ex-voto tablets and portraits, most of them
amateur photographs of couples, First Communion groups, and
even weddings; hundreds of names have been scratched on the
walls: all this has been done to obtain the saint's blessing. The
Moulin de Boly is situated in the poorest part of Lourdes, below
the level of the old town, shut in by the crumbling old houses that
surround it and cut off from the light of the sun by a kind of
architectural tunnel through which comes an offensive, fetid
breeze. The façade of the house has been scraped clean, repointed
and smartened up; [8] in 1844 it was practically a blind wall, cracking
and oozing moisture. The house was extremely damp on account
of the rainy climate of Lourdes and the Lapaca brook which ran
beneath the mill and was eating away the foundations.

We know all that is essential to our purpose about the Soubirous
family, together with several details of the sort that are not un-

[8] It would be unfair to emphasize certain "restorations" and shop signs in
Lourdes where the mere name of Soubirous is all a commercial enterprise requires. The miracle of Lourdes is one thing, and its commercial exploitation is
quite another. But religious-minded people cannot help finding it all intensely
shocking.

common with people who have always lived in the same village and whose reputation was well known before the event. Nevertheless, careful investigation enables certain errors to be corrected. The father, François Soubirous, a miller, was a rough, peasant type who was fond of saying that he never had any luck; it was generally asserted that he had never done much to deserve any. From his youth up he was unsettled, going from one employer to another, a jack-of-all-trades rather than a real craftsman, who did as little work as possible. When he was still quite young he married Louise Casterot, Boly's daughter, whose dowry was her father's mill. Here at any rate was a chance. But it was of no avail; very soon he was bankrupt. It must be borne in mind that in those days, the time of Louis Philippe, a bankrupt was commonly looked on as a man disgraced; people would point him out in the street; some of them committed suicide. Now Soubirous was not merely a bankrupt but a man whom no one wished to employ, save out of charity; at the time of the apparitions he existed on casual, seasonal work, lowly tasks that, practically speaking, he had to beg for.

There was probably no more harm in this man, nor perhaps was he any lazier than another, but his misfortunes had embittered him. He was forever dwelling on his ill luck; sometimes at the local tavern banging the table with his fist he would expatiate on the good fortune that had passed him by. His wife, who was of the lower middle class in Lourdes, had become his companion in distress. She was somewhat uncouth, but hard working, and never spared herself; between two confinements she would undertake all sorts of menial work, even the most laborious. For the rest, she was a humble housewife with all the qualities and defects of her condition. Like many poor people she was improvident; she was talkative and welcomed all the gossips of the district to her home, would often forget the time for meals and, when there was some in the house, liked to offer her neighbors "a drop to drink." [9] Of course she was devout, like all the women of Bigorre.[10] In point

[9] One of the reasons, it was asserted, for the bankruptcy of the mill was the Soubirous' excessive generosity. They entertained their customers and kept open house for them. The profits from the flour were turned into meat and wine, in other words, were wasted.

[10] The district round Lourdes.

of fact this couple was an object of pity or contempt at the time their daughter, whom they called Bernadette after her godmother, was born. And it would have required a great deal more than good luck to set them on their feet again.

Good luck did not come. On the contrary ill luck dogged them. Little Bernadette grew up in an atmosphere of hardship, suppressed quarreling, bitterness, and complaining bordering on despair. She was at first put out to nurse at Bartrès, a village some two miles from Lourdes. A few years later she was again sent to this out-of-the-way village to look after the sheep for the Lagüe family. There she had her first catechism lessons from young Father Ader, who became fond of her. Occasionally her father went to see her there and inquired after her health; on one of his brief visits he was quite startled at her credulity.[11] She returned to Lourdes bringing back with her memories of a thatched sheepfold, a good parish priest, a rustic church, and the first symptoms of asthma and tuberculosis which, gradually gaining a hold on her frail body, tormented her with fits of breathlessness and bronchial troubles. A doctor was consulted. He prescribed the usual treatment: rest, sunshine, hygiene, and nourishing food. The cheapest of these remedies would have cost more than her father earned for the support of his whole family.

At the age of ten Bernadette looked like a child of seven. At fourteen she seemed scarcely ten years old. This assertion is made on very good grounds; there is a photograph in existence, taken shortly before the apparitions, which, very fortunately, has not been touched up like those of St. Therese of Lisieux. In this photograph Bernadette is standing, with five companions, in the second row; five companions who, obviously, are of the same age, more or less; all five look more like young women than little girls. Except for one, they are all dressed in black, in their best clothes; decked out in all their finery, they are posing with all the serious-

---

[11] She was leading her sheep home and one of them had a green stain on its back. "Look," said her father, "it's all the grass she's eaten coming out through her back." Bernadette began to cry. "Is she going to die of it?" she sobbed. That little incident should not be seen as anything more than an example of childish simplicity. When she was at the Nevers convent, Bernadette, in telling the story, added, "Why, I didn't even know what it was to tell a lie."

ness the occasion required. It might well be asked what Bernadette was doing in their company, by what special favor she had been allowed to be photographed with them. For if these sturdy, well-filled-out girls, one of them especially, already have something of the grown-up about them, Bernadette with her veil and her shawl hiding the shabbiness beneath looks like a little beggar girl, several years younger. And the astonishing thing is that she alone is smiling. She alone is not posing; keeping an entirely natural attitude, she faces the camera with a look of amusement. She is by far the prettiest, the most pleasant to look at, with an indefinable air of childishness and something rather affecting about her charming face; she has, too, a slightly derisive expression as if she cared not a rap for the honor done her by the photographer and the solemnity of this moment which has frozen the others into a conventional pose.

This photograph will be mentioned again for it provides such unrivaled testimony to Bernadette's youth that without it there would be perhaps an irreparable gap. Leaving aside for the moment the question of Bernadette's presence in this group of the daughters of tradesmen, as likely as not druggists or hardware merchants, our attention may dwell on this picture of a sickly, half-starved child who was yet of happy, vivacious disposition, a child of poverty accustomed to getting the better of it, who looked on the bright side of life. This little girl, who was allowed to appear in the photograph by special favor but with an obvious effort to conceal the poverty of her clothes, gave promise of being a good-looking young woman, pretty above the average, endowed by nature with delicate features—perhaps, in the future, a very beautiful woman. But she was still a child. Everything about her proclaimed privation, hunger, the want of even elementary comfort. She was the daughter of the bankrupt Soubirous. She was the poorest child in Lourdes, the poorest child perhaps in the whole of France.

This is no exaggeration. At the time this photograph was taken the Soubirous family had long been out of the Moulin de Boly. In spite of its tumble-down state, its sweating walls, crumbling staircase and draughty rooms, it was too fine a house for the bankrupt.

E

Turned out of the mill, the Soubirous sought other accommodation in the village. They were directed to the only one befitting their condition, which seemed to be ready waiting for them, the one which nowadays is frequented by crowds and at whose threshold no one, whether believer or unbeliever, can forbear to pause, unable for the moment to pass by, his heart heavy with compassion and tears in his eyes. It was the jail.

For it was indeed the jail—the Lourdes prison. Lourdes possessed a municipal lockup in the Rue des Petits Fossés. Originally a warehouse, it had been disposed of by its owner because of its dilapidated and insanitary condition; it was no longer serviceable for the storage of goods, but in the reign of Louis Philippe, and then of Napoleon III, it was considered good enough for habitual criminals, and for some years the delinquents of the district—the thieves, fire-raisers and murderers—were locked up in it. But after a time the public conscience was pricked: these men's crimes might be very great but they hardly deserved a fate like that, to rot in this filthy cavern, a prey to tuberculosis. A petition was organized and the authorities were stirred to action: an order from the Prefect decreed the closing of the prison. There was no thought of pulling it down, it was left to fall down of itself. And then someone in Lourdes—unfortunately it is unknown who it was—suddenly had the idea that the prison could still be of some use. He sought out Soubirous and told him to go and live there "with his brood." The village heard of what had occurred and signified its approval. The lockup was not fit for criminals, but it was considered a veritable godsend for the Soubirous family and their consumptive daughter.

So Soubirous moved his furniture and together with wife and children took up residence in the lockup. Moving house for him simply meant that he transferred himself and his family there, for it was many a long day since this bankrupt had possessed any furniture save a bed and a dresser. They entered the building, went along a dark and noisome passage and arrived in a hovel measuring some nine by twelve feet. There were no windows, only, of course, holes with bars—the prison bars—across them looking out on the lane. Bed and dresser were moved in, mattresses thrown on the floor, and the whole family camped there as best it could. For a table they made use of the crumbling ledge beneath one of the barred openings, and from it ate their first supper there— black bread and maize porridge—amid the dirt and the dust. They had a roof over their heads, but that was all. To keep out the cold and the rain, Louise Soubirous hung pieces of old cloth in front of the holes in the wall.

In our own day, even if Lourdes did not attract pilgrims and tourists for reasons which have stirred the whole world, I am among those who believe that it should be visited just to see the lockup, and the evidence it adduces of the living conditions of a nineteenth century poverty-stricken family: father, mother, and four children, one of whom was ill. That lockup by itself is worth a pilgrimage. The village has been transformed and has become a town dominated by a double basilica and resplendent with fine houses and luxury hotels; policemen on their little raised platforms direct the traffic and wave on the Buicks, Packards, and Lincolns; electric signs and arrows show the way to the grotto and the over- head railway; an immense airfield is projected where four-engine planes flying direct from London and New York may land. The grotto with its approaches and precincts has gradually swallowed up and destroyed the landscape of fields and cottages.

Bernadette's birthplace, the Moulin de Boly, has been tidied up and gives its visitors an appearance almost of daintiness. But nothing could alter the lockup. It has been made into a chapel— the shrine of Poverty, as Madame Colette Yver so beautifully puts it—with an altar and a statue of Our Lady above it surrounded by three other statues—Our Lady, St. Bernadette as a peasant, and as a nun; on the walls, everywhere, ex-voto tablets jostle one another. But in spite of it all it remains essentially unchanged, haunting and unforgettable, the prison. The barred window is still there, though it no longer overlooks a lane; the sill, on which the Soubirous ate their black bread, its grimy, greenish stone still crumbling away, is there yet. Here are the broken, blackened walls of affliction and of death itself, and within them, through adversity and the wish of the village, dwelt these six poor folk whose sole crime was lack of money. There they dwelt and there they came near to dying, and the continual, confused murmur of the crowd, of these millions upon millions of men and women, can never succeed in muting the râle of the young Bernadette, racked with pain at night on her mattress, or in dispelling her mother's despair as she got up to tuck her in and comfort her, imploring her to be good and not to wake her brothers and her sister.

The fate suffered by this little girl can hardly be expiated save by an all-embracing gesture of forgiveness. It is a heartbreaking experience for anyone who enters this hovel, sees these walls, and can cast his thoughts back to the photograph of that village group in which Bernadette found strength and grace to smile. We can imagine her leaving the group of her companions—when the photographer threw back the black veil which concealed him behind his camera—and running, skipping along the street to her mother to tell her that a fine picture had just been taken; and it would be good indeed to know that on that day at least there was something of a treat in the hovel. But we can be very sure that there was none. On that day as on all the others Louise Soubirous wondered anxiously what she was going to give her children to eat. Their father had sought work, in all humility, from door to door, only to be rebuffed and snubbed. "He couldn't shift for himself, he's only got what he deserved." They dared, all of them, to judge this man who had managed his business badly, but no one knew his quality of soul, nor that in a very short time he would refuse piles of gold. He had been despised for so long that in the end he was distrusted: "Fancy giving work to a rogue like that, given half a chance he'd steal!"

The chance occurred ("I told you so!" was the village's reaction). At the end of 1856 a building contractor pulled down a ramshackle house on the corner of the Rue des Petits Fossés. When the work was completed a beam was left leaning against the Soubirous' wall. It was a heavy beam of old wood; there it remained all the winter, five months in the rain and snow; on March 22, 1857, came a return of intensely cold weather; the children were coughing, Louise was in despair; François could bear it no longer. He caught up his bush hook, chopped off some chips and made a fire. The next day someone at last noticed the old beam standing there, moss covered and rotting. But who had been chipping at it? François Soubirous was arrested, taken to the police station and thrown into prison—the new prison, of course. He stayed there a fortnight, at the end of which they decided to kick him out; he could go and be hanged somewhere else. A fortnight for a few chips of wood. He went back to his own prison.

François Soubirous returned home more embittered than usual, crushed by the weight of his misfortunes. The story of the beam had gone the round of the village, and now the miller Saci was telling anyone who would listen how one of his sacks of flour was missing. The consequence of all this was that no work could be found anywhere. The family in the old prison had previously not enough to eat; now they began to starve to death. The youngest, Jean-Marie, was observed going into church, scratching wax off candles and quickly gobbling it up. When sometimes some lean provision of food was obtained, the starving children forced open the dresser door to get their hands on it. And Bernadette's parents, awakened often by her wheezing and coughing, recalled the doctor's dictum that unless she were given plenty of nourishing food she would not survive.

Bernadette's illness was not their only worry in her regard; the village gave additional reasons for commiserating—sheer hypocrisy this—with the bankrupt on possessing such a daughter. There was indeed no question of her morals. The most that could be urged against her was a certain lack of cleanliness, she was not very tidy, inclined to be verminous (though living in such a hovel she can hardly be blamed for that). Her manners were engaging and she was so extremely gentle that it is tempting to give the word its out-of-date meaning with its implications of a certain nobility. Strange though it is in the case of a little girl so extremely poor, Bernadette was "well born," as well as being pleasant, affectionate, willing, polite to a degree rare among her kind and by no means a prude [12] though entirely opposed, of course, to loose talk (she was angry if anyone swore in her presence). All the same,

[12] Someone met her one day carrying a baby in her arms. "This is my little brother," she said, "I'm looking for mother to suckle him."

these quite considerable qualities could not disguise a very serious shortcoming; Bernadette, it was asserted, was stupid; but stupid was hardly the word for it. She could not understand when matters, the more difficult portions of the catechism for example, were explained to her. This accusation was to follow her all her life. Many years later, at the Lourdes orphanage and at the Nevers convent, this "total lack of intelligence" was imputed to her. If it was objected that, on the contrary, Bernadette possessed a certain native wit and attempt to prove it was made by quoting any number of her actions, remarks, or sallies—whether from firsthand knowledge or from report—the answer was always the same: see the report drawn up by the Fathers of Garison which was published in the *Journal de la Grotte* on April 30, 1869.

"Bernadette Soubirous spoke without being at all moved; she gradually showed a little more animation, but her joy was never expressed with real warmth" (the good Fathers are obviously not referring to her ecstasies). "She was really quite insignificant. In this child there was no versatility of mind or variety of imagination; she could never shed her reserve; hers was not the pleasing manner of speech which would have drawn great crowds to belief in the visions and no one was less capable of arousing enthusiasm. . . ."

This pen portrait hardly rings true in comparison with the photograph. A face cannot lie. Bernadette's likeness, permanently recorded by the negative, gives a far greater impression of intelligence, of a certain mischievousness, than those of her companions, even though they probably understood their catechism lessons very well. But it is a fact that everyone in Lourdes considered Bernadette "insignificant," "common," [13] or "backward." [14] She had never been able to learn the French that they tried to teach her at school.[15] She was the despair of her mistresses. She herself agreed that she was stupid. "What a fool I am," she ex-

[13] Father Pomian.
[14] Dr. Dozous.
[15] At the time of the apparitions the Pope's nephew, Rafaele Cinnasi, interrogated her in French. To his question, "Did you really see Our Lady?" she answered, "Yes with my eyes," saying *avec mes œils* whereas the plural of *œil* (an eye) is *yeux.*

claimed, "it's quite true I'm an absolute fool!" Nor should her well-known remark, uttered a year before her death at the convent, be forgotten: "If Our Lady could have found a greater fool than I, she would have chosen her."

Her father, François Soubirous, shared the general opinion about his daughter. He had been born under an unlucky star; he was doomed throughout his life to bear several crosses. Bernadette, his sickly, backward child, was one of them. And as he watched her growing, smiling, weeping, suffering before his eyes, did he ever, it may be wondered, ask himself what would be her future? For the time being, the present absorbed his whole attention. Sufficient unto the day was the evil thereof.

It is related that a short time before February 11, 1858, François Soubirous earned a meager franc (about twenty cents) by undertaking a job that no one else would do; he collected the dirty linen at the hospital—the used, discarded dressings and pus-sodden lint—and carried them in a basket on his shoulders to the Lourdes rubbish dump which was situated behind the grotto at Massabielle. It is said that on the same day a dealer in the village, one Alexandrine Baron, offered Bernadette a penny to pick up old bones and scrap metal for her. Father and daughter make their first appearance in history as rag and bone pickers.

Rubbish and dead wood and old rags, and then, soon afterward, the sovereign miracle of humility; the child of a poor man, the poorest child in France who is ordered to eat earth and obeys, on her knees, with not a flicker of revolt, without a murmur; such humility requires no comment, not a word, nothing else but silence will suffice.

III

We examined a photograph, and leaving it now, turning over, as it were, the pages of an album, we look at another more bewildering, more extraordinary than the first. This time Bernadette is portrayed alone.

Representations of the little visionary of Lourdes are, it must be confessed, as various as they are execrable. St. Sebastian had his Mantegna, Giotto achieved immortality by painting St. Francis; our own times furnish nothing better for insertion in prayer books than dreadful illustrations of the picture post card genre. From time to time, fortunately, some obscure photographer with his ancient apparatus secures an immortal picture.

I wonder if the village photographer of Lourdes by recording Bernadette Soubirous' image for the second time knew that he was effecting something more than a priceless document, that he was achieving something which was not far off a work of art. No one can say when exactly or on what particular occasion this second photograph was taken.[16] It matters little, it is enough that it was taken after the visions and not, like the first, before them. The fact that Bernadette is posing by herself is itself significant proof, for this time her vain, plump companions in their Sunday best no longer feature in the picture. The whole rather ludicrous band has made off, scared away by the manifestation of the supernatural; Bernadette in dress shawl and veil remains alone, holding the forefront of the field. But she no longer appears as the gay, smiling little girl who, poor as she was, entirely dominated the situation and looked as if she could hardly contain her laughter or restrain herself from playing some prank. This second picture shows a mature human being, facing the camera with an unwavering gaze that seems not of mortal man; it is the look of one who has been for an instant in touch with the Unknowable and the Infinite.

No engraving, no painting, no image of Bernadette whether on paper, canvas or wood is to be compared with this amazing photograph; its technical perfection far surpasses all the most sensational results obtained by modern picture hunters and all the connoisseurs of back-lighting and soft focus. There are no "frills," no attempt to stage the subject or to study the angle and plane of presentation; the artist intrudes not at all, he has confined his activity to focusing the image and pressing the shutter, and succeeds in showing the futility of all the progress and research since Daguerre. This village photographer did not even trouble to hang a back

[16] It was taken, probably at a relative's house, three years after the apparitions.

cloth behind his subject, he arranged no scenery, there were no properties to encumber him. Bernadette is portrayed sitting there quite naturally on a chair which is concealed by the folds of her long black dress; the toe of one shoe is just peeping out. Quite naturally, too, her rosary is held tightly between her joined hands. Her long, delicate fingers are interlocked. Her shawl, held in place by a hidden pin, comes down to her wrists partially hiding her blouse and its sleeves. Her head is almost entirely covered by a veil, but her hair, parted in the middle, just peeps out beneath it. This veil, as is customary in that part of France, comes down to her waist. Between veil and shawl emerges the face with its unwavering glance.

Bernadette's face in this picture has nothing in common with that other, taken some time before, almost, it seems, on the spur of the moment. Nor is it in any way like those from other sources, showing us a Bernadette imbued with angelic sanctity, all drawn or painted with the date 1858 carefully in prominence; these pictures depict a "pretty-pretty," affected, mincing little creature. But what is surprising in this Rembrandt-like photograph is its tragic appearance. The face it portrays bears the seal of a superhuman fate. It makes one pause and examine meticulously, with intense emotion, every detail of the picture: the wide, full, intelligent forehead, the ideally regular eyebrows, the perfectly shaped nose, the faultless lips, the flawlessly oval-shaped mouth. It is no longer a face that we are examining, but a mask of amazing beauty, in which can be discerned no influence of heredity, education or environment. Bernadette might have come into the world just at the time when the great Event seemed entirely to refashion her mortal clay. The visionary of Lourdes, withdrawn from the ordinary circumstances of her life, freed from the uncertainties of this earth, seems to appear from some sphere unknown, belonging to the afterlife or a prenatal existence entirely outside our ken. And then comes the realization that her eyes are piercing because she is not seeking us; they are fixed solely on an interior spiritual world. From all other pictures of Bernadette there look out at us those fine large eyes of hers, fully expressive of all that is gentle and kindly, dreamy and somewhat pathetic; but here her gaze contemplates a secret world, a world of suffering and mercy. Better than any lesson, any sermon or homily from the clergy, it teaches the Christian the tragedy of grace and solitude, that there is no fate more fearful for a human being than to be chosen by God for a special purpose.

Father Peyremale, the parish priest of Lourdes, as we have seen, at the outset adopted an attitude of prudence bordering on skepticism. At the beginning of the apparitions, he supposed, like many others, that Bernadette was just another deluded young girl to be classed with all those girls and children of that century who claimed to have experienced communication with the supernatural. On the other hand the "miracle" of Bourriette, the quarryman, had certainly shaken him a little; shortly afterward he was told of three cases in his parish, Marie Daube, Bernarde Soubie, and Fabien Baron who had risen from their beds and spurned their crutches after applying water brought them from the spring.

Father Peyremale's first real connection with the "Lourdes affair" occurred when the district authorities decided to shut Bernadette up in a mental asylum. At this point the parish priest suddenly decided on action. His disbelief was by no means weakened, but this powerfully built country priest, though something of a rough diamond, was kindly, and he loved a fight; all at once he realized what was going on: on one side was authority and on the other a poor fourteen-year-old shepherdess without support of any kind. Almost instinctively he rushed to the help of the harassed child. He realized what confinement would mean to Bernadette, particularly in those days when science was making no headway in the treatment of madness, when lunatics of all categories were shut up for the remainder of their lives without consideration of their condition. Besides, he was sure that Bernadette was not mad. He knew her well, had kept her under close observation for the preceding fortnight, and taken counsel with his assistant, Father Pomian, who was her confessor; even if she was suffering from a passing aberration or was simulating ecstasy—that, he considered, was insufficient reason for her to exchange the prison where she lived for the padded cell.

Baron Massy had given orders to the mayor for Bernadette's immediate arrest and her transfer to the asylum at Tarbes. Father Peyremale crossed the Rubicon. He called at the town hall and secured an interview with the mayor. "I will defend this child with my life," he told him. "Please inform the Prefect," he went on, "that his police will find me before her door, and that they will cross the threshold only over my body."

A country parish priest, supported by his flock, is not to be resisted. The order for Bernadette's arrest was not carried out. But Father Peyremale was now confronted with other problems. In the first place he must safeguard Bernadette against future danger of this kind, and then, too, she must be rescued from the slum in which she dwelt. For the prison was beginning to give scandal; the devout were growing indignant at the destitution of the visionary; and yet to improve the lot of her family, or even to provide them with a certain security and comfort, would cause a still greater scandal. There was only one thing to be done. The Lourdes infirmary took in boarders. Father Peyremale installed Bernadette there. Now for the first time in her life, perhaps, she had enough to eat. She was taught reading, writing, and sewing. Strict orders were given that she was not to be questioned or disturbed in any way but treated just like an ordinary inmate lost in the throng of her companions.

This was no abduction, nor was it a plot, with Bernadette for center, to manufacture the legend of Lourdes. Father Peyremale's behavior, in this respect, is beyond reproach. He continued to harbor considerable doubts about the authenticity of the visions and, indeed, held himself to be personally outside the whole affair. The "miracles" happened to occur in his parish; that was all. He informed the competent authority, that is, his bishop, of the course of events. On July 28, 1858, Bishop Laurence wrote telling him that a commission of inquiry had been set up and asking whether he would not only give evidence before it (as, of course, he would) but also be its chairman. Father Peyremale replied, strenuously refusing this position of honor. He would confine himself, he said, to welcoming the committee, giving evidence, introducing Bernadette to it, and praying that all might be made clear.

On November 17, 1858, almost four months to the day after the last apparition of the Lady, the ecclesiastical committee of inquiry arrived in Lourdes, settled into its quarters and began its work. Its first care, obviously, was to summon Bernadette. As may well be imagined the investigators were very curious to see this sickly fourteen-year-old child who was brought before them, though it was by no means the first time that a committee of inquiry interrogated a visionary or a miracle worker—as was pointed out, the nineteenth century is full of them—and the whole series of questions was ready prepared, bristling with snares and traps of all sorts. The case of Bernadette was studied from beginning to end, from her earliest infancy right up to her revelations; the slightest features of her character were investigated—even her practical jokes and childish pranks as a girl at school were brought up against her. Directly the committee came to the apparitions at the grotto they showered questions on her.

"What was the secret the Lady imparted to you?"

"If I told you, it would be a secret no longer."

"And if our Holy Father the Pope himself were to ask you?" After some hesitation, Bernadette replied:

"But the Pope's a man, too, I should tell him nothing."

"What prayer did Our Lady tell you to say?"

"The Glory be to the Father."

"Why not the *Pater* and *Ave?*" [17]

"I did what she told me."

"Why did you eat grass? Only animals eat grass."

"But you eat salads, don't you?"

"Why did you kiss the ground?"

"The Lady told me to do so for the conversion of sinners," Bernadette replied.

So the interrogation went on, broken off now and then for the investigation of side issues and to receive the evidence of others: the inhabitants of Lourdes and its district, doctors and even chemists and geologists on the subject of the spring; finally Bishop Laurence himself required from Bernadette for the last time a

[17] This was a catch question: the Blessed Virgin, praying with Bernadette, would not address herself.

complete account of the apparitions. Bernadette complied and the committee thereupon declared its sittings concluded.

Three years went by before the Church, by the mouth of the bishop of Tarbes, pronounced judgment.[18] Bernadette was still at the infirmary. It seemed likely that the verdict would be published in August, 1861. But when the time came the silence was not broken; the diocesan authorities maintained their guarded attitude. At last, on January 18, 1862, Bishop Laurence published a pastoral letter in which he recognized the reality of the apparitions of Lourdes.

There was a great outburst of joy in the whole district and throughout France; and also a wave of anger. The first official pilgrimages began and, at the same time, attacks on the part of skeptics and unbelievers. Lourdes became simultaneously one of the important places of Christendom and a perpetual scandal to all those who recoiled before any manifestation of the supernatural.

Bernadette, meanwhile, remote from these controversies and outbursts of enthusiasm, carried out her task to the end and accomplished her destiny to the last.

It is recorded that Bernadette, who was still at the infirmary, had to endure the visits of numerous persons—on an average of twenty a day—and that she was confronted with one who showed, to say the least, bad taste. The mother superior of a convent arrived with a complete outfit for a nun which she made the little shepherd girl try on, dressing her up, combing out her hair, showing her the effect in a mirror. "Our habit suits you, doesn't it, my dear? You would be much happier with us than anywhere else, wouldn't you?" It is to the credit of the ecclesiastical authorities that they pointed out to this mother-superior-turned-dressmaker the impropriety of her conduct and quickly showed her the door.

As a matter of fact Bernadette for some time past had shown a desire to be a nun. Here again there is no question of her being

18 The ecclesiastical commission waited five years before making up its mind about La Salette; one year was enough for the apparitions of Pontmain, but thirteen were to be required for Fatima.

forced to go away, and no one could imàgine for a moment or dare
to say that it was a more or less mysterious disappearance like that,
some years later, of Lucia of Fatima. By the public expression of
her wish to be a nun Bernadette remained true to her destiny. No
one, in the end, was in doubt what her final choice would be. Just
for a month or two it was noticed at the infirmary that she formed
a certain attachment to some of the things of this earth. She was
susceptible to the attractions of fine clothes and endeavored to be
smart; after all, such an attitude is easily understood in a young
girl who until then possessed nothing but rags. Historians who like
details of the sort may mention with a smile that two or three
times Bernadette was caught in front of a mirror in the act of
trying a blouse with leg-of-mutton sleeves or the effect of a bit of
ribbon. At the most it was a venial sin, and well might be no sin
at all. This phase of concern for her appearance did not last long
and was but a prelude to her coming great renunciation.

Bernadette was a peasant and so remained all her life. Peasants
feel very strongly the ties of their native soil and their family; the
little shepherdess of Lourdes fainted when she had to leave her
parents. This occurred in 1866 when Bernadette was twenty-two.
The poor, hunger-stricken child, who had "encountered" Our
Lady at Massabielle, by this time had grown into a serious though
very pleasant young woman who was no longer ignorant. She had
learned to read and write French; her neat writing was admired
as well as her faultless spelling and the elegant turn of her sentences; nothing was left, so it seemed, of the little ragpicker of
days gone by. But there remained unfortunately something of her
wretched past, of the dreadful heritage of the disused prison;
tuberculosis had taken hold of this defective constitution. On
July 4, 1866, then, Bernadette who shortly before had said farewell
to her relations and to the grotto left Lourdes definitively for the
convent of the Sisters of Charity of Nevers.

She set out, it could be said, at the height of her fame. That very
year, during the celebrations held in the crypt, it had been necessary to protect her from the excited fervor of the crowds. She was
leaving now a Lourdes that was transformed, a village that was
turned into a town, peopled with believers who never dreamed of

questioning the truth of the apparitions. Everyone, the authorities to the ordinary village folk, Father Peyremale foremost among them, had "come over" to Bernadette; morally and materially speaking she had made the fortune of this district of Bigorre. We saw how François Soubirous had most creditably refused the money that he might well have taken; in the end, however, he accepted another house, went back to his trade, and in a few years had become a prosperous miller. But as the coach bore Bernadette away from Lourdes and her family, from its back window she could gaze on the walls of the new sanctuary beginning to rise above their surroundings; she could contemplate, too, the crowd of worshippers which daily collected at the grotto to pray fervently for miracles without number. The decision rested entirely with her; she could have remained in her own district, an object of praise and admiration, with every sort of earthly success at her feet. But she scorned this royal road.

All the convents in France had vied with one another to receive her. It might well be thought that further fame awaited her at Nevers, but to do so betrays misunderstanding of the church's plans for Bernadette and the dearest wish of this twenty-two-year-old young woman whom her own village called "the saint."

This book is concerned with the study of miracles; complete and detailed biographies of the miracle workers are somewhat outside its scope. I may be pardoned, therefore, for not devoting a long chapter to Bernadette's life at Nevers. On the other hand, some mention must be made of the conditions which governed her reception and her life there and the circumstances of her last years, which were spent at the convent. At Nevers there awaited Bernadette the humility of her childhood days. On arrival she made the acquaintance of the superior, the Mother General, Josephine Imbert, and the novice mistress, Mother Marie-Thérèse Vauzou, in whose particular charge she was. Mother Vauzou has been the object of fierce criticism couched, not infrequently, in ill-considered and extremely blunt language. She has been blamed, even by her fellow nuns, for the treatment of Bernadette. But before passing judgment on her it is necessary to go back to that historic day when the Sisters of Charity admitted that "vessel of election," the little shepherdess who had *seen* the Mother of Christ: a sacred trust it no doubt was, but also a somewhat formidable one, for these nuns' first duty was to incorporate Bernadette into ordinary community life; in the event every effort was made to do this, and—after all the nuns were only human—there was a tendency perhaps to overdo it. Particular stress was laid on humility and passive obedience.

Bernadette was welcomed with an eager curiosity that may be imagined and the nuns, we may well believe, even in their dreams were obsessed by the arrival of one already acclaimed a saint by popular estimation. At first her youth, her impulsive, natural turn of character and speech caused some surprise. On her way to the convent she had wept; on arrival she underwent an abrupt change and appeared full of gaiety, inquiring about the games played by the novices, especially about their skipping game "because I am very fond of holding the rope for the others." From the outset, two parties, if I may so speak about life in a convent, were formed at Nevers; on the one side were the professed nuns, very much on their guard where the "saint" was concerned, and on the other, the novices who from the first took her part and held her in great affection. Bernadette, on entering the convent, lost her name and became Sister Marie-Bernarde. She had to lose even the memory of her fame and the great stir that she had caused throughout the world. It was considered proper, therefore, to entrust her with suitable manual tasks; at first she was sent to scrub the stone floors and afterward to do the washing up.

From these tasks she was transferred to the infirmary, first as infirmarian, then as a patient; last of all, she acted as sacristan, concerned, that is, with the altar linen and the decoration of the sanctuary.

There is abundant evidence about Bernadette's life as a nun—most of it the direct testimony of the nuns themselves; we could almost follow her month by month but that, I repeat, lies outside the scope of this book. We should, however, note the essential points of the severe measures of discipline that were adopted in her regard. It was forbidden to speak to her about Lourdes, or to treat her differently from an ordinary nun. These measures were maintained even when illness was ravaging the little nun's body; no special favor was granted her, except that after a hemorrhage had recurred on several days running, she was allowed to take her vows and received the veil as a professed nun, and even then, when it seemed that she was recovering the Mother General exclaimed, "You little ninny! I believe you knew you weren't going to die and you didn't say so. If you are not dead by tomorrow, I shall take your veil away from you." These cruel words give some clue to the sort of treatment Bernadette received. A Sister of Charity could write, many years later, "It was not very pleasant to be Bernadette at Nevers."

This evidence concerning Bernadette's life in the convent is, of its very nature, controversial, and the opponents of the supernatural are within their rights in rejecting it when an attempt is made to prove the authenticity of the miracles of Lourdes by citing the views of the nuns of Nevers about them. No one knows if among the Sisters of Charity there were any to be found who doubted the reality of the apparitions; the plain fact that the great majority of them were convinced of this reality is of no value to the impartial historian. But the psychological evidence provided by the anecdotes of Bernadette's convent life and her sayings there cannot be rejected out of hand. It exists in considerable quantity and indicates an uncommon degree of humility. A postulant arrived at a time when Sister Marie-Bernarde was with the superior and asked immediately to be allowed to see Bernadette. The superior, turning towards the visionary, indicated her with a gesture. The postulant gazed at her for a moment. "Oh," she exclaimed, "is that all?" "Yes," replied Bernadette, laughing, "that's all!" A little later a nun asked her, "Who do you think you are?" "Who am I?" answered Bernadette. "Why, Sister, what do you do with a broom when you've finished with it?"

"Well, you put it in a corner behind the door."

"Exactly. That's what I am, a broom."

Numerous trials served only to strengthen this humility. One of the hardest occurred at the public ceremony for the profession of the Sisters (October 31, 1867). On that day the Bishop of Nevers, Monseigneur Forcade, came to the convent to announce the desti-

F

nation of the Sisters who were to be sent to undertake various work in towns all over France. He read them out, one by one, but Bernadette was not in the list. "And what about Sister Marie-Bernarde?" he asked at the end. "Oh, as for her, Monseigneur," replied the superior, before the crowded congregation, "we hardly know what to do with her. She's good for nothing." This public insult had been pre-arranged; it was an additional trial which, we are told, though it made Bernadette turn pale at the time, a moment or two later she had apparently forgotten.

It was said that she could not meditate. "Indeed I can't," she agreed, "I can only pray." But that did not prevent her spending long hours absorbed in thought, especially when she was left free to sit in the garden at a spot where there stood a statue of Our Lady—the only one that appears to have found favor in her eyes.[19] "Every day," she wrote in a letter to Lourdes, "I go in spirit to my dear grotto at Massabielle and make my pilgrimage there." Although she was living retired from the world she sometimes received news from it. The most distressing was that which told her of the death of her mother, followed quickly by that of her father. The Soubirous parents had not enjoyed their new-found prosperity for long. Both died within a short time of each other and both with every sign of genuine piety. (François Soubirous, particularly, had greatly changed; he was discovered on several occasions kneeling before a picture of his daughter and so lost in prayer that he was unaware of the presence of others.)

News of one sort and another trickled through to Nevers; the most startling concerned the miraculous cures. Occasionally, too, the turmoil of the outside world beat against the walls of the convent; pilgrims assembled with the hope of catching a glimpse and possibly of even touching the visionary, and, as formerly at

[19] Bernadette disliked exceedingly and even laughed at all statues of Our Lady of Lourdes. "It's a shame," she asserted, "to dare to make such a caricature of the holy Mother of God!" From an aesthetic point of view it can hardly be denied that she was right; her good taste was admirable and in this case more reliable than that of the Curé d'Ars. It is true, of course, that she had *seen* Our Lady. "Oh no!" Bernadette exclaimed, "she's not a bit like these dreadful things."

Lourdes, the crowd had to be held at bay for fear the clothes would be torn from Bernadette's back. The rule of the Order, of course, entirely forbade such noisy manifestations. The most that was finally permitted was that certain women visitors, friends of the community, were enabled just to see Bernadette in the parlor. In addition to the Bishop of Nevers, only two men enjoyed this privilege—one was another prelate for whom a special arrangement was made whereby Bernadette, summoned by a novice, appeared motionless for a few seconds at the window giving on the garden, ostensibly to pick a flower, and the other was a young seminarist who obtained permission to speak to her. She smiled at him very charmingly, called him "young man," made him promise to serve God with all his heart, and foretold that he would have to undergo intense spiritual struggles and physical sufferings. I do not include, of course, the community doctor who, on more than one occasion, was called to see the little nun in the throes of illness.

One of the professors of the Medical Faculty of Paris, Dr. Voisin, expressed in public his views on the "Lourdes affair" and taught his pupils that the "pathological liar Bernadette Soubirous" had been placed out of harm's way in the Nevers mental hospital. The community doctor had no difficulty in refuting these assertions; he invited his colleague to undertake the journey, promising that, as a special favor, he should be received by Bernadette herself. Dr. Voisin did not reply. At this time (after 1870, and the terrible year that Bernadette spent on her bed of sickness) the question arose in men's minds: why did not the visionary of Lourdes, stricken with tuberculosis, ask for her own cure at the grotto? And at Nevers, too, the question was asked; the visionary replied in the negative, merely repeating the words that Our Lady had said to her: "I promise to make you happy not in this world, but in the next. The spring is not for me," she added. The disease, however, continued to make headway, and Bernadette's resistance in spite of her weak constitution caused general astonishment. On several occasions she was thought to be on the point of dying and was given the Sacraments; she appeared to possess unsuspected physical resources, the consequence, probably, of her peasant ancestry, of being used in her childhood to hardships, and, in the last place, to her frugal, temperate habits.

When the time came when it was quite obvious that Sister Marie-Bernarde was soon to die, the need was felt, so to say, to "tidy up" her case. Surely, it was thought, the visionary of Lourdes could not die without revealing at least a part of her secret. In the first place she was studied from the religious and theological viewpoint: there was some discussion about how much she had struggled against evil, and on the other hand, how far God had worked on her soul. It was an entirely ecclesiastical question and does not concern us here. More especially, and from another point of view, there was some anxiety about the secrets that Our Lady had entrusted to her. It seemed unthinkable that Bernadette should take them with her to the tomb. She maintained silence about them before the commission of investigation; it was now decided to question her on the subject for the last time.

So, when she was *in extremis,* a second commission appeared in Nevers; this time its function was not to establish the authenticity of the apparitions, but to demand the secret which, it was commonly supposed, concerned the means of gaining heaven. Bernadette, who was nearly on the point of death, received the commission with her usual kindness and simplicity, but was no more willing to disclose her secrets than on the previous occasion. Requests couched in the most solemn manner could not make her speak. The investigators were obliged to confess themselves beaten and withdrew extremely vexed and not a little edified. They had received from Bernadette one final reward: she had described once again for their benefit the whole series of apparitions, she had repeated verbatim the words of Our Lady, except, of course, the "secrets," and in addition they had been privileged to behold what all who saw it assert was the wonderful sight of Bernadette making the sign of the cross. It was a gesture graceful and beautiful beyond human ken; thus, said Bernadette, the Lady had taught her to make it. A precise description is nowhere to be found of this sign of the cross which, save for the ineffable impression it produced, was made in the ordinary way. It was, as it were, inherent testimony to the apparitions of Lourdes. Bernadette never afterward signed herself in any other way.

On April 16, 1879, at a quarter-past three in the afternoon, Sister Marie-Bernarde, in the world Bernadette Soubirous, died at the convent of Nevers. Her last words were: "Holy Mary, Mother of God, pray for me, a poor sinner . . ." She repeated the words "poor sinner" and then came the end.

For three days the body lay in the chapel; it was then buried in the convent garden inside an oratory dedicated to St. Joseph. The inscription on the tombstone read as follows:

HERE LIES
IN THE PEACE OF THE LORD
BERNADETTE SOUBIROUS
IN 1858 AT LOURDES HONORED WITH SEVERAL APPARITIONS
OF THE MOST HOLY VIRGIN
IN RELIGION SISTER MARIE-BERNARDE
WHO DIED AT NEVERS
AT THE MOTHER HOUSE OF THE SISTERS OF CHARITY
ON APRIL 16, 1879
IN THE 36TH YEAR OF HER AGE
AND THE TWELFTH OF HER RELIGIOUS PROFESSION

Thirty years later, on September 22, 1909, the body was exhumed for the purpose of the beatification process; it was in a state of perfect preservation, dull white in color, the mouth slightly open, showing the teeth, the eyes closed, slightly sunk in their sockets; the arms still showed the veins in relief. The body was washed before being put back in the coffin. On April 18, 1925, a second exhumation took place in accordance with the rubric. The body was again found intact save for some desiccation of the chest and an accentuated brownish coloring of the face (which was attributed to the washing at the previous exhumation). When the bottom right rib was removed (to be sent to Rome) a small portion of the liver came away on the scalpel; placed on a piece of white linen it left a reddish stain. Nowadays the body of Bernadette Soubirous is exposed to full view, enshrined in the convent chapel at Nevers. The visionary of Lourdes is dressed in her habit as a nun, her face, turned slightly to one side, is covered with a thin coating of wax. Her hands are crossed as if in prayer. The sanctuary is open to the public and pilgrims without number visit it.

IV

At this point it is proper to examine more closely the elements of the miracle of Lourdes: we shall study first the *authenticity of the apparitions,* then the *spring,* and finally the *cures* attributed to it.

1. AUTHENTICITY OF THE APPARITIONS

About the authenticity of the apparitions we have Bernadette's evidence and no other; strictly speaking, if we apply the old maxim *testis unus, testis nullus,* it is valueless for that reason.

Contrary to what happened, or what is supposed to have happened, at La Salette, Pontmain, and Fatima, in this case we possess the statement of only one visionary. One of the first results of this is our inability to confront her statements with those of others, to cross-check them, to consider them in isolation before collating them with other statements to detect contradictions or similarities. Our only possibility is to interrogate Bernadette and detect her in the act of self-contradiction; it is clear, therefore, that under these conditions, all the child has to do is to keep to the same carefully learned story. It should be added that her story never varied over a period of many years.

Bernadette asserted that on eighteen occasions she was the witness of a supernatural apparition. There are four possible hypotheses: (1) *She was telling the truth;* (2) *She was lying;* (3) *She was mistaken;* (4) *She was deceived by others.* We can examine this last hypothesis first.

Several authors have assumed that Bernadette was deceived by the clergy or the inhabitants of Lourdes who were anxious to start a concern which materially and spiritually should be profitable to religion. Some have repeated the story ascribing the whole affair to a hoax perpetrated by a local woman. Camille Flam marion goes so far as to name her. This Madame P., who in 1858 was living at Lourdes with a Lieutenant Garido (of the 42nd regiment of the line), is supposed to have played the part of Our Lady at Massabielle for the sole purpose of hoaxing a credulous shepherdess. Investigation brought to light that on February 8, 1858, three days, therefore, before the apparitions, Madame P. had given birth to a daughter; consequently it seems obvious that she had nothing to do with the apparitions.

Contemporary newspapers, on the other hand, among others *Les Débats, Le Siècle, Le Lavedan,* in their opposition to a supernatural explanation of the events of Lourdes, all maintained for some time that the whole thing had been staged. They relied on a letter alleged to have been written by the Procurator-General Falconnet, of Pau, to the Procurator Dutour of Lourdes. This letter dispatched at the end of 1857 gave warning that there was "a plot afoot in Lourdes to produce certain manifestations of an alleged supernatural, miraculous nature." But it should be pointed out that the existence of this letter has never been proved; it was never found in the municipal archives, and the first mention of it occurs several years after the event; finally, and this is certainly the essential point, Monsieur Falconnet himself never alluded to it. Although he was entirely opposed to a supernatural explanation, in writing to his minister in Paris he confined himself to remarking, "The legal authorities here have watched the affair very closely with a view to instituting a prosecution, but there were no grounds for doing so. The position is entirely unlike that of Rose Tamisier who fabricated a miracle. In this case the child is the victim of hallucination, but sincere. She has certainly seen, or thinks she has seen, something."

Father Ader remains to be considered. A good deal of ink has flowed concerning his part in the affair, and Émile Zola wrote at length about him. Father Ader was parish priest of Bartrès at the time when Bernadette was a shepherdess there; she was a member of his catechism class. More important still, he took a particular interest in her and was very fond of her; he was even heard to say, "I find the appearance of this little girl exceedingly moving. I believe that the children of La Salette must be just like that."

This is an instance, then, of remarkable intuition or else it is the starting point for the fabrication of the miracle of Lourdes. Some time before the apparitions at the grotto, Father Ader had been moved to another parish; there is no evidence that he was ever in touch with the Lourdes clergy and, in any case, he took no part at all in subsequent events. Moreover, it is difficult to imagine him informing Father Peyremale of his proposed plot, taking into account what we know of the latter and his extreme unwillingness to believe Bernadette at the outset. Father Ader will be mentioned again in connection with Bernadette's alleged hallucinations.

Before we leave this theory (that Bernadette was deceived by others) the possibility of a plot by the Soubirous parents must be considered. It should be noticed that not one of their contemporaries advanced this theory, although it is an obvious suggestion to make. The Soubirous were poor and naturally desired to improve their wretched position, but it seems, surely, that to adopt methods of this nature would have been somewhat beyond their intelligence or the means at their disposal. It was no direct advantage to them to publish abroad the sanctity of their daughter—they were not hotelkeepers in the district like Rose Tamisier's cousin—and all they could hope for as a result would have been gifts in money or in kind from the devout. But it has been seen how energetically they refused such gifts, almost, on occasion, to the point of exaggeration. Bernadette herself, one day, so far lost her temper as to strike a visitor who had left a golden louis on the table. On some days the amount of these gifts would have been enough to provide a certain degree of comfort; if the whole affair was a plot by the Soubirous for their own advantage, the temptation to profit by it would surely have proved too strong. But the Soubirous, on the contrary, remained poor for long years afterward, and although in the end they enjoyed a certain measure of prosperity it was only obtained by means of loans raised in the normal way when they were told by the clergy that they should live in a manner befitting their position. There are no grounds at all for suspecting the integrity of this family. And what opinion are we to form of the *duplicity* of a child who, to enrich her family, was willing to agree to the sacrifice of her own life and pass the rest of her days in a convent?

Was Bernadette lying? At the outset this was the generally accepted opinion. Biographers as keenly sympathetic as Madame Yver record that this was the view of the women of the town. To suspect lying in such circumstances is a natural and instinctive reaction.

Was Bernadette untruthful? Perhaps she was, but only in the way of all other little girls of her age: in other words she was fond of practical jokes and playing pranks, a characteristic without which she would have been abnormal. After all, a young girl of fourteen—even a future saint—cannot be expected to display that complete adhesion to reality which is reached by few even in riper years. The Lourdes apparitions coincided with Bernadette's reaching puberty, the age at which pathological disregard of the truth is common. Bernadette's case was the subject of long and careful investigation on this point, and it must be admitted that if falsehood is present her case is exceptional, and to all intents and purposes an impossibility. In this respect she should be compared with the large numbers of children who have been convicted of lying on matters relating to mystical phenomena.[20]

Whatever a child's ability to lie—and it is very generally quite considerable, far greater than an adult's—it cannot withstand such a daily inquisition as that undergone by Bernadette. The usual motives for lying are vanity and the desire to astonish, to make people talk about oneself. Now the first thing that is remarkable about Bernadette is not merely her profound humility but the conviction, expressed by her whole personality, that she has done nothing out of the ordinary. At no time was she perceived to play a part, or to give herself airs, or in any way seek publicity for herself. She gave an account of the apparitions only if constrained, if obliged to, she avoided inquisitive people, she hid away at home during the celebrations in the crypt when the crowd acclaimed her and when she needed only to appear to be the object of their adulation. No objection of even the most harmless vanity can be urged against her; not the smallest gesture, the slightest

20 Cf. Chapter 5, on the "epidemic" of Beauraing.

word of hers, is open to criticism on this score, and in the whole record of the events of Lourdes not one witness is to be found who mentions anything of the sort.

At Fatima on the day when "the sun danced" a Portuguese journalist recorded that the visionary Lucia spoke dramatically about the end of the war; in Bernadette's case there was never anything like that. Did she lie for the sake of lying? It should not be forgotten that Bernadette never contradicted herself. She underwent arduous and distressing interrogation (among others at the hands of the Imperial Procurator when all sorts of traps were laid for her) and never once made a mistake; not once was she upset or did she appear obviously to wrestle with her memory. Either she was sincere or else she possessed an exceptionally gifted brain. Was it a case of secondary personality? That could hardly have been a permanent condition. Bernadette was at the mercy of a running fire of questions every day, without warning. In the Procurator's office, as in the orphanage recreation yard where her playmates despite the prohibition clamored for her story as they skipped over the rope she held, no one ever caught her up. She always narrated the facts quite straightforwardly, as if they concerned an ordinary occurrence, a chance encounter. She never even boasted that the Lady had addressed her with the formal *vous* instead of the familiar *tu* and had spoken so courteously in asking her to make the fortnight's pilgrimage to the grotto. Later reflection produced the same reaction in her as in others, predominantly one of astonishment. She never confused one apparition with another. Lastly, her account never varied, and the story she told in her fourteenth year was, point by point, identical with the one she told on her deathbed.

Furthermore, even those who believe that Bernadette was a liar are forced to yield to reality: this "lie" determined her whole life. Once again Bernadette fulfilled her destiny. We can agree with Pascal that witnesses who suffer for their testimony are worthy of credence; in the same way those who surrender their whole lives in accordance with their testimony are equally to be believed. What child who from mere vanity or in play had told a lie would be willing to prove it by entering a convent? Children grow up.

Life as it opens out before them causes them to forget their day-dreams. Organic and psychological development stand in the way of the make-believe and inventions of childhood days. The up-holders of the lie theory are obliged, on a final analysis, to assert that Bernadette was her own first victim; that, in other words, she came finally more or less to believe her own story. From that point we are led quite naturally to consideration of another hypothesis, that of hallucination.

Was Bernadette insane? Charcot thought so, but there is a very considerable body of evidence against him. Bernadette showed none of the signs of madness, quite the contrary in fact. Here again there is no case on record of an insane person who at some time or other did not give evidence of it.

Was she a dreamer, a mystic, unbalanced? She was accused of being unable to meditate—but what does that imply save inability for, or even dislike of, abstract ideas? Hysteria? There was no clinical evidence of it (Zola was so far put to it as to label her an *abnormal* case of hysteria). Did she suffer from hallucinations? This too was asserted by Zola; in his view the ideas put in her mind by Father Ader and Father Aravant (another parish priest of Bartrès) were the origin of Bernadette's later "mystical" inventions. But he furnishes not a particle of proof for all this.

Some semblance of proof might possibly be gleaned from Bernadette's statements at Nevers toward the end of her life. Three or four years before her death, Bernadette, or rather Sister Marie-Bernarde, used to say the rosary for an unknown sinner whom she called the Great Sinner and for whom she wished to obtain divine mercy. Who was this great sinner? It might possibly be imagined that he was one of these priests, inventors of the Lourdes myth (finally recognized as such by a hallucinated young woman who had now recovered her wits), if the visionary herself had not answered the question by stating that she did not know who it was, but was merely praying for the "greatest sinner of all" in accordance with her belief in the communion of saints.[21] A few days

[21] There is another explanation. One of the secrets communicated by Our Lady to Bernadette at the grotto might have been the name of this great sinner, whom Bernadette could possibly save by praying for him.

before her death, we are also told, Bernadette was a prey to acute doubt regarding her own salvation. That again was probably due to her humility, her feelings of unworthiness about the favors she had experienced of which, there is every reason to believe, she was reminded by the Sisters of Charity whose motives in this case were questionably . . . charitable.

What conclusion may be drawn from all this? I must repeat that there is no question here of taking sides. If two or three theories have been rejected in this study of the case of Bernadette Soubirous, it has been done because historical accuracy requires it, and, it should be added, these theories have also been rejected by opponents of a supernatural explanation. The hypothesis of mystical delusion must not be treated lightly. On the one hand, those who uphold a miracle as the only tenable explanation dispute this hypothesis by emphasizing the obvious and very considerable points of difference between Bernadette and ordinary cases of delusion (such as her absence of anxiety or agitation, her being able to foretell the date of the apparitions, her lack of any sign of mental deficiency or persecution mania, etc.); on the other hand, those who favor a rationalist explanation put it forward as the only possible argument. But the field of speculation is too wide and the matter can never be settled definitively. For my part I believe that the Lourdes question contains other mysteries, and the following chapters are not exactly intended to contradict this statement.

2. THE SPRING

In the first place, we will avoid any quarrel about words. The existence of the *spring* which began to flow at Lourdes on February 25, 1858, has been denied; it has been explained as humidity and water oozing out. We can be categoric about it, since the geologists allow us to be so, with no bias of opinion or belief. It is definitely a spring, unanimously acknowledged as such, what is called in the local dialect a *houn*: this is the word used by Bernadette who asserted that she had it from Our Lady who told her to go and wash in this *houn* and drink at it.

This spring flows out exactly at the bottom of the fourth stratum of the left vertical wall of the rock of Massabielle through several separate orifices, imparting a distinct gyratory movement to the sand it there encounters. Its rate is, as has been mentioned, 85 liters a minute, or upward of 120,000 liters a day. The force of the spring is a material factor in causing it to flow out into the open; in fact it has been found that two-thirds of the *houn* runs into the Gave through an underground channel. The force of these waters would necessarily have led to their seeking an outlet in the open air in accordance with the elementary laws of physics.

The miracle consists then, not in the appearance of the spring, but in the date of its appearance and the fact that it coincided with Bernadette's announcement, together with her choice of position at which to scratch the earth with her fingers. In short, if this spring had appeared on any other day, or if Bernadette had never existed, the occurrence would have been considered entirely natural and would have passed practically without notice.

The water of the spring at Massabielle was analyzed as early as 1858; a second analysis, identical in result with the first, was carried out in 1934. The following results were published:

QUALITIES:
    Clarity: clear
    Odor: none
    Color: colorless
    Taste: none
    Keeping properties: good

GENERAL ANALYSIS (all figures expressed in milligrams per liter of water):
    Organic matter, estimated in oxygen: 1.2. Acid solution: 1.2. Alkaline solution: 1.2. Ammonia and ammonia salts: none. Nitrites: none. Nitrates: HNO_3. Traces: Chlorine: NaCl: 15.

HYDROMETRY AND ALKALIMETRY:
    Total hydrometric strength: 13. Constant hydrometric strength: 8. Total alkalinity: as $CaCO_3$: 148

MINERAL ANALYSIS:

> Residue at 110°: 194. Lime (as CaO): 90.7. Magnesia, as
> MgO: 7.6. Sulphuric acid (SO$_3$): 7.8

CONCLUSIONS: Chemically this water has the composition of a
drinking water of good quality.

In 1915, on the recommendation of Monseigneur Schoeffer,
bishop of Tarbes, the Lourdes spring was examined for its possible
radioactive properties. These were found to be practically non-
existent (scarcely 0.7 millimicrocuries of radon at the point of
emergence).

Since 1928, finally, the water from the Lourdes spring has been
subject to bacteriological examination. Two specimens were taken
from the part known as the men's bath in the pool and were found
to contain various bacilli originating from sick persons, including
staphylococci, colon bacilli, pyrogenetic bacilli. The water was
then injected intraperitoneally and subcutaneously into guinea
pigs. This inoculation was found to be harmless (note that water
taken from the Seine and injected under the same conditions produces serious symptoms resulting in death).

It follows that water from the Lourdes spring is of normal composition but possesses the particular property of complete harmless-
ness in a polluted state, so that, with medical approval, permission
has been given for it to be drunk even when the sick have bathed
in it. It is, in fact, a natural water possessing properties superior
to those of sterilized water though neither its chemical composition
nor its radioactive properties justify the attribution to it of particular hygienic or curative qualities.

3. THE CURES AT LOURDES

We have come now to a fundamental chapter of this study. It
is not specially concerned with Lourdes but includes all places
of pilgrimage where healing of souls is joined to another and as
a rule less secret form of healing, the healing of bodies. Lourdes
constitutes the primary example.

The cures at Lourdes, like all those recorded at the places in the
world visited by Our Lady, are presented for our consideration together with a great quantity of conflicting evidence. Volumes have

been written about them; they have been the cause of heated controversy, and books exciting world-wide interest, Dr. Carrel's
especially, have been produced about them. All this commotion is
easily understood, for the whole question of miracles is involved.
Proof that these cures are miraculous is proof of the invasion of
the natural order by the supernatural; to show the invalidity of
this claim, on the contrary, although it does not amount to a denial
of the possibility of miracles, certainly restricts it to a considerable
extent.

Christian opinion, of course, attaches only secondary importance
to bodily healing, for it sees in grace granted to a soul the greatest
of all miracles. Bodies, whether cured at Lourdes or not, remain
mortal none the less; a miracle, merely an incident taking place
in time, is no bar to growing old or death. But it would be rash to
maintain that belief in the cures of Lourdes has not strengthened
many a Christian in his faith and has not been the means of conversion of more than one atheist. It is true that "God does not
love a doubting Thomas," yet Christ vouchsafed to let him touch
His wounds. And it was not from mere whim that the Son of God
healed the paralytics and the blind.

The healing spring of Massabielle demands our attention and
provokes our questions. For in this place is to be found, visibly and
tangibly, the frontier between the natural and the supernatural.
Here the Unknowable makes bold to assert that the earth is partly
its province. Thither, in the company of all those thousands who
are tossed about between faith and doubt, we must now penetrate,
and as a beginning can consider the story of this strange region
set halfway between heaven and earth.

V

At the beginning of the apparitions of Lourdes no one contemplated the possibility of curing the sick at Massabielle; during
these first days interest was concentrated on the fact of the revelation which was then occurring. The first incident we encounter
which shows that the possibility of cures was beginning to be

realized took place one or two days before the spring began to flow; someone in the crowd accompanying Bernadette drew her attention to a child of her own age, blind from birth. Bernadette, on the impulse of the moment, ran up to the blind child, hugged her to her breast and kissed her warmly. No miracle occurred; the child remained blind at the time and afterward. It is quite possible that Bernadette never thought for a moment that she could restore her sight. Nevertheless, it is not unreasonable to believe that on that day the crowd experienced a vague feeling of disappointment; for the first time a heartfelt desire had found expression. Supplication, entreaty, remained silent, but before long it was to make itself heard and its voice was to reach to the end of the world.

In all times the supernatural or unexpected emergence of a spring has been considered as a miracle with a practical purpose in view. The spring has a meaning, it answers a need. When Moses by striking a rock caused a spring to flow, it was to quench the thirst of his people dying for want of water in the desert; sacred history and *The Golden Legend* are filled with chosen beings whom a spring, gushing out at a given spot, preserves from some fearful suffering. The annals of Lourdes inform us that on the afternoon of February 25, 1858, peasants took water from Massabielle in bottles and flasks; one of these flasks was used in the cure of the quarryman Bourriette. The next day a curb was built confining the spring and converting it into a pool, a bathing place, and sick people were at once brought there and immersed in it.

Bernadette, it should be noted, at no time besought Our Lady to effect miraculous cures, at no time did she even raise the question. But fifty-nine years later Lucia dos Santos's first care was to appeal to the Lady of Fatima for this material intercession; the little Portuguese visionary insisted at length, almost ponderously, until Our Lady answered yes or no. She did so precisely because Lourdes had become part of history—a revelation of this sort without miracles could no longer be imagined. Lourdes had created a fashion.

The first cures at Massabielle not only surprised the inhabitants of the district, they raised vast hopes not always inspired by supernatural or disinterested motives. Lacade, the mayor, as we have seen, thought of taking over the spring as his personal property, giving it his name and placing an order for labels to be fixed to bottles of the water; the worthy mayor scented a profitable piece of business; he had not the slightest belief in a supernatural intervention, but he wondered whether by chance the village under his charge might be situated on land likely to produce a medicinal, curative spring. "Take the cure at Lourdes and regain your health." Unfortunately, the first analysis of the water destroyed all his hopes; the doctors declined to allow any medical properties to be claimed for it. The worthy Lacade had perforce to burn his freshly printed labels lest he be accused of illegal practice of medicine, charlatanry or even worse. And there ended his dreams of palatial bathing establishments, casinos and all the rest.

The report of miraculous cures at Lourdes was bruited abroad, therefore, quite early. It coincided with the appearance of the spring. Even before the last of the apparitions the sick began to throng to Massabielle. Bernadette encountered them the whole way along as she went to the last of Our Lady's visits. The agitation caused by these cures was one of the pretexts used by the authorities for fencing off the grotto; but this pretext proved a double-edged weapon and turned against those who invoked it. Faced with the threat of a riot in Lourdes—and what a riot! the lame, the paralyzed, the blind, the dying—Napoleon III ordered the fence to be taken down and gave permission for bathing in the sacred water and for supplies of it to be taken away.

The sequel is not difficult to guess. Following the example of Dr. Dozous, who was on the spot, other doctors began to interest themselves in these supernatural cures. There were only a few years of indecision during which the cures remained unauthenticated and then, in 1863, recording of them began. Every year saw an increasing number of doctors at Lourdes—the number of sick increased out of all measure. In 1876 three Little Sisters of the Poor founded the *Hospitalité de Notre-Dame du Salut* intended to receive the disabled; in 1882 the first *brancardiers* (stretcher-bearers) made their appearance, under the command of the Comte de Combettes du Luc. In 1885 Monseigneur Dillère, bishop of Tarbes, set up the *Oeuvre de l'Hospitalité de Notre-Dame de Lourdes* (Charity Hospital), and in 1912 a second municipal hospital was opened under the care of the Sisters of Charity of Nevers. Meanwhile, in 1884 was established the *Bureau des Constations Médicales* (Medical Investigation Office—B.C.M.) in the charge successively of Doctors Maclou, Boissarie, and Vallet.

Nowadays, and indeed for the last half century, Lourdes has been very well organized on the medical side. It is a health center of world-wide importance, but with this difference that the sick only pass through without receiving treatment from the hundreds of doctors who take part in the pilgrimages. No one "takes the cure" at Lourdes other than supernaturally, and the only actual treatment given there is confined to the necessary dressings and injections. In addition, following many another, I can add the following evidence seen with my own eyes: the term *sick* is not entirely exact. In half the cases at least *dying* is the appropriate term. To anyone who happens to be in Lourdes, at the season of the great national pilgrimages for instance, the place appears like an immense pathological museum wherein are collected together the hopeless cases from all countries. A professor of the Paris Faculty of Medicine admitted that he encountered every year at Lourdes more cases for his clinical notebook than he would ever have found in the course of a lifetime in his Paris lecture room. Lourdes is the capital city of suffering.

Between 1888 and 1910 the Assumptionist Fathers compiled statistics of 2,973 miraculous cures in Lourdes, an average of 135 a year. G. Bertrin arrives at the figure of 3,962 between 1857 and 1917, an average that is, of about 78. Between 1926 and 1938 the average falls to about 10; 19 in 1926, 14 in 1933, 6 in 1932. These statistics do not mean that there are less miracles at Massabielle as the years go by, they merely record the decrease effected immediately when purely nervous diseases were declared inadmissible for examination, when the B.C.M. severely tightened its precautions in order to leave no possible loopholes for discussion.

What diseases are cured at Lourdes? And, firstly, what are the signs by which the B.C.M. recognizes supernatural intervention in a cure?

Skeptics have the advantage when they demand the one cure that is never granted: the regrowth of a missing limb. But, apart from this phenomenon which has never been observed, it can be said that all diseases are capable of cure in Lourdes. To substantiate a miracle, the B.C.M. requires one of the five following signs of which it has made an absolute rule and in the absence of which it refuses to pronounce an opinion:

(1) Absence of a curative agent. (2) Instantaneousness of the cure. (3) Suppression of convalescence. (4) Abnormality in the method of cure. (5) Recovery of the use of a function without the action of the appropriate organ which remains incapable of performing it.

Each of these five characteristic signs has been exemplified at Lourdes on several occasions, and Dr. Vallet and the doctors assisting him at the B.C.M. have recorded the cases in their various books. Before mentioning here certain particular cures, it will be useful to fix the limits of discussion by stating the one law governing the miraculous cures of Massabielle.

In fact, it was for long imagined that there was no such law. And it appears indeed that none obtains with regard to the sick and the method of their cure. Here chance is triumphant, divine chance, assert the believers. Children are cured as well as the old, the lax have an equal chance with the fervent; in many cases he who prays for himself receives no answer, while the prayer of a third party may provoke a miracle. It is not always necessary to go to the grotto and, in many cases, sick persons at a distance of hundreds or thousands of miles away have had their supplications granted, after drinking Lourdes water, or having uttered a simple prayer. In the last place, more than one "miraculous" cure has been known where the sick person had not even asked for it; one of their associates or helpers prayed for them, sometimes without letting them know for fear of receiving an uninterested or wrathful answer.

Nor is there any law governing the stages of a cure. Sometimes patients declare themselves cured at the spring itself; sometimes they only become aware of it during the return journey after experiencing varying degrees of disappointment while in Lourdes.

The cures in Lourdes are "silent ones" (Dr. Vallet). Frequently the cure does not take place at the first visit but at the following one, or perhaps at the third or fourth. Yet for all this the sole law does exist and can be enunciated in this way: at Lourdes, as in all other places of pilgrimage, miracles do not operate *contra naturam* but *praeter naturam*. In short, a miracle is not irreducibly contrary to nature (as, for example, if a missing limb grew again) but accelerates its rate of functioning to an extraordinary degree, fights disease and works in conjunction with it, causing it in the minimum period of time to pass through all the stages between illness and health.

But are such occurrences really miracles in the absolute sense of the term? The time has come to give examples which will talk louder than any moral or metaphysical considerations.

I have chosen two examples from among the most famous and the most keenly discussed: the case of John Traynor, the severely wounded Englishman of the 1914–18 war, and that of Marie Biré, known as the blind woman of Vendée.

THE CASE OF JOHN TRAYNOR

John Traynor, of the diocese of Liverpool, England, a British ex-marine, arrived in Lourdes for the first time on July 22, 1923, accompanied by Doctors Azurdia of London, Denis Flynn of Liverpool, and James Marley of Walterley. He made this pilgrimage by his own wish; it was his last hope of obtaining some measure of relief in his suffering, and a bed was already reserved for him at the home for incurables at Mosley Hill.

John Traynor had been seriously wounded three times during the war. His case showed the following clinical picture: frequent epileptic fits, monoplegia and amyotrophic condition of the right arm, partial paraplegia, loss of control of the vesical and ano-rectal sphincters, convulsions, loss of memory, vertigo. To these symptoms it must be added that as the result of an operation there was an aperture in the skull and hernia of the dura mater. John Traynor was completely disabled, classed as incurable, and regarded by the medical profession as a regular pathological museum piece.

On July 25, 1923, Traynor, lying flat on a stretcher, was present at the procession of the Blessed Sacrament when, as the benediction was given, he experienced an extraordinary feeling of well-being; at that moment his paraplegia disappeared. His reflexes were restored. He got up and was able to walk without difficulty. On July 27th the doctors of the B.C.M. recorded that he had recovered use of his right arm and feeling in his lower limbs; the aperture in his skull was partially resorbed and he himself had removed the protective plate from it; lastly, no epileptic fit had occurred for the last two days. Nevertheless, the B.C.M. was careful to come to no decision at once; a year later Traynor's doctors declared their patient entirely cured, and quite free from epilepsy. Traynor reported himself again at Lourdes and brought with him definitive and convincing proof of his cure; this completely disabled man had gone back to his work as a truck driver. Since that date he has always enjoyed excellent health.

THE CASE OF MARIE BIRÉ

This case goes back to August 2, 1908. It was observed and described by Doctors Lainey, Mairiaux, and Hibert.

Since February 25, 1908 Madame Biré had been blind as a result of optic atrophy on both sides, accompanied by a state of extreme general debility. She had expressed the wish to be taken to Lourdes and arrived there on August 4th, together with her daughter and some persons from her village. During the night of August 4–5, she had a fainting fit, and another on the next day, just as the Blessed Sacrament was carried past her on its way back to the Church of the Rosary. When she came to herself, Marie Biré realized that she had recovered her sight. She was taken to the B.C.M. where she underwent various medical tests of which the following embodies the findings:

Right eye: greyish white pupil, central vessels almost imperceptible, remainder of the fundus normal.

Left eye: greyish white pupil, central vessels contracted to one-third normal caliber. Madame Biré is suffering from white atrophy due to cerebral causes. This extremely serious condition is recognized by all authorities to be completely incurable.

It will be realized, therefore, that though Marie Biré remained *organically* blind, she could see and distinguish clearly persons and objects about her as well as read the small print in newspapers. In fact, cure of the function took the place of, or rather preceded, cure of the organ. A year later Madame Biré returned to Lourdes and was certified by the same doctors to be in possession of two eyes in perfect condition. In 1933 she was still alive and although quite elderly her sight was excellent. Her case is one of the most puzzling of all those that have occurred at Lourdes; it has been the subject of medical theses and scientific reports in all parts of the world.

It is incontestable that these two famous cases—showing spontaneous restoration of tissue, recovery of a function independently of the cure of the affected organ—require an explanation that science has been unable to provide. To these a round dozen other cases could be added which have also caused considerable stir throughout the world: the child Mieuzet, Louise Jamain, Elisabeth Delot, Father Lochet, etc. In the one year of 1937 the doctors of the B.C.M. admitted eight cures as supernatural. Among the diseases or disabilities concerned may be mentioned: a case of angina pectoris due to coronary atheroma, a case of total paralysis of the right lower limb and hemianesthesia of the side, a case of sub-acute malignant endocarditis, and finally a case of tuberculosis involving both kidneys and the bladder.[22]

All those cases represent the results of one year only and we may well trust the doctors of Lourdes when they tell us that they rejected many other quite probable cases on account of some want of proper certification or merely because the cure, although complete in spite of its hopelessness from a medical point of view before the pilgrimage was undertaken, had required several weeks or months to become effective and did not show therefore the spontaneity laid down for a miracle.

That, then, is the field open for discussion though it must be made clear at the outset there can be no question of the genuine

---

[22] Without drawing any conclusions from the fact it may be pointed out that in that year all the miraculous cures were of women.

sincerity of the doctors at the B.C.M.; [23] indeed any possibility of fraud is excluded; the doctors at the B.C.M are controlled by the documents with which they work. Patients come to them with medical certificates signed by other doctors and in two or three days they themselves must send these patients on to other colleagues, generally unknown to them. Moreover, it is the certificates of these unknown doctors that attest the fact of a cure. In addition, the doctors at the B.C.M. are the first to draw attention to any cases of possible deception. The likelihood of fraud is always borne in mind.[24]

Admitting the good faith and honorable character of the doctors at the B.C.M., together with the reality of the extraordinary cures, we are obliged to approach the question of miracles without hope of finding a solution on a natural plane.

Obviously the Christian doctor as doctor does not discuss the presence of the supernatural at Lourdes, Fatima, or elsewhere. As a doctor he may be disturbed by the appearance of phenomena which are contrary to the scientific teaching that he received, but he can record them happily and with calm assurance. True, the scope of a miracle is thus reduced to a reinvigoration of nature, as has been noted, or to the abrupt arrest of a process which would otherwise lead to an early death. In most cases the patient has already been given up by the doctors; very frequently, too, he has so far given up hope himself that he comes to implore his cure at Lourdes only for the sake of his family which he must support or for an addition to his span of life that he may praise God by his

23 Dr. Maïocchi, in his excellent *Souvenirs d'un chirugien* (*A Surgeon's Memoirs*) which has recently appeared, while denying the miracles of Lourdes is careful to acknowledge the entire good faith of the B.C.M. in whose sessions he took part for a month.

24 Two such cases occurred, for example, in the same year of 1937; both were immediately detected by the doctor of the B.C.M. There should be added also, for their anecdotal qualities, some of the quainter reasons for making the pilgrimage to Lourdes. For instance there was the case of the young woman quoted by Dr. Vallet; she came before the doctors at the B.C.M. in perfect health but greatly upset because she was not up to the average in height—four feet ten inches—"Do you think," she inquired, "that Our Lady will make me grow?"

good works. One woman who was miraculously healed at Fatima had even asked Our Lady not to cure her if by her survival she ran the risk of falling into a state of mortal sin. The Christian doctor can but rejoice at such things and approve wholeheartedly. For him science has limits which are known in practice; where they end, there God begins.

The unbelieving doctor for his part must seek some explanation and is glad to entertain the two that are open to him: the psychical origin of disease, and the continual progress of science which sooner or later will be in a position to record miraculous cures as merely natural phenomena.

"Faith which heals" is Dr. Fiessinger's formula. It would be useless to dwell on it at length for it is an adequate expression of what he means. The Lourdes spring is not medicinal; it is healing in the sense that the word is understood of all those many free lances of science who in nearly all cases work by suggestion and frequently with the help of some kind of water. The most recent instance is the healer of Menton who is credited with restoring to paralytics their freedom of movement. Doesn't Oriental science employ similar methods in certain cases? But that does not mean that Lourdes should be closed. In Dr. Fiessinger's view, on the contrary, it should be carefully studied and, in short, be incorporated into medical science.

That is a revolutionary proposal for a doctor. In other times—and not so very long ago—its author would have been the target for the full wrath of the profession. For upward of fifty years Lourdes was a forbidden subject, and for a candidate to choose it for a doctoral thesis was to make quite sure of being relentlessly failed. All that was tolerated was a passing reference or two, provided, of course, that a denial of miracles followed as a consequence. The most striking example of ostracism for this reason is Dr. Carrel's experience. Alexis Carrel was convicted of admitting in scientific research certain ideas regarding the miraculous; in effect he was turned out of his laboratory and sought asylum in the United States. There he was welcomed by the Rockefeller Institute and his subsequent discoveries are well known. Carrel has given free expression to the theories of his younger days in his celebrated book *Man the Unknown*. The following extract is well worthy of quotation for it manifests an entirely honest intellectual approach. The reader will discover in it no trace of prejudice, nor yet an act of faith which oversteps the strict bounds of science. Here we have an elementary, straightforward statement of fact.

"The author knows that miracles are as far from scientific orthodoxy as mysticity. . . . But science has to explore the entire field of reality. He has attempted to learn the characteristics of this mode of healing, as well as of the ordinary modes. He began this study in 1902, at a time when the documents were scarce, when it was difficult for a young doctor, and dangerous for his future career, to become interested in such a subject. . . .

"In all countries, at all times, people have believed in the existence of miracles, in the more or less rapid healing of the sick at places of pilgrimage, at certain sanctuaries. But after the great impetus of science during the nineteenth century, such belief completely disappeared. It was generally admitted, not only that miracles did not exist, but that they could not exist. As the laws of thermodynamics make perpetual motion impossible, physiological laws oppose miracles. Such is still the attitude of most physiologists and physicians. However, in view of the facts observed during the last fifty years this attitude cannot be sustained. The most important cases of miraculous healing have been recorded by the Medical Bureau of Lourdes. Our present conception of the influence of prayer upon pathological lesions is based upon the observation of patients who have been cured almost instantaneously of various affections, such as peritoneal tuberculosis, cold abscesses, osteitis, suppurating wounds, lupus, cancer, etc. The process of healing changes little from one individual to another. Often, an acute pain. Then a sudden sensation of being cured. In a few seconds, a few minutes, at the most a few hours, wounds are cicatrized, pathological symptoms disappear, appetite returns. Sometimes functional disorders vanish before the anatomical lesions are repaired. . . . The miracle is chiefly characterized by an extreme acceleration of the processes of organic repair. There is no doubt that the rate of cicatrization of the anatomical defects is much greater than the normal one. . . .

"Today, any physician can observe the patients brought to Lourdes, and examine the records kept in the Medical Bureau. Lourdes is the center of an International Medical Association, composed of many members [upward of 3,000 in 1939]. There is a slowly growing literature about miraculous healing. Physicians are becoming more interested in these extraordinary facts. Several cases have been reported at the Medical Society of Bordeaux by professors of the medical school of the university and other eminent physicians. The Committee on Medicine and Religion of the New York Academy of Medicine, presided over by Dr. F. Peterson, has recently sent to Lourdes one of its members in order to begin a study of this important subject."

This extract is very much to the point. The relations between science and miracles have evolved in three stages: (1) Faith will not allow science to deny the supernatural; (2) Science as it develops will not allow faith to encroach on its own province; (3) Faith and science collaborate or, at least without mutual embarrassment, study the problem together. Obviously each may be imbued with the ulterior motive of influencing the other. Nevertheless it is a good thing for these opposing views to meet and Lourdes provides them with an admirable meeting place. Year by year, before the grotto at Massabielle, an increasingly fruitful exchange of ideas takes place. There has been time for the heat of argument to subside. The ardent search for truth among men of good will, free from all bias, continues untiringly against a background of the prayers of the sick, the hymns of the pilgrims and the long-drawn, continuous murmur of sorrow and mercy which arises endlessly from this place where the Spirit breathes.

The pilgrim in good health, one of those who from curiosity, who "once in a lifetime" would see Lourdes, will hardly, I imagine, hurry off straight from the station to the B.C.M. Even if he has gone hoping particularly to be present at a miracle (rather as if he were at a theater, eager to see what he believes is a regular occurrence), or if his so-called pilgrimage to Lourdes is really just a commonplace holiday or sight-seeing trip for the beauty of the spot, I do not give him long before being torn out of himself, carried away on the great wave of suffering which through streets bordered by hotels, handsome residences, bazaars and the quaint houses of the old town, sweeps on to the grotto. Even the glaring shop signs will not detain him for long. He will spare hardly a glance for the Gave. But as he enters the territory of the grotto, seething with silent humanity, he will have no eyes for anything but the sick—the kings of Lourdes as a journalist called them—for here is the kingdom of suffering made royal and all powerful, supported by thousands of its eager servants.

At such a moment the whole question of the possibility of miracles is relegated to the background. Our isolated traveler, driven at first by his curiosity, now drops his stand-offish attitude and the somewhat contemptuous reserve with which he has surrounded himself; he realizes that he is no longer self-sufficient but, whether he likes it or not, is part of that immense wave which impels him to the grotto. The most aggressive of egoists feels himself at one with the cripples, the paralytics, the epileptics, and the blind: even an unbeliever feels tempted to pray. It is not pity—or if it is it does not last for long—for pity is an ambiguous sentiment, fluctuating between good and bad, and often degrades both giver and receiver. Pity is not Christian. But what Lourdes teaches us —irrespective of all philosophies and beliefs—is the infused light of charity. Earthly events are powerless against it. There may be there at the grotto some robust sight-seer watching one of the sick, almost at death's door. And after a short time it is impossible to tell whether the sight-seer prays for the sick man or the sick man for the sight-seer; the great brotherhood of Lourdes has moved their hearts. It may happen that a mere spectator will witness an occurrence more pathetic than anything that he had, almost unconsciously perhaps, expected to find: he intercepts the glance of one of the sick following another with his eyes and praying for him to be cured. Such a sight is never to be forgotten. It is like seeing the face of Bernadette herself: "the spring is not for me but for others"—the spring exists, it flows out from the ground and works miracles only because I decline to make use of it.

That refusal, that self-denial is the only trail that mankind has been able to blaze through the undergrowth surrounding the Unknown to lead him straight to God. It is the path leading straight to the Interior Castle. The features of the Curé d'Ars show plainly this tremendous and complete denial of self. Any man of lesser stature, like Napoleon, Caesar, Alexander, or Hitler, may well achieve his ends so long as he possesses his soul in patience; only the saints have that supreme strength which consists in not desiring. To act throughout a lifetime, and at every moment of it, directly counter to desire, self-interest, hunger and thirst, is the characteristic of such as Jean-Marie Vianney and Bernadette. And Bernadette's features are, so to say, a composite picture of all those millions of faces dedicated to a great renunciation of self. My thoughts are drawn to the last picture taken of her, after those two others, before and after the visions, when she posed for a photographer. This third and last photograph was taken at Nevers and is as unlike the other two as they are different from each other. Bernadette no longer appears as the merry child, unaware of her future destiny, nor yet as the visionary lost in contemplation of her tragedy as the chosen one of heaven; in her nun's habit, her face framed in the white wimple, she proffers a peaceful smile, which is the sign of understanding attained. "All is well," she seems to say. In spite of all the controversy and heated debate concerning Lourdes, the arguments and insults that blare forth, *all is well,* I have accomplished my mission. All else is irrelevant. The deathless silence that fell as the brambles parted before the grotto and the terrible wind blew without moving leaves or water was to herald God's message to men.

Fatima

or the Age of Mary

*Who is she that goeth up by the desert, as a
pillar of smoke of aromatical spices, of myrrh,
and frankincense?—Canticle of Canticles.*

THIS book, as has been explained, is not written in chronological
order. Lourdes deserved the special attention that was paid to it,
but it is only right to mention here that the miracle of Lourdes
was not an isolated event, and that it belongs, not to a trilogy as
Emile Baumann asserts, but to a tetralogy, and that, following
chronological order, La Salette should come first, then, after
Lourdes, Pontmain and Fatima.

Although miracles seem to occur following no determinable
rule, without being amenable to any law, there does appear to
be a fundamental rhythm that can be discovered sooner or later
by the writer who studies these phenomena. The signs change,
the intercessors—if I may venture to use the expression—take
duty in turns. We might almost speak of cycles and estimate their
length at about three centuries. Thus there is the cycle of the
Holy Spirit (an angel, a dove appears to the favored one), the
cycle of Christ (as He was seen by Francis of Assisi, Teresa of
Avila, as He spoke by the mouth of Ursula Benincasa), and lastly
the cycle of Mary. No one will deny that at the present time we
are in the age of Mary, for she it is who appears in the supernatural occurrences of our epoch. She it is who seems to be delegated
from on high to deliver a message to mankind.

Our Lady's influence was found at all periods and this theory of cycles is, of course, only a rough approximation. Already in the seventeenth century she had appeared in the neighborhood of La Salette to an obscure peasant woman, Benoîte Rencurel to whom she gave a message about events of those days and from whom she exacted a promise, as she did afterward at Lourdes, to build a church. Notre-Dame du Laus, built with the pennies of the poor, is standing testimony to this miracle. Yet if one miracle can be compared in importance with another on the basis of the stir it caused in the world, the miracle of Laus has left little mark in the memory of man. At the same period the miracles of Christ —both visions and stigmata—made a far more lasting impression on men's minds.

In the two cases also the message seems to differ. Joy and ecstasy are the principal marks of a vision of Christ; those of visions of Our Lady are tenderness, the desire to warn men of a danger threatening them and to tell them of the necessity for penance. "And cast the tears from your eyes, unbeknown to God, over the souls of the damned." That naïve, moving prayer to Saint Anne by the poet Tristan Corbière might be made to Our Lady if we could imagine that for a single instant she could be hidden from God; a Christian's mind and heart need another explanation— intercession besought and granted.

On September 19, 1846, Our Lady of La Salette, appearing to the shepherdess Mélanie, spoke of the punishment that would be meted out if men did not amend their lives. This apparition of La Salette has also caused considerable discussion. As regards the cures that it has led to, it is a less important miracle than that of Lourdes, but though Bernadette seems to echo Mélanie's strik- ing account, it is the latter which excels for its sheer beauty.

"It seemed as if the moving light increased or rather became concentrated all round the most holy Virgin to prevent my seeing her any more. Thus the light took the place of those parts of the body which disappeared from before our eyes; or rather it seemed that the body of my Lady changed into light as it melted away. The ball of light rose gently upwards. I cannot say whether the amount of light diminished as it rose, or if it was merely the distance which caused the light to grow fainter as it moved farther away until it disappeared altogether."

In addition to its beauty this account is also extremely precise. To use a term from the cinema we might say that it was a kind of miraculous "fade-out." Surprisingly enough the visionaries at La Salette were also extremely observant. The "shock" they experienced—imagine the effect on a child who sees heaven come to visit the earth—by no means dulled their visual or mnemonic faculties. Mélanie seems almost to let us touch her vision. In the same way she passes on to us word by word what Our Lady said, that speech by the "beautiful Lady" which we reproduce here, for the time being without comment:

"If my people will not submit, I shall be forced to let go my Son's arm; it is so strong and heavy that I can no longer hold it up.

"With all your prayers and works you can never make up for all the trouble I have taken on your behalf.

" 'I gave you six days to work and kept the seventh for myself, and men will not grant it to me.' It is that which makes my Son's hand heavy.

"The wagon drivers cannot swear without using my Son's name. It is both these things which make my Son's hand so heavy.

"If the harvest is ruined it is your fault. . . . Well, children, you will pass on my message to my people."

At La Salette Our Lady, as afterward at Lourdes, entrusted the children with a secret. As at Lourdes, the miracle consists in the apparition itself, though Lourdes shows a certain evolution: the choice of place, firstly, which is more accessible and better adapted for crowds than La Salette. Then, as we have seen, there is the spring and the cures and, lastly, the dogmatic importance of the message. That is the order from a human point of view, from the divine it is the other way about. At Pontmain the evolution is more marked still. It is no longer one or two children who are privileged but four.

The apparition at Pontmain took place on the evening of January 17, 1871, between a quarter to six and a quarter to nine.

Any account I could give would pale beside that which the bishop of Laval inserted in his pastoral letter of February 2, 1872. The bishop's style reflects the recent occurrence of the events he describes; he writes with obvious emotion.

"At first one child left the barn where he was working with his brother, 'just to see what the weather was like,' as he put it; then the younger brother and presently two little girl boarders at the Sisters' school, and, like the boys, aged between ten and twelve, taken there without being told what was happening, all asserted that they could see in the air above the house, situated opposite the barn, a tall, beautiful lady (*une grande belle dame*) in a long blue dress sprinkled with golden stars and wearing on her head a golden crown.

"At the children's loud enthusiastic exclamations people started to gather round from all sides and soon more than a third of the population of the little village, their worthy parish priest at their head, were assembled at the spot where these wonders were reported.

"In the attentive, excited crowd opinion was divided. Although some believed, the majority doubted or refused all belief in the constantly reiterated statements of the children. Suddenly, while the canticle of Mary's humility and faith, the *Magnificat*, was being sung, a long white band began to unroll beneath the feet of the beautiful Lady and an invisible hand began to form in large letters of gold [1] these words: MAIS PRIEZ, MES ENFANTS (But pray, my children). Other hymns followed, and to the children's delighted gaze other letters appeared which they spelled out and repeated time after time, vying with one another to be the first to finish; these letters falling into position after the first that had appeared completed the previous sentence by adding: DIEU VOUS EXAUCERA EN PEU DE TEMPS (God will hear you in a short time). A full stop, shining like the sun, came at the end of the line. It seemed that all was over. By no means. The invisible hand continued its mysterious task: the inscription, going on to the second line, was completed by these moving words: MON FILS SE LAISSE TOUCHER (My Son allows Himself to be moved).

[1] In capital letters, specified the visionaries.

"The astonished, attentive crowd was praying in silence. Then a voice was raised; it was Sister Marie-Edouard starting the hymn *Mère de l'Espérance* (Mother of Hope). Suddenly the beautiful Lady, whom all present took to be the glorious Mother of God, raised her hands, which previously had been stretched out toward the children, and slowly moving her fingers, looked at them with indescribable tenderness.

"But shortly afterward came an unexpected contrast. The crowd had begun the hymn "Sweet Jesus, now the time has come, our sorrowing hearts to pardon," when the Lady's face became clouded with sadness. She was holding in her hands, before her breast, a red cross bearing on it a figure of Christ also in red with, above it, a white band on which stood out in red letters the name JESUS CHRIST. At the same time she moved her lips and seemed to pray.

"That was the last stage of the great event, and while at the parish priest's bidding the people were saying their night prayers, a sort of blue veil came slowly up from the Lady's feet and gradually hid the vision from view. Only the crown remained for a moment and then that, too, disappeared; the apparition was over; it had lasted nearly three hours."

The bishop's pastoral letter is not confined merely to the apparition; it also relates events which occurred after the vision and are, as it were, its justification.

"On the very day that these astonishing things happened at Pontmain the advance guard of the Prussian army had reached the neighborhood of Laval and the next day, from a distance of only a mile and a quarter from the town, could be heard the last of the heavy gunfire (the last, at any rate, in our part of the country) of the terrible war which has soaked our unhappy land in blood and covered it with so many ruins. Three days later, the enemy army, scattered over the region between Mayenne and the eastern part of the district, began to fall back on the Maine-et-Loire and the Sarthe. Finally, on January 28th, the two warring nations signed an armistice and preliminary peace terms. This occurred exactly on the eleventh day after that when the white band shone with its letters of gold displaying those blessed words:

H

'God will hear you in a short time.' We mention these facts without drawing any conclusion from them, but no one who has considered them in connection with the occurrence at Pontmain can have failed to be struck by the coincidence we have just pointed out, that decisive events followed immediately after those occurrences." [2]

What was the meaning of that MAIS (but) in letters of gold on the white band? Perhaps it was merely a conjunction. It connected Pontmain with La Salette. The sentence begun twenty-five years before was thus completed; the MAIS was like a rainbow of peace stretching from La Salette and Lourdes to Pontmain.

"Rainbow" is the word used, too, by Emile Baumann.[3] Thus the nineteenth century witnessed three miracles. If it is true that the number three possesses some peculiar significance, the golden full stop "shining like the sun" would seem, in its turn, to mark the end of a cycle. Two of these three miracles were, in wonderful fashion, complementary in meaning: Pontmain was connected with La Salette; Lourdes, by the emphatic nature of its message, seeming to confirm the dogma of the Immaculate Conception, stood out prominently. There seemed to be no more to be said. But after the nineteenth century was to follow a period of horrors and of wonders. After the war of 1870 came another with its terrible slaughter. But incredible marvels were about to occur; the age of Mary was moving to its climax, reaching to its zenith with the most sensational and spectacular of miracles, the phenomena of Fatima.

I

About forty hamlets clustering, at an altitude of some 1,200 feet, in a hollow of the Serra de Aire and comprising about four thousand inhabitants form what is called the village, or it would be better to say the parish, of Fatima in Portugal; it is situated in the province of Santarém at a distance of sixty-two miles north

[2] Quoted from *Notre-Dame de Pontmain* by Canon André Roulleaux.
[3] *Histoire des Pélerinages de la Sainte-Vierge* (Paris: Albin-Michel).

of Lisbon. The rather unusual name of the place is explained by an event in history, or possibly a mere legend, which goes back to the twelfth century. In 1158, Portugal, like Spain, was overrun by the Moors. One of the heroes of the war of liberation, Dom Gonçalo Hermingues, came upon and took prisoner a party of young Moslems, of both sexes, who, after a banquet, were amusing themselves in the valley; as reward for his exploit he besought the king, Alfonso, for the hand of one of his prisoners, Fatima, the daughter of the vali of Alcazar. Fatima agreed to marry him, was converted, and lived for some years with her lord. She died, it is said, in her prime, having bequeathed her Arab name to Dom Gonçalo's estate and her Christian name, Oureana, to the county town which became Ourém.

In 1917, like all the other parishes of Portugal, Fatima consisted merely of a collection of peasants and mountain folk all affected to a large degree by the world war. For a year past Portugal had thrown in her lot with the allies. The European war was only the exterior cause of the misfortunes of the country, for within it a conflict almost as serious divided the population into practically equal parties. The political evolution of Portugal had been largely influenced by a philosophy imported from abroad, and her position at that time was by no means unlike that of France some years before at the time of the separation of Church and State. Church and State were in open opposition; the Masonic lodges were attacking the religious orders; the freethinking propaganda was beginning to find its way into the country districts which until then had been well known for their attachment to Catholicism; lastly, those in power, entirely won to the new ideas, were doing their utmost to destroy in an underhand way the traditional faith of the country. Taking into account the climate and the heat of passion that it engendered, it was by no means impossible that Portugal would become another Mexico, proscribing and persecuting her priests as has been described, for instance, by Graham Greene in his well-known novel *The Power and the Glory.*

Fatima, in spite of its proximity to the capital, was cut off from all this turmoil, possibly because it was difficult of access in the

natural isolation of the mountains; it remained an island of peace
where men were too long acquainted with one another for hate
to take root among them. The families living in the parish had
been settled there for several generations, in some instances from
time immemorial; the bonds between them were forged from many
acts of kindness done, frequent commercial dealings, a sharing of
joys and sorrows in common, and marriages between next door
neighbors or cousins. This was the case in the hamlet of Aljustrel,
with its upper and lower parts, rocky pathways, fields of wheat
and maize divided by low walls, like those they call *plou* in Brittany; every family maintaining its own privacy yet practicing
generous hospitality; whitewashed houses with tiled roofs, and on
the walls inside devotional pictures and plaster statues; an orchard
and a paddock for the sheep. Two men living there were brothers-
in-law, Antonio dos Santos at lower Aljustrel and Manuelo Pedro
Marto at the upper village. Manuelo had married for the second
time Olimpia de Jesus, a widow with two children; she bore him
nine more children, the youngest being Francisco (born on June
11, 1908) and Jacinta (born on March 10, 1910). Manuelo Pedro's
sister Maria Rosa, wife of Antonio dos Santos, had brought one son
and four daughters into the world. The youngest was Lucia de
Jesus who was born on March 22, 1907.

In May, 1917, therefore, Lucia was ten, Francisco nine, and
Jacinta seven—three children of more or less the same age. By
reason of their parentage it is not surprising that they behaved
like brother and sisters, and they were generally to be found in
company. Their parents, who were on very good terms, sent them
off every day to look after the sheep together. The children preferred that to going to school. There is little to be added. Lucia,
Francisco, and Jacinta were, or seemed to be, ordinary children.
No one could have expected that they would be the heroes of the
most extraordinary miraculous adventure of the century.

Fatima began, like Lourdes, with a child letting out a secret. On
Sunday, May 13, 1917, at seven in the evening, little Jacinta Marto
ran to meet her mother on the Aljustrel road. She flung her arms
round her (a mark of affection, it was noticed, that was unusual

with her) and, stammering in her excitement, blurted out, "Mother, I saw the Blessed Virgin today in the Cova da Iria!"

Her mother untwined the child's arms and looked at her.

"Whatever are you saying," she exclaimed. "Are you mad?"

"But it's true!"

"*You* saw the Blessed Virgin? But you aren't a saint!"

"Mother, I promise you it's true, please believe me." And the child went on: "We must go back to the house and Francisco and I are going to say the rosary. The Blessed Virgin asked us to."

The mother, dumbfounded, allowed herself to be led off through the dusk. Francisco was already at home with the other children. He seemed at first rather astonished and somewhat annoyed that his sister had told their secret; but she held out her rosary and both at once began their prayers. A quarter of an hour later their father came in and that was the scene that met his eyes. Seeing his wife there on her knees he opened his mouth to put a question. Jacinta interrupted him:

"We must say the rosary every day. The Blessed Virgin wishes it."

Finally they all sat down to supper: the father, mother, eight children, together with two visitors who had come to spend the Sunday, a brother-in-law, and a nephew. Olimpia served out the soup and then, when all had begun their meal, started to question her daughter. Jacinta, not in the least embarrassed, gave an account of the events of the day just as they are related below. There was much astonishment and not a little derision; they all turned to Francisco and began then to question him. Francisco merely said, "It's true," and would add no more.

By this time it was half-past eight, too late to decide, as was obviously indicated, to go down to the other end of the hamlet to the Dos Santos's house and demand from Lucia confirmation or denial of the story. The children were put to bed. The grown-ups spent an hour or two discussing it all and then they too retired for the night. But the next morning, directly she was up Olimpia ran down to Maria Rosa.

"What did your daughter tell you yesterday evening?" she demanded.

"My daughter? Lucia?" was the reply. "Why nothing at all. What's happened?"

"Oh, thank God for that! It's only some foolishness of my children's. But how in the name of fortune could they make up a story like that?"

"What story?" asked Maria Rosa.

So Olimpia told her tale. Maria Rosa shrugged her shoulders; she had heard nothing of it before. But perhaps if she questioned Lucia carefully . . . That was it, question Lucia, perhaps they could find out from her what had put that tale in Jacinta's and Francisco's heads. "Ah well," Maria Rosa said to herself, "after all if Lucia has anything to tell me, she's sure to do so." But when Olimpia had gone Maria Rosa, for one reason or another, postponed questioning Lucia until later. Possibly there were more urgent tasks to be seen to; the housework, for instance, would not wait.

Francisco, on that Monday, May 14th, had managed to warn Lucia and to tell her that Jacinta had spoken. Lucia, worried and annoyed, found her little cousin and reproached her for what she had done. Jacinta admitted it and striking her breast remarked, merely, "There was something there which prevented my keeping silent."

A whole week went by, during which Maria Rosa dos Santos from embarrassment, annoyance, or anxiety did no more than observe her daughter. She was one of those mothers who take a certain pride in enjoying the confidence of their children while doing nothing to provoke it: between mother and daughter there should be no secrets. But by the end of the week Lucia had said nothing and Maria Rosa could bear it no longer. In addition the Marto parents had urged her every day to try to discover the truth. She summoned her daughter and openly questioned her. Maria Rosa's impatience and curiosity entirely overcame her usual maternal delicacy.

"Jacinta says that with Francisco and you she saw the Blessed Virgin. What about it?"

"It's quite true," Lucia answered.

"Why didn't you tell me about it before?"

"We had decided to tell no one," replied Lucia. "Jacinta didn't keep her promise, but as you've asked me about it today I tell you, it's true."

Maria Rosa was by no means satisfied with this answer; she was a believer and practiced her religion but was less inclined than Olimpia to admit such supernatural phenomena. So, like the wife of the miller Soubirous on a similar occasion, she could scarcely refrain from hitting her daughter. She managed, however, to confine herself to a blunt request.

"Anyhow at least keep quiet about it," she ordered, "and go on keeping quiet. Don't start a scandal about our family." As if, indeed, scandal was something that could be avoided.

Scandal, in fact, was already making its round in Aljustrel where, as may well be imagined, the other Marto children, perhaps their father, and in any case the two Sunday visitors had not been backward in spreading the news; the whole hamlet, soon the whole parish of Fatima knew all about it; it caused a fine chorus of jocular remarks, ridicule and scorn. Maria Rosa could not bear it. In her distress, fearing what people would think and that the family would be pointed out in the street, she decided to confide in the parish priest, Father Manuel Marqués de Ferreira. This priest, like many in Portugal, bore the title of Father Prior as the parish at one time had been the site of a priory. He observed approaching him a woman in tears who did not trouble to tell him the facts, supposing (rightly as it happened) that they were already known to him.

"What trouble!" she began at once. "Things like that happen only to us!"

That is the continual complaint of the poor. Father Ferreira looked at her thoughtfully.

"Trouble, you say," he replied. "Are you quite sure, Maria Rosa? If your daughter is telling the truth—suppose she is for a minute—it would be, rather, a great happiness, a blessing, wouldn't it now?"

"A blessing?" puzzled the woman. "A blessing to have a daughter who tells lies?"

Her anger flared up. She hurried back home, found her daughter busy with the housework and this time gave her a sound whipping.

"It's the first time you've lied to me," she cried, "and it is going to be the last. Come with me. We'll go round to all the houses and you shall tell the neighbors you were lying."

Lucia said nothing and did not move. But her refusal was not exactly disobedience. Maria Rosa threatened her with prison. But just at this moment the door opened and Olimpia walked in. She had come to remind her sister-in-law of something which would greatly increase her distress and anger.

"They say that they saw Our Lady," she announced. "And they say that she told them to return to the Cova da Iria on June 13th. What do you mean to do about it?"

"Lucia is not going. I shall stop her," replied Maria Rosa. "What about you? I hope you'll . . ."

Olimpia shrugged her shoulders.

"I don't know," she answered, "I think I shall let Jacinta and Francisco go there. Don't you see, supposing it were true!"

Supposing it were true . . .

What is the Cova da Iria? The word *cova* means a dale, a hollow, a basin; Iria means Irene. There was a Saint Irene who died in the district about A.D. 652. The "dale of St. Irene" looks like an enormous natural amphitheater nearly a mile in diameter; it provides pasturage for sheep and is connected with Aljustrel by a stretch of moorland known as the Charneca. Fatima is about a mile and a quarter from the Cova da Iria. In 1917 the Santos family owned a portion of partly cultivated land there on which grew some evergreen oaks and olive trees. It was therefore an obvious place for Lucia and the Marto children to lead their flocks.

What happened there on May 13th? The following is an accurate reconstruction of the events of that day according to the account given by the three children:

Lucia, Francisco, and Jacinta reached the Cova da Iria at about midday. As has been mentioned, it was a Sunday, and so they had first been to Mass and then were sent to look after the sheep. As they were to stay in the Cova for the rest of the day, they had been provided with a meal packed in a little basket. With that impatience common among children they began on their meal at once. When they had taken some of the edge off their appetite, Lucia pulled a rosary out of her pocket and began to pray; Francisco and Jacinta followed suit. All three children were devout. And so they prayed on their knees for some time in the shade of an olive tree, and then, as they usually did, decided to play at building houses. That, too, is common enough with children. When the house was built (a few small stones with pine branches on top) they pretended that it was a chapel where they could go for sanctuary and to do penance. Just then, although the sun was shining brightly in a uniformly blue sky, there was a flash of lightning. "There's a storm brewing," cried Lucia, "we must go back."

The children got up and began collecting their sheep together. When they had gone about thirty yards, a second flash streaked across the sky and rooted them to the spot. It was not exactly like a flash during a storm, but rather a bright light which surrounded them and which all three imagined to come from the right, for they all turned in that direction instinctively, and without speaking to each other. There, on their right, encircled, like them, with a blinding light, a lady more resplendent than the day was looking at them.

"Don't be afraid," they heard, "I won't hurt you."

The "Lady"—or rather the "girl," for so they called her at first, as Bernadette did—seemed to be eighteen at the most. "She was dazzling light" Lucia was to say later. But they could clearly make out her clothes and her face. The "girl" was wearing a long white dress coming down to her feet, and tied at her neck with a golden cord; a white, gold-embroidered veil covered her head and shoulders.[4] Her feet rested on a cloud. Her hands, joined before her

[4] In a letter written to Bishop da Silva of Leiria in 1937, Lucia dos Santos added the following lines to the original description of the apparition: "It seems to me, that if I could paint—without being able to paint her as she is, which is impossible since one cannot even describe her with words of this earth— I would clothe her with a dress as simple and white as possible, and a 'mantle' falling from the top of the head to the edge of the robe. And since I could not paint the light and beauty that adorned her, I would suppress all, except a fine gold fillet on the edge of the mantle. This ornament shone on the background of light, like a ray of the sun, shining more intensely than the rest. This comparison is far, indeed, from the truth, but I cannot express it better." Quoted by Canon C. Barthas and Father Gonzaga da Fonseca, S.J., in *Our Lady of Light* (Milwaukee: Bruce Publishing Co., 1947).

breast, held a rosary with white beads. Lucia was the first of the three children to come to herself after the ecstasy caused by the vision. The dialogue that then took place, as Lucia afterward recounted it, is here set down.

LUCIA: "Where do you come from?"

THE VISION: "I come from heaven."

LUCIA: "Why have you come here?"

THE VISION: "I have come to ask you to be here six times running at this same time on the thirteenth of each month. In October I will tell you who I am and what I want."

LUCIA: "You have come from heaven . . . And shall I go to heaven too?"

THE VISION: "Yes, you will go to heaven."

LUCIA: "And Jacinta?"

THE VISION: "Yes."

LUCIA: "And Francisco?"

THE VISION: "Yes. But first he will have to say many rosaries."

As the apparition uttered these words she turned toward the little boy with a look of maternal pity and love. It was possibly at that moment that Lucia noticed a strange phenomenon: Francisco had heard nothing save the questions asked by his cousin. But Jacinta heard, though she said nothing herself. Nor did she do so during the whole time the apparition lasted; the dialogue continued, as it had begun, solely between the "girl" and Lucia.

The whole of this dialogue was not revealed at the outset by Lucia or Jacinta; and there was also, as at Lourdes, at this first vision, a secret that was not to be revealed. In 1940, however, at the instance of the bishop of Leiria, Lucia dos Santos wrote down certain additional words (the reader is hereby warned: throughout the history of the miracle of Fatima, from 1917 to our own day, he will encounter successive revelations, some of them of an astounding nature). The additional words were as follows:

THE VISION: "Will you offer sacrifices to God and accept all the sufferings that He will send you in reparation for the many sins which offend His Divine Majesty? Will you suffer to obtain the conversion of sinners and to make amends for all blasphemies and offenses committed against the Immaculate Heart of Mary?"

Lucia, in the name of all three, answered with great fervor that they would.

THE VISION: "Then you will have much to suffer, but the grace of God will help you and be your continual strength."

With these words the apparition opened her hands, causing a beam of light to be thrown towards them; the three visionaries fell to their knees, saying fervently "O most holy Trinity, I adore You! My God, I love You!" The apparition spoke for the last time, recommending the children to say the rosary. Then "all at once," "straight up," she disappeared into the sunlight.

The vision had lasted for an indefinite time, the dialogue for about ten minutes. Some authors assert that on this first day Lucia asked the vision a question about two little girls who had recently died at Fatima; the vision is supposed to have answered that one of these little girls was in purgatory and the other in heaven. It seems also to emerge from the account given by the children that Francisco (who, I repeat, heard nothing) did not at once see the vision; after some minutes, and only when he had said his rosary were his eyes able to behold the apparition. In any case, when the children recovered from their ecstasy their first care was for their flock which, while the watchers were otherwise engaged, had strayed away. As they rounded up their sheep, Lucia, Francisco, and Jacinta kept on saying: "What a beautiful lady! What a beautiful lady!" They talked it over and came to the conclusion that it would be better to say nothing about this vision. Lucia insisted on silence. "Not a word," she insisted, "not a word to anyone, like last year."

Like last year: the meaning of that sentence will be made clear in a later chapter.

Francisco promised to hold his tongue, so did Jacinta. But Jacinta, we know, found it too much for her.

II

Five more apparitions were to take place at Fatima and in the exact order that Lucia said they would occur: June 13, July 13,

August 19,[5] September 13, and October 13. The precision of this order should be noticed; there is no possible room for discussion on the point, unlike what happened at Lourdes, for example (the vagueness about February 26, 1858). For the moment it is important, following the documents, to draw up a list and, in some sort, a report of these visions. It will be done as clearly and as baldly as possible in accordance with the declarations of the visionaries themselves and of other witnesses. But the reader should bear this preliminary warning in mind: there is a certain peculiarity about the miracle of Fatima which may well confuse him and that renders our account of it more complex.

The revelation of Fatima was not divulged all at once, but in stages. That was due, as at Lourdes, to the secrets confided to the children by the vision; but, unlike what happened at Lourdes, several of these secrets have not been kept. Since 1917 Lucia has revealed several of them to the ecclesiastical authorities; and it is extremely probable that she will continue to reveal others up to the day of her death. How does she reconcile disclosure of these secrets with her promise of silence? The answer is quite simple: unlike Bernadette, Lucia dos Santos *promised* nothing, and Our Lady never explicitly required such a promise of her; certain words she has hidden in her heart, she says, because she is sure that Jesus—not His Mother—requires her not to repeat them.[6] What have been revealed, in short, are but half-secrets that in the absence of a strict command may be told when there is some certainty that they ought to be. A later chapter will enlighten the reader about the way in which Lucia gradually revealed her secrets. At the present moment the difficulty must be faced whether to mention them at the proper time, in chronological order, or to incorporate them into the accounts of the visions as they were imparted; to make for easier reading and to avoid constant reference back the second method has been chosen, but care has been taken to distinguish between what was immediately published and those sentences of the dialogue which were kept secret at the time but are so no longer. What Lucia kept secret in

---

[5] The postponement was due to material causes.
[6] "I am not a prophetess," she adds.

1917, therefore, is here so marked. Whatever is unmarked was published at the time of the apparition.

1. THE SECOND APPARITION

(*June 13, 1917*)

Olimpia Marto and her husband decided to allow Francisco and Jacinta to go to the Cova de Iria, but in spite of their children's repeated requests, they refused to go there with them. In the end Maria Rosa dos Santos allowed Lucia to go, but decided to remain at home herself. At nine o'clock in the morning, Lucia, Francisco, and Jacinta set out, while the Marto parents went off to the fair at Porto de Mos. It was the feast of St. Anthony of Padua, known in Portugal as St. Anthony of Lisbon.

About sixty people went to the Cova out of curiosity. One of them contributed the following evidence which has been added to the chronicle of Fatima:

"At the time agreed upon the three children arrived. Kneeling down in the shade of a large evergreen oak they said the rosary. . . . Afterward Lucia got up, arranged her shawl, the scarf over her head and her clothing, as she might have done to go into a church. Then she turned towards the east, awaiting the vision.

"She was asked if there would be long to wait. She said not. The two other children asked for another rosary to be said. At that very moment Lucia made a gesture of surprise. 'Look, there's the flash,' she cried. 'The Lady's coming!' Followed by her cousins she hurried down to the foot of the slope to the evergreen oak of the first apparition.

"I could hear quite well what Lucia said to the vision, but I saw nothing and could not hear the answers. Yet I noticed one remarkable thing; it was the month of June and the trunk of the tree was covered with long young shoots. Now at the end of the apparition, when Lucia declared that the Lady had departed in the direction of the east, all the branches of the tree came together and bent in that direction, as if the Lady in leaving had trailed her dress over the top of the tree."

On this occasion the vision and the dialogue had lasted ten minutes. This is what was said:

LUCIA: "You asked me to come back here, my lady, what do you want of me?"

THE VISION: "I desire you to learn to read so that I can tell you what I want."

Lucia asked for the cure of a sick person that one of her mother's neighbors had recommended to her.

THE VISION: "If he is converted, he will be cured in the course of the year."

LUCIA: "Will you take all three of us to heaven soon?"

Secret:

THE VISION: "Yes, I shall soon come to take Jacinta and Francisco. But you must remain longer here below. Jesus wishes to use you in making me known and loved. I wish to spread devotion to my Immaculate Heart throughout the world."

LUCIA: "Then I must stay here all by myself?"

THE VISION: "All by yourself! No, my child, I shall never abandon you. My Immaculate Heart will be your refuge and the way which will lead you to God."

With these words the Lady, as at the first apparition, opened her hands wide. A heart pierced with thorns appeared in the right hand. Then the vision vanished. The children said the rosary; the spectators, the Litany of Our Lady. Gradually they all dispersed and went home.

2. THE THIRD APPARITION
(*July 13, 1917*)

The events of July 13th began with a heavy interior trial for Lucia dos Santos who for a whole month had been subjected to the contradiction and ridicule of her family and the neighbors. Some continued to maintain that she was lying; others said that the apparitions were due to the devil and that she was his protégée. Lucia was quite prostrated, hardly knew what to do and at first made up her mind not to go to the Cova da Iria; then an invisible force—she used the same expression as Bernadette—impelled her forward, and decided what she should do. On her way she shouted to Francisco and Jacinta and told them to come with her. Manuelo Pedro Marto and his wife Olimpia accompanied them. From that day onward they believed in the reality of the visions.

There was now a dense crowd of about five thousand people massed at the Cova. At midday Lucia, who was praying, uttered a piercing cry and fell to her knees. The others present, though they saw nothing, followed her example. At first Lucia remained silent and Jacinta was obliged to intervene:

"Go on, speak," she urged. "The Lady is there to talk to you."

Lucia repeated the first question of the previous interview.

LUCIA: "What do you want of me?"

THE VISION (*repeating her previous words*): "I want you to learn to read. You must come back here on the thirteenth of next month. You must recite the rosary every day. Say it to obtain the end of the war. Only the intercession of the Blessed Virgin can obtain this grace for men."

LUCIA: "Who are you? Will you tell me your name and work a miracle so that everyone will believe" (in the reality of the vision).

THE VISION: "Continue to come here every month. In October I shall tell you who I am and what I want. *In October I shall work a great miracle* so that everyone will believe you."

LUCIA: "I have some other requests to make. Would you please cure X . . . , the poor cripple, convert the family X at Fatima, and take to heaven soon the sick man . . . of Atonguia?"

THE VISION: "I shall not cure the cripple nor relieve him of his poverty, but he must say the rosary every day with his family. The sick man of Atonguia must not lose patience; I know better than he the proper time to come for him. Others will obtain many favors in the course of the year, but they must say the rosary."

At this point those present noticed that Lucia's face gave an extraordinary impression of sadness; her eyes filled with tears, she sighed deeply and cried out in terror. For some time she said no word but seemed absolutely exhausted as did the other two visionaries; silence, hardly broken by the muttered prayers of the crowd, reigned in the Cova da Iria.

Secret:

THE VISION: "Make sacrifices for sinners and say often, especially when you make a sacrifice, 'O Jesus it is for love of You, for the conversion of sinners, and in reparation for sins against the Immaculate Heart of Mary.' "

Once again the Lady opened her hands. Lucia's account continues: "The rays of light reflected seemed to penetrate into the earth and we saw what seemed to be a great fiery sea in which were immersed demons, all black and burned, and souls in human form like transparent glowing embers. They were raised in the air by the flames and fell down in all directions, like sparks in an immense fire, without weight or equilibrium, with loud cries and groans of pain and despair, making us shudder and tremble with fear.

"The demons could be distinguished from the humans by their horrible, repellent shapes as of terrible unknown animals, and were transparent like burning coals.

"This vision lasted only a moment and we must thank our kind heavenly Mother for having prepared us beforehand by promising to take us to heaven. Otherwise I believe that we should have died of fright."

THE VISION: "You have seen hell where the souls of poor sinners go. To save them Our Lord wishes to establish in the world devotion to my Immaculate Heart. If you do what I have told you, many souls will be saved and there will be peace.

"The war which began in 1914 is drawing to an end, but if men do not cease offending God, in the next pontificate a worse one will begin.

"When you see a night illuminated by a great and unknown light, know then that this is the sign given you by God that the punishment of the world by war, famine, and persecution of the Church and the Holy Father is at hand. To prevent this I shall come to ask the consecration of the world to my Immaculate Heart and the Communion of reparation on the first Saturday of the month.

"If my requests are heeded, Russia will be converted and

there will be peace. Otherwise Russia will spread her errors in all the world, causing wars and persecutions of the Church. Many good men will suffer martyrdom, the Holy Father will have much to suffer. Many nations will be wiped out. In the end my Immaculate Heart will triumph. The consecration to my Immaculate Heart will be made, Russia will be converted, and a period of peace will be granted to the world.

"When you say the rosary, add at the end of each decade: 'O Jesus, forgive us our sins, save us from the fire of hell, and lead all souls to heaven, especially those who need Your mercy most.' "

(At this point was revealed a secret that has not been divulged.)

THE VISION: "Tell this to no one, but you may tell it to Francisco."

LUCIA: "Do you want anything more of me?"
THE VISION: "No, I want nothing more."
LUCIA: "Nor do I."

The vision smiled and then faded away as usual. Those present, as they prayed, thought they could see a small white cloud encircling the children. In addition the sun seemed to give less heat and to have lost some of its brilliance. Then the cloud dispersed and the light of the sun returned to normal.

3. THE FOURTH APPARITION

(August 19, 1917)
Called the Apparition at Valinhos
preceded by the first public phenomenon

For three months, reputedly supernatural phenomena had been taking place at Fatima and the local newspapers had mentioned the fact; curiosity and the comparative nearness of Lisbon combined to draw an increasing number of spectators to the Cova. On the morning of August 13th the number of pilgrims was estimated at some twenty thousand persons. From the early hours of the morning—some had spent the night out of doors—they were

I

waiting round the evergreen oak of the apparitions for the arrival of the children. At midday it was announced that they were not coming.

They had been abducted by the sub-prefect of the province, who took them to Ourém where they were questioned once in the town hall and once in the prison.[7] They returned to Fatima two days later, when the crowd had dispersed, to hear that this crowd had witnessed the first prodigy to occur in public. The following is a summary account of it:

The twenty thousand pilgrims in the Cova da Iria heard a clap of thunder at the time at which the apparitions usually occurred; at the same instant, it was asserted, they saw a flash of light in the sky and then a small cloud formed above the tree and remained there for about ten minutes, and then seemed to disappear in the sky. In addition some there claimed that they had seen Our Lady; but it was quickly pointed out to them that they were mistaken and in the end, for the most part, they admitted it good-humoredly enough. In spite of what had occurred, all said and done, the day was a disappointing one.

Four days later, Lucia, Francisco and Jacinta, accompanied on this occasion by another of Marto's children, João, who, however, was not favored with the vision, all went, not to the Cova, but to a place called Valinhos between the hill Cabeço and Aljustrel. Abruptly there occurred the usual atmospheric disturbance and once again, though unexpectedly for no "appointment" had been made, the Lady appeared. Once again, too, she spoke and complained of the harsh treatment undergone by the children (whom she called her friends).

THE VISION: "Because of the wicked men and their sectarianism, the miracle promised for October will be less striking. But you will have to go to the Cova da Iria on the thirteenth of the two following months. Will you promise me that once more?"

LUCIA: "I promise to do so myself and on behalf of Jacinta and Francisco. . . . People have left offerings of money at the Cova on a table put there by C. . . . She has requested me to ask you what is to be done with this money, there are 13,450 reis."

[7] See below, p. 124.

THE VISION: "This money should be used to celebrate the coming feast of Our Lady of the Rosary. For that occasion two processional stands must be bought, one gilded and the other silvered. You, Lucia, will carry the first with Jacinta and two other little girls, all dressed in white; Francisco with three little boys, all in white, will carry the other. What money remains over may be used to build a little chapel."

LUCIA: "I have been asked to implore you again to cure some sick people" (she named them and mentioned their diseases and infirmities).

THE VISION: "Some of them will be cured in the course of the year. But that is of less importance than prayer and mortification. Pray, my children, pray very much, and make sacrifices for sinners, for many souls are lost because nobody makes sacrifices and prays for them."

The vision smiled and vanished. João tried in vain to see it. Instinctively the children cut off the branch on which the apparition's feet had rested. Jacinta seized it. She took it back to Fatima in her arms and encountering Maria Rosa dos Santos showed it to her. Witnesses who were present at this meeting have asserted that this branch of holm oak gave off a delicate, pervasive perfume.

4. THE FIFTH APPARITION

(*September 13, 1917*)
Second and third public prodigies

The crowd of onlookers constantly increased; on September 13th there were between twenty-five and thirty thousand of them. The children arrived at the Cova at noon, passing down a lane in the crowd, with spectators on either side endeavoring to touch their clothes as they went by, or to recommend intentions to be passed on to the Lady. They knelt down. The sky darkened. A witness declared, "It was as if dusk had fallen very quickly and I thought I could make out the stars, as if it were really nightfall."

"Look!" cried the crowd in unison. Thus was heralded the second public phenomenon, known as the prodigy of the ball of fire. The evidence which follows is quoted from the testimony of Father João Quaresma, the future vicar-general of Leiria:

". . . to my great astonishment . . . I saw, clearly and distinctly, a luminous globe coming from the east and moving to the west, gliding slowly and majestically through space. With my hand I motioned to Monsignor Gois who was standing next to me, and who had been making fun of me for coming. Looking up he too had the good fortune to see this unexpected vision.

"Suddenly this globe, giving off an extraordinary light, disappeared from my sight and Monsignor Gois, also, saw it no longer. But there was a little girl near us, dressed like Lucia and of about the same age, who continued to cry happily, 'I see it! I see it! Now it's coming down towards the bottom of the hill.' "

It was, in fact, a luminous globe and according to the assertions of those who saw it [8] oval in form with "the widest part underneath." "A sort of celestial airplane," Canon C. Barthas wrote afterward, in the light of this evidence. Meanwhile the children were in ecstasy and Lucia was speaking with the apparition.

THE VISION: "You must say the rosary. Say it to obtain the end of the war. Come here without fail in a month's time, on October 13th next. I promise to return in October with St. Joseph and the Child Jesus."

LUCIA: "I have been asked again . . ." (here followed the list of the sick of Fatima and district who wished Our Lady to obtain their cure).

THE VISION: "I will cure some of them, but not all, because Our Lord does not trust them."

LUCIA: "You asked for a chapel. The people here also want to build one."

THE VISION: "That is good. Half of the alms received may be used for this chapel."

"She is going!" cried Lucia at this point. Those present heard her; but just at this moment, and indeed for the last few minutes, some of the spectators had been distracted by a further phenomenon, the second public prodigy that day, a shower of flowers.

---

[8] How many saw it? And how many gazed at the sky in vain, astonished at the shouts of their neighbors? It is impossible to say. It may be pointed out that among those who saw nothing were many priests, including Canon Manuel Nunès Formigão who, under the pseudonym of Vicomte de Montelo, had already questioned the children by order of the Patriarch of Lisbon.

This was an even more striking phenomenon than those which went before and heralded in some sort the great miracle promised for October 13th. This shower of flowers took place not only on September 13, 1917, but twice more at least—during pilgrimages to Fatima on May 13, 1918, and on May 13, 1924. On this second occasion occurred an event unique in the history of miracles: the shower of flowers was recorded on a photographic plate. This photograph, which has been frequently reproduced, was taken by the Portuguese vice-consul to the United States of America, Antonio Rebelo Martins. The back of the original bears attestations signed by Father Carreira Ramos, Father Carreira Poças, and J. L. Ribeiro; their signatures were authenticated by Pedro Dias, notary at Leiria.

This photograph of the miracle has been published in newspapers all over the world; the original is kept under seal. To return, however, to September 13, 1917: Following the evidence closely, an attempt must be made to describe this mysterious shower which shortly preceded and then coincided with the conclusion of the apparition.

It was a fall of white petals, which "like round, shining snowflakes floated down towards the earth, in a strong beam of preternatural light." Contrary to all the laws of perspective these petals or flakes became smaller as they fell; the larger they were, the higher they were in the sky, and the farther away from the earth. They vanished, directly people tried to touch them, leaving no trace; some of them just brushed the heads and shoulders of persons in the crowd. This phenomenon moved the spectators to such an extent that some of the priests present, whom the Patriarch of Lisbon had prudently ordered to maintain an attitude of strict neutrality both of word and bearing, fell on their knees, said the rosary and, forgetting what they had been told to do, united with the crowd in their fervor. The three little children did not seem particularly surprised at this further miracle; by this time they appeared to have grown accustomed to manifestations of the supernatural and all their efforts were directed at getting out of the throng surrounding them. Gradually the sky cleared, or it would be better to say, perhaps, emptied. The crowd began to disperse and peasants were to be remarked who were talking about the grape harvest which they had left in order to make the journey to the Cova. Lucia, Francisco, and Jacinta rejoined their parents and together they hurried home again. The fifth apparition was over.

"October 13th, a whole month to go," exclaimed Lucia dos Santos. October 13, 1917, was to see the promised proof. She had more than thirty days before her, days of waiting, anxiety and hope.

III

At this point in the narrative, between the penultimate apparition and the day of the great prodigy which was to make Fatima the Lourdes of the twentieth century, it is necessary to pause and record certain facts which though they are no part of the miraculous occurrence itself are yet bound up with the events of these first five months. The three children's behavior before the first investigators, both of Church and State, should especially be studied. The latter, in fact, was the first in the field, but it is convenient to begin with the ecclesiastical representative.

When Canon Manuel Nunes Formigão, delegated for this purpose by the Patriarch of Lisbon, arrived in Aljustrel, he found that the parish priest was as prudent about and as skeptical of the whole affair as, fifty-nine years previously, Father Peyremale had been at Lourdes. Like Father Peyremale, Father Ferreira refused to give an opinion. He was torn between doubt and the temptation to believe in the visions, and confined himself to playing an unobtrusive part which consisted mainly in preserving Lucia dos Santos from the severe thrashings with which her mother daily threatened her. For in September, 1917, Maria Rosa, impulsive as ever, did not yet believe that her daughter had seen the Blessed Virgin. Yet it was on Lucia that Canon Formigão paid his first visit; quite naturally he considered it opportune to question first the eldest of the children who was, moreover, the only one to have the privilege of converse with the apparition.

It so happened that Francisco and Jacinta were both at Maria

Rosa's house before Lucia came in from working at the grape harvest. The Canon was welcomed with all politeness by the mistress of the house and at once began his interrogation. Both questions and answers have been published at length and more than once. Here it will be sufficient to indicate those matters about which the children's answers agreed and those about which they differed or seemed to do so.

Obviously they agreed about the dates of the apparitions, the precise spot at which they occurred and the abnormal atmospheric phenomena. There was entire agreement also about the duration of the apparitions and the indelible impression of beauty left by the vision. With an ingeniousness that was quite intentional the investigator tried a comparison; mentioning a young woman of the hamlet well known for her beauty, he asked if the lady was still more beautiful. "Oh yes," came the answer, "a hundred, a thousand times more beautiful, there's no comparison!" Estimates of the age of the Lady showed some variation. "She might be fifteen," Lucia asserted on this occasion, whereas two months before she had put it at eighteen. It is true, of course, that children have rarely any clear idea of the age of grown-ups. To a little girl of ten there is not much difference between fifteen and eighteen, both seem to her quite a fair age.

The apparent childishness of question and answer should cause no astonishment. For instance Canon Formigão asked the three visionaries—separately, of course, taken without warning, and with no possibility of communicating with each other—if the Lady wore earrings. Jacinta answered "No"; Lucia said that she did. Later on Lucia amended her evidence and mentioned again the golden border to the Lady's mantle which, catching the rays of the sun, might have given the impression of two earrings. In which hand did Our Lady hold her rosary? In her right hand according to Lucia, and this was Jacinta's answer too, but when the question was repeated she hesitated. All three children asserted that the apparition wore neither sash nor ribbon. Lucia was a little upset when the investigator asked her if, in obedience to the Blessed Virgin's request, she had started to learn to read. "No," she replied, "I have not begun yet."

"Is that how you obey the Lady?" demanded the Canon. Lucia remained silent.

The investigator decided after a certain time to put two questions which, it may well be imagined, he had with difficulty refrained from asking before. Both, it seems likely, were suggested to him not by his own intuition or as the result of ingenious deduction but by certain rumors current in Fatima which must have originated from the children themselves. The first question (to Lucia) was, "But why should you learn to read since, so it appears, you are going to die in a month's time?" Lucia bridled at once: *she* was not going to die in a month, the Blessed Virgin never said anything of the sort. The Canon insisted no further, but there are grounds for supposing that the first secret (cf. above) even then had not been very well kept. Probably one of the visionaries had vaguely mentioned approaching death—early death and the reward of heaven had been promised to Francisco and Jacinta—and by tackling Lucia on the subject Canon Formigão chose mistakenly that one of the three who was to survive the others. What would have happened if he had put the same question to Francisco and Jacinta? But he did not do so, having made up his mind no doubt that the rumor was incorrect.

The second question, too, appeared to be derived from some disclosure by the visionaries. Lucia again was asked, "Is it true that you saw the Blessed Virgin last year?" We know nowadays what this question concealed, and it will be explained here in its proper place; Lucia's words on the way back to Aljustrel, after the first apparition, will be recalled: "Not a word, not a word to anyone, like last year." Directly she heard Canon Formigão's question Lucia turned pale. But once again in all innocence he had framed his question badly and instead of setting a trap, as he expected, had proffered a helping hand. "No," replied Lucia, "no, it's untrue, none of us saw the Blessed Virgin last year." And she told the truth. As with the previous question the Canon did not insist although all he had to do was to put another, very simple question to cause Lucia very considerable embarrassment.

Perhaps Canon Formigão had a shrewd idea that behind that

little peasant's bulging obstinate-looking forehead was concealed a whole collection of secrets which, he considered, it would be wrong for him to penetrate too quickly. That first day's interrogation sufficed for him to gain the children's confidence. He was on excellent terms with them when he took his leave; he feared to worry them any more to no purpose, bearing in mind the trials they had already endured. Actually neither his gentleness nor the harshness exhibited by the representatives of the law succeeded in entangling them in a mass of contradictions which lying could have caused. Neither kindness nor unkindness influenced their answers.

At Ourém there was a notorious anticlerical, Arthur d'Oliveira Santos, by name, who owned a small factory for metal pipes which was known as the Progressive Metalworks, while he himself was commonly called "the Tinker." Political machinations of the time had made him the administrator of the provincial council. This Oliveira Santos was a common enough type of local politician, boisterous, a victim of persecution mania, who passed quickly—a little too quickly perhaps—from thought to action. In 1918, a year after the events of Fatima, therefore, relieved of his functions by the Sidonio Païs ministry, he contrived a bomb to polish off his opponent. Unfortunately for Oliveira Santos the bomb exploded in his hands as he was filling it. Indeed his clumsiness was on a par with his violent nature.

By treating Oliveira Santos here somewhat ironically, at least we have not depicted him in too dark colors nor made an object of overwhelming hate as has been done in some quarters. The Tinker of Fatima seems to have been primarily a man of impulse, dominated by his anti-religious fanaticism and living in a district which was in general opposed to his "progressive" ideas. After the third apparition d'Oliveira Santos, with all the authority of his post of provincial administrator, decided to put a stop to all this religious "nonsense." He summoned Lucia with her father and interrogated her, endeavoring to make her disclose her secrets. Then, having failed to obtain anything from her, dismissed her after making her sign (with a cross: she could not write) a formidable looking statement. He added that he would shrink from nothing to prevent her returning to the Cova da Iria, from nothing, he reiterated, "not even death."

On August 13th, as Lucia was getting ready to go to the Cova, where not only the Lady but also the crowd of pilgrims desired her presence, she was told that the Administrator required to see her and was awaiting her at the Marto's house where he was already questioning Francisco and Jacinta. In fact he was trying his best to dissuade them also from going to the Cova, making use of threats and cajolery by turns. Faced with the children's obstinacy he pretended to give way. "All right, then," he exclaimed almost merrily, "since you obviously mean to go on working miracles, at least you shall do so in my presence. I'm like St. Thomas; I ask nothing better than to believe, but I must see first. Jump in my carriage, I'll take you there." Manuelo Marto refused. It was decided to leave on foot, calling at Father Ferreira's rectory en route. There, bringing new tactics to bear, the Tinker at last managed to whisk off the children. He got them into his carriage, the horse was whipped up, and off they went not towards the Cova but to Vila Nova de Ourém.

At Ourém the children were given something to eat, and an attempt was made to win them over with candy; but Lucia, Francisco, and Jacinta still desired as much as ever to go and see the Lady, and furious at their determination d'Oliveira Santos decided to strike a decisive blow. He ordered the children's arrest and they were locked up in a room. An old woman, "a great enemy of priests," was sent in to them; she did her very best to find out their secrets, but quite in vain. A day and a night passed. The next day the children were taken to the Council offices where they were alternately threatened or promised rewards; money was spread out in front of them. In the afternoon, finally, they were thrown into jail. They were left to stew there for some hours with ordinary criminals, who, it should be said, comprised about a dozen relatively harmless thieves and drunkards. At 5 P.M. d'Oliveira Santos came in to them.

"As you won't make a clean breast of it all," he announced, "you'll have to die!"

For the next hour the Administrator behaved odiously. He seized hold of Jacinta shouting, "You're first, you'll be burned alive!" And she was taken away. Francisco's turn came next: "The fire's alight and the oil's boiling," he was told. Then Lucia. She was to be dropped in the cauldron with the others, he told her. However, in the end the children were all together again and passed the night in the Tinker's house. He was now a much worried man, at his wit's end to get the better of these obstinate children. On Tuesday morning their interrogation was a mere form and the Administrator had given up hope of ever discovering anything; he decided to take the children back to their homes. On arrival at Fatima he noticed a gang of youths prowling about the village street armed with hefty clubs which seemed to portend rough treatment for him. In the nick of time he noticed the parish priest and made a point of exchanging a few words with him. Popular annoyance calmed down. Lucia, Francisco, and Jacinta went back to their parents and the Tinker saved his skin by paying a round of drinks for everyone at the village café.

This tragicomedy, it must be emphasized, should not be used to make capital for either side in the discussion. The miracle of Fatima transcends this storm in a village teacup and the blunders of a wretched politician. It is true, of course, that the general public fastens on these unimportant details of a great adventure and, as has been shown, feeling ran high in Portugal. The Portuguese anti-clericals were much given to dynamite. At this period they had a penchant for the somewhat outmoded terrorist tactics of bomb throwing. On May 6, 1922, four of their bombs were meant to destroy the chapel—the *capelinha*—which had been built on the site of the apparitions. A little later there was the story of the young man of Lisbon who journeyed to Fatima with one of those charming objects in his pocket; he, too, intended to destroy the sanctuary; at the last moment one of his relatives substituted a rosary for the bomb; the story ends with the youth's conversion. The supporters of the miracle were no less noisy in their enthusiasm. One day—October 13, 1919—the pilgrims at the Cova were startled by what seemed like several rounds of heavy gunfire: a regular salute of twenty-one guns. It was only one of Our Lady's grateful clients expressing his joy and gratitude by letting off crackers. He was a fireworks maker by trade.

So we must be careful not to dramatize the events of August 13, 1917. On the other hand, the atmosphere of violence in Fatima at this time should not be minimized; the behavior of the Tinker playing the bogieman—though to threaten children of seven, nine, and ten with boiling oil was, all the same, extremely cruel—can be put down as an exaggerated or improper expression of the prevailing temper. "No man is a prophet in his own country," and the little visionaries of Fatima were not as a matter of course prophets in their own village. When Maria Rosa dos Santos was told that her daughter had been taken off by the Administrator, her only answer was, "So much the better! Now the Blessed Virgin can look after her!" As formerly at Lourdes so at Fatima it was good form for the smart women of the parish to throw doubt on the sincerity of the children and to jeer at the pious folk who were ready to believe in the miracles.

Several priests made the journey to Aljustrel in order to make the acquaintance of the children and question them and also, no doubt, to form their own private opinion about the phenomena, though maintaining the prudent attitude required by the Church. Many of these priests returned home convinced that "the finger of God" was to be detected in these events; one such was Father Faustino Ferreira (namesake, merely, of the parish priest) who afterward pleaded the cause of Fatima with the bishop. On the other hand there were priests who did not scruple to cry fraud, and some were to be seen making fun of the children, laughing at their answers and nudging each other during the interrogations. Both sides stoutly maintained their viewpoint. The parish priest of Fatima, as may well be imagined, was besieged with questions. His attitude was mentioned at the beginning of this part. Everyone was expecting him sooner or later to come out on one side or the other and many of the villagers had determined to follow his lead. But he never adopted a definitive attitude, at any rate in public. The fact is that he was entrusted with the preparation of a report for the bishop at Leiria about the apparitions in his parish and he delayed—or at least there was considerable delay—in its presentation. Then, two years after the apparitions, just when the devotion to Our Lady of the Rosary was beginning, he requested, and was granted, another parish. Or perhaps he was obliged to move.

On August 15, 1917, the youths with clubs in their hands, waiting for the Tinker, had observed Father Ferreira in conversation with their opponent and, on that score, found his conduct questionable. "If he's siding with the enemies of the Faith," they exclaimed, "he'd better go!" For some were inclined, quite naturally indeed though erroneously, to turn Fatima into an article of faith, a sort of proof by novel means of the existence of God. "The Church has no need of Fatima," it was later proclaimed by the ecclesiastical authorities; "Fatima is inconceivable without the Church." Nor had God or Our Lady any need of Fatima. But crowds often stand in need of miracles, even though they afterward deny them or forget them. In a country rent asunder as Portugal was at that time, rightly or wrongly Fatima had a certain probative value. If the marvelous events at the Cova were refused credence, then Portugal would follow its course, be transformed into another Mexico, a godless country; belief in these events would lead, on the other hand, to a revolution in the opposite direction and to the definitive and irretrievable rout of all the "Tinkers" in the country.

There was another more serious side to the question. This partisan attitude could, if expectations were not fulfilled, easily degenerate into implacable hatred. From May onward peasants were to be found in Fatima—and among them, no doubt, the youths with the clubs—who went about saying to all and sundry that they believed the children had not deceived them, "but," they added, "they have made a tremendous fuss about a great miracle which is to occur on October 13th; if nothing happens, they'd better look out for themselves." Simple notions of that kind can sway whole crowds. Others were heard to say in addition that after all the three visionaries were only children and no harm should come to them, and then went on to declare, "Their parents will have to suffer, for if there is no miracle, that can only mean that they have contrived the whole thing."

On the morning of October 13th, a neighbor sought out Olimpia Marto and told her, "If the Blessed Virgin doesn't work a miracle today, you and your children will not be alive this evening."

IV

October 13, 1917, dawned at last. It was the dawn of one of the most historic days for the Church in this century. On this occasion it was no mere eighteen or twenty-five thousand spectators who hastened to the Cova, but seventy thousand pilgrims who came on foot, on bicycles, in carts, by car, or got off the train at the Chao de Maças station. In this enormous crowd were to be found doctors, professors, special correspondents from the Lisbon newspapers, and news photographers. All through the night this great mass of humanity maneuvered into place, hung about, prayed, or slept in the open air since there were no inns. At the first light natural instinct turned all eyes to the sky. It was covered with low clouds. Rain was on the way.

In all probability neither the Martos nor the Dos Santos slept much that night. The last fortnight had been particularly trying for them; unceasingly, tiresome importunate callers knocked at their doors, demanding the children, who were sometimes forced to hide themselves in the fields to escape their tormentors. In the end they had to be sent away from Fatima. They were put in the charge of a woman, Cruz by name, at Reixeida, a neighboring village; but she was hardly more successful in shielding them from the attentions of the curious. When she returned the little visionaries to their families, she could not restrain expression of her fears.

"The Tinker wanted to burn them alive. Poor children! It will surely come to that if there's no miracle!"

At the last moment sensational, alarming news flashed through the assembled crowd. The Masonic Lodge, it was reported, had decided on action. Action, obviously, meant the perpetration of a bomb outrage; at midday, so the rumor went, the time when the apparitions were due, two bombs would explode near the

children, blowing them to pieces and with them the famous evergreen oak, not to mention those spectators nearest them. Of course,
it was only a rumor but there was just the possibility that it might
be true. Terrorists do not always reflect beforehand on the possible
consequences of their actions, nor do they necessarily understand
that violence is not the best way to convince the masses. There
were some unbelievers who asserted that the Blessed Virgin ought
to thank them for providing her with the opportunity of working
a miracle: "She must want the children to live," they sneered.
"All she has to do is to stop the bombs going off! Let her change
the dynamite into flowers."

At the beginning of this momentous day it might have been
said that the children were about to undergo trial by fire. This
abrupt impression of time rolled back and the return of those
medieval trials by ordeal is not the least extraordinary feature of
that morning of October 13th. It is no exaggeration to call their
position a tragic one. Supposing that the long awaited miracle did
not occur, even if the disappointment of the crowd did not cause
it to go to extremes, and the Cova was not the scene of violence,
if no blow was struck, no insult uttered—and there was reason
to believe that matters would not pass off so quietly—even so, it
meant the complete ruin of the Marto and Dos Santos families.
These humble peasants had never desired this tremendous experience which had made them not its beneficiaries but its victims. All sorts of anxieties already weighed heavily upon them;
not the least was the threat of legal proceedings by their neighbors whose fields adjacent to the Cova had been trampled on and
ruined by the crowds; some of these fields were under cultivation
and their crops were now destroyed. The peaceful atmosphere of
Fatima had gone for ever. During the apparitions in July and
August pickpockets had operated among the crowd. If the final
outcome of this day were failure, the Marto and Dos Santos families, who had already sold some of their flocks, would have no
other resource but to leave the district, always supposing they
were given time to get away.

What was the attitude of Lucia, Francisco, and Jacinta at this
difficult moment? They seem to have been entirely without fear.

When in the prison at Ourém the Tinker threatened them with death, the three children met persecution with prayer; Jacinta had even had the touching thought of fixing a medal to the jail wall and one of the ordinary prisoners, moved by this gesture, had helped her knock in the nail for it. Now she and her brother patiently awaited the time to set out for their meeting with the Lady. Lucia was no more anxious than they. "We'd better go to confession," urged Maria Rosa, "because I'm sure the crowd will put us to death this evening." Lucia replied that she was willing to go to confession with her mother, but not because she was frightened. "The Lady promised me a miracle and she will keep her promise," she concluded.

It is difficult to decide which is the more moving, the thought of these children or that of their parents, simple, modest, peaceful, sturdy peasant folk fulfilling a destiny beyond their comprehension. Like love, the marvelous strikes where it wills; it singled out Soubirous the miller, and now it was the turn of these Portuguese peasants. Maria Rosa did not insist, but she put on her Sunday clothes to go to this extraordinary festival; at the other end of Aljustrel the Marto family, too, were dressing up in their best clothes. The visionaries' brothers and sisters had not yet made up their minds to go with them. Some of these older children were incredulous of the whole affair, but in the end family solidarity prevailed.

As the three children left their homes heavy drops of rain began to fall.

It was about half-past eleven when excited murmuring from among the crowd denoted the arrival of the children. Right up to the last moment there had been some fear that the Tinker would repeat his maneuver of August 13th; it was known at this moment that the great event awaited by all could now freely take place.

The three children appeared; Francisco in a little black coat, Lucia and Jacinta in blue dresses with white shawls which had been garlanded with artificial flowers by a devout woman of Pombalinho. On their heads all three wore wreaths of flowers, soon, unhappily, to be ruined by the rain. Francisco led the way.

At one point Jacinta started to cry because they were going too fast for her. Francisco and Lucia slowed down and let Jacinta walk between them. When they arrived in the Cova, in front of the evergreen oak, Lucia abruptly told the people to close their umbrellas.

It was an order given in a voice which though not loud commanded obedience; it was passed on from one group to another and rapidly complied with. Half an hour passed by in waiting and prayer. Suddenly, just as it happened at the previous apparitions, Lucia exclaimed, "There is the lightning!" Maria Rosa had just time to shout, "Look properly, my child, make no mistake," before Lucia and her cousins fell to their knees.

THE DIALOGUE AND THE MULTIPLE VISION

There came a small white cloud and a very bright light. The Lady appeared, her feet resting on the oak which some devout people had decked with ribbons and flowers.

LUCIA: "Who are you, my lady, and what do you want of me?"

THE VISION: "I am Our Lady of the Rosary, and I wish a chapel to be built here in my honor."

LUCIA: "What else do you want, my lady?"

THE VISION: "I wish you to continue saying the rosary every day as you do already. Great events will soon occur. The war is nearing its end and the soldiers will soon be home again."

LUCIA: "Again I have been asked to make requests of you and I have still many things to ask you."

THE VISION: "I will grant some favors, but not others. Men must amend their lives and ask pardon for their sins." (Here the voice became sad, almost pleading in tone.) "Men must no longer offend Our Lord who is already offended too much."

The Blessed Virgin said no more, but as on previous occasions opened her hands; there occurred now the multiple vision as it was witnessed by Lucia and later described by her. This vision did not appear from between Our Lady's hands but in the sky which she indicated and toward which the children immediately began to gaze. Lucia described this vision as follows:

"I saw St. Joseph and the Child Jesus by Our Lady's side. Next,

K

I saw Our Lord blessing the crowd. Then Our Lady appeared, dressed like Our Lady of Sorrows but without the sword in her heart. Lastly, I saw her dressed in another way, I don't know how to describe it, but I think it was as Our Lady of Mount Carmel. She was dressed in white with a blue veil and held a scapular in her hands."

Jacinta's and Francisco's account: "We saw the Holy Family but nothing else. The Child Jesus was in St. Joseph's arms. He was very little, not more than a year old. Both were dressed in red, not dark—but pale—red." [9]

Lucia, then, was looking at the sky, or, to put it more accurately, at the sun. But she was not alone in doing so. At that moment the seventy thousand spectators in the Cova da Iria had eyes only for the sun; it was Fatima's great moment, the miracle promised by Our Lady, the famous solar phenomena, one of the most amazing miraculous manifestations of all time.

The Solar Phenomena
Cova da Iria, October 13, 1917, from 12:05 P.M. to 12:15 P.M. [10]

The rain stopped abruptly, and in scarcely a minute the last clouds had dispersed. The sun appeared: it was not golden but looked like a silver disc. It seemed to be surrounded by another disc whose color the spectators could not state beyond saying that it was dazzling, though they acknowledged that this effect might have been due for the moment to the sudden appearance of the sun in a sky which until then had been overcast.

The sun remained motionless for an instant and then, as abruptly as it had appeared, began to tremble. It almost looked as if it was shaking itself. It stopped trembling and then began to spin round, shooting out on all sides rays of light which changed

[9] The children later added more precise details to this account at their next interrogation (by Canon Formigão). St. Joseph and the Child Jesus were near the sun (Jacinta). He did not reach St. Joseph's waist (Francisco and Jacinta). St. Joseph's right arm could not be seen (Jacinta). The Child Jesus was small, quite little, the size of little Deolinda de José das Neves, who is not yet two (Francisco and Jacinta). The Blessed Virgin shone so brightly that she dazzled me. Now and again I had to rub my eyes (Lucia).

[10] Solar time.

color. These rays were, in turn, red, blue, violet, and green; they colored the spectators' faces. The sun stopped spinning, and stood still in the heavens; then it began to spin round, again throwing out colored rays of even greater brilliance. It then stopped spinning for the second time.

A moment passed and then the spectators received the impression that the sun detached itself from the sky. Literally, it seemed to jump in space. It zigzagged about from east to west and then, as if quite eccentric and, in some sort, crazed, it fell from the sky, plunging towards the earth and giving out unbearable heat. At this moment the feelings of the crowd were divided between wonder and fear. From all sides shouts went up. "Take pity on us! Have mercy on us! It's the end of the world!" The sun came to rest for a third time. Then it zigzagged its way up into the sky and, so to say, back into its usual place. The sky was clear again and with no sign of cloud.

The spectators suddenly realized that their clothes were dry once more. The solar phenomena had lasted for ten minutes.

It is hard to imagine that anyone, believer or atheist, would not wish to have been present in the Cova da Iria on October 13, 1917, and, sharing the thrill of the crowd, to have witnessed this extraordinary spectacle. Failing that, we can at least still examine the evidence of those who were there; for the purposes of this book the testimony of one such witness has been chosen because the facts are related with patent impartiality, the witness himself is entirely reliable and his evidence besides its attraction for us by reason of its obvious accuracy contrives to capture the atmosphere, the prevailing tone of that memorable day.

Among the journalists who rushed to Fatima was a representative of the Lisbon daily *O Seculo*, Avelino de Almeida; he was not a mere reporter but the editor of that newspaper. The fact that he should have taken the trouble to be present to report the proceedings, an assignment which ar.y member of the reporting staff could have carried out, shows clearly enough the importance attached by public opinion to the apparitions at Fatima. *O Seculo* was an avowedly left-wing paper and hostile to the Catholic religion.[11]

Senhor de Almeida, as a conscientious journalist, was not satisfied with arriving at the Cova da Iria just as the children were making their way towards the oak tree. He went to Fatima the previous evening and, having observed the prevailing state of the district, sent a preliminary article written somewhat ironically and with an eye to picturesque detail. It was a sequence of facts observed on the spot: he depicted the congested roads with the inns few and far between, reported the edifying or mockingly humorous conversations of the peasants, setting it all down higgledy-piggledy, and merely pointing out, in conclusion, that in his view the "miracles" of Fatima would not be unprofitable for the Church and for trade. This article appeared in the morning edition of *O Seculo* on October 13th just as Senhor de Almeida was making his way to the Cova da Iria accompanied by an American friend of his, Miss Judal Ruah. Both of them had been obliged to spend the night at Ourém where they had experienced great difficulty in finding lodging.

The second article begins with incidents and facts, the result, once again, of personal observation—a group of peasant girls chaffing the "saint," Lucia dos Santos, a description of the storm and how the spectators' clothes clung to their bodies. The rest of the article deserves quotation in full for every detail is of importance and helps to convey the "atmosphere."

"The road to Leiria overlooks most of the moor of Fatima where, it is said, the Blessed Virgin appeared to the little shepherds of Aljustrel. Pilgrims and tourists parked their vehicles along this road. Someone counted upward of a hundred motorcars, and as many bicycles, and it would be impossible to enumerate the various kinds of horse-drawn vehicles blocking the road. Among the motors the motor coach from Torres Novas could be noticed; its passengers comprised people from all grades of society.

"The pilgrims massed . . . round the small evergreen oak which, the shepherds assert, was chosen by the vision for a pedes-

[11] De Almeida was a member of the Lisbon Masonic Lodge.

tal. It could be regarded as the center of a wide arena on the slopes of which the rest of the spectators and the devout had taken up positions. Seen from the road the general effect was quite incredible. There were groups of prudent peasants gathered under their gigantic umbrellas, unpacking their scanty food supplies to the accompaniment of hymns and decades of the rosary. No one minded walking in the sticky clay to obtain a closer view of the tree over which a rough archway with two hanging lamps had been constructed.[12] Group echoed group in singing the praises of the Blessed Virgin. Suddenly, a bewildered hare, escaping towards a wood, attracted the attention of half a dozen shepherd children; they headed it off and killed it with their sticks.

"And what about our three little·shepherds? Lucia, ten years of age, the visionary, and her young companions, Francisco, nine, and Jacinta, seven, had not yet arrived. Their presence was reported about half an hour before the time announced for the apparition. The children, wearing garlands of flowers, were led to the spot on which the arch stands. The rain beat down unceasingly, but no one lost hope. On the road, latecomers arrived by car. Groups of the faithful knelt in the mud, and Lucia asked them, ordered them, to close their umbrellas. The order was passed from group to group and carried out at once without opposition. Many, very many, it might be thought, were in a state of ecstasy. They were deeply moved, and their parched lips no longer prayed; there were some in a swoon, their hands held in an attitude of prayer and their eyes moist; they seemed to be in touch with the supernatural. . . .

"The little girl asserted that the Lady once again had spoken to her, and then the sky, which was still overcast, began suddenly to grow lighter from above; the rain stopped and it could be seen that the whole landscape, rendered still more gloomy by this autumn morning, was about to be bathed in light by the sun. . . .

"Solar, not legal, time was followed by this crowd. . . . Ac-

---

12 The "little archway" was the work of some devout inhabitants of Aljustrel who had also decorated the trunk of the tree with flowers. It was destroyed during a "raid" by the freethinkers of the district soon after October 13th.

cording to many of the pilgrims the miraculous manifestation, the visible sign which was promised, was about to occur. Then we witnessed a spectacle that was unique, and incredible for one who did not see it. From the road above, where the cars were crowded together, and there were several hundred persons standing, the immense crowd was seen to turn towards the sun which appeared, free from cloud, at its zenith. It looked like a dull silvery plaque . . . as if an eclipse had occurred. Then a tremendous shout went up and we could hear the spectators near us crying out, 'A miracle, a miracle, a marvel!' To the astonished eyes of this crowd, whose attitude takes us back to biblical times and who pale with fear, with bared heads, looked at the blue sky, the sun trembled, made abrupt movements never seen before and outside all cosmic laws. The sun 'danced,' to quote the term used to describe it by the peasants. Standing on the running board of the Torres Novas motor coach an old man, with a gentle but energetic air, looking towards the sun, shouted out the Credo from beginning to end.

". . . I saw him then speaking to those standing round who had kept their hats on; vehemently he besought them to bare their heads before so extraordinary a proof of the existence of God. Similar scenes took place at other points. A woman, tears in her eyes and almost choked by emotion, shouted out, 'How dreadful! There are men still who will not remove their hats before so amazing a miracle.'

"At once people began to ask each other if they had seen anything, and what they had seen. Most acknowledged that they had seen the trembling and the dance of the sun; others, however, said that they had seen the smiling face of the Blessed Virgin herself, swore that the sun rotated like a firework wheel, that it had come down so low as to scorch the earth with its rays. Another claimed that he had seen it change from one color to another.

"It was now almost 3 P.M. The sky was clear and the sun followed its course, shining with its usual brightness so that no one could bear to gaze at it directly. What about the three shepherd children all this time? Lucia, she who spoke to the Blessed Virgin, from the shoulders of a man who carried her from one group to another, proclaimed with dramatic gestures that the war was over and that the soldiers would soon come home. But even news like that could not increase the joy of those who heard it. The heavenly Sign was all they thought of, though there was much curiosity to see the two little girls with their garlands of roses. Some sought to kiss the hands of the 'little saints,' and one of them, Jacinta, was nearer fainting than dancing. . . . Peddlers hawked post cards with portraits of the children and other cards showing a soldier of the Portuguese Expeditionary Corps calling on the help of his Benefactress for the safety of his country—and even a picture of the Blessed Virgin supposed to be the likeness of the vision. They did a roaring trade. . . . The crowds dispersed quickly and without incident. And the priests? Some had appeared on the scene, but they were among the curious spectators rather than the pilgrims eager for heavenly favors. One or other of them, perhaps, did not succeed in hiding that look of satisfaction which so often appears on the faces of those who are triumphant. It remains for those competent to pronounce on the macabre dance of the sun which today at Fatima has drawn hosannas from the hearts of the faithful and has naturally impressed—so I am assured by reliable witnesses—freethinkers and others not interested in religious questions, who had come to this spot which henceforward will be famous." [13]

This article, telephoned from Ourém the same evening, October 13th, appeared in *O Seculo* on October 15th under the headline: *Amazing phenomenon: How the sun danced at Fatima at midday.*

It earned for its author bitter attacks on the part of unbelievers and he was even accused of having been "paid by the priests." The considerable extracts quoted above appear to leave no doubt of his impartiality and perfect sincerity. De Almeida did not deny that he had witnessed a strange atmospheric phenomenon; [14] but he managed to keep his wits about him and continued, even after the "prodigy," to notice what was happening all round him. His account of the event bears the mark of a personal experience.

13 Quoted by C. Barthas and G. da Fonseca, *op. cit.*
14 The expression "to the astonished eyes of this crowd," judging by the context, is obviously no more than a turn of phrase.

Only certain awkward or uncompleted sentences betray rapid composition in the telephone kiosk at Ourém. In every line can be read the sincerity of an honest man.

To return to the solar phenomena, it is obviously beside our purpose to consider the theological controversy that it caused, and to determine whether God, for a moment, upset cosmic laws or whether He miraculously influenced the senses of the pilgrims at the Cova. Did the phenomena really occur or not? That is the whole question. And in the first place were any of the phenomena observed elsewhere than at Fatima?

Yes and no. No observatory in the world, on October 13, 1917, recorded anything in the least resembling a solar disturbance. The archives of the meteorological institute at Lisbon record on that day: "Storms in the morning, showers; bright periods from 1 P.M. to 6 P.M." [15] But the phenomena were observed outside the Cova, none the less, according to the testimony of Ignatius Lourenço Pereira. He was nine years old in 1917, and witnessed the "dance of the sun" in his village street, some six and a quarter miles from Fatima. To this must be added the testimony of the poet Alfonso Lopes Vieria who observed it from a distance of some thirty-one miles. His evidence has been quoted and discussed more frequently because of the greater distance involved, but Pereira's seems to be the more valuable evidence because the little boy of nine, as he then was, was not the only one to be favored with the sight. He declares that the whole village witnessed it and that even "the schoolmistress rushed out of the school, followed by all her pupils, into the village street to see the sight." It may be mentioned that Vieria became a well-known Catholic writer and that the little Pereira was later ordained and became a missionary in India. So it seems that a sight of the prodigy was granted as a special grace to certain persons of great piety who were unable to go to the Cova.

There is hardly need to dwell on certain miracles of a more private nature which occurred on that day, and on which the Church, with her usual caution, has not pronounced. There was thus the cure of a tuberculous peasant woman who, present in

[15] Legal time.

the Cova, recovered her health after standing three hours in the rain, when to all normal expectation she should have met her death. The great majority of the seventy thousand pilgrims and tourists claim to have witnessed the solar phenomena. There were a considerable number of conversions. What these conversions were worth, and how long they lasted, is not for us to say; it lies beyond both our knowledge and our purpose. But it is quite certain that among the spectators of the prodigy many changed their outlook, their ideas, and their lives. It is no less certain that the anticlericals of the country pursued their campaign of religious persecution. But Christ said that even a miracle would not convince the "generation of vipers." The atheist reply, and "explanation," depended on "collective psychosis and hallucination." It was the sole method of reducing the phenomena of the Cova to a scientific basis.

For it was obviously not a case of one of those verifiable facts, an eclipse or an atmospheric mirage. The prodigy was the exact opposite of an eclipse; the absence of cloud when the "dance" took place excludes any idea of a mirage. At first the unbelievers were delighted that the Lisbon observatory and those of the rest of the world had recorded no solar disturbance; but they were not long in regretting that they were not dealing with a properly observed phenomenon neatly labeled by the scientists. Such a hypothesis would be absurd, of course (for if the dance of the sun had occurred in the natural order, it would have meant the end of the world), but it would have provided them with an opportunity of putting down the miracle of Fatima as a mere if rather astonishing coincidence. We saw how the spring of Lourdes, gushing forth beneath the fingers of Bernadette in ecstasy, might, strictly speaking, remind us of that great law of coincidence, of which we still know so little; but at Fatima even this would explain nothing at all. The great miracle of the Cova is of a type hitherto unknown in the history of religions. It only faintly resembles Josue's prodigy. It must be admitted, therefore, if a materialist explanation is to be given, that seventy thousand persons were mistaken, and thought they saw something under the influence of collective hallucination, that they were all the victims of some colossal suggestion the like of which is also without parallel in history.

A few years ago a crowd of about a thousand peasants of Aveyron (department in the south of France), suffering from one of those "epidemics of miracles" deriving from that fantasy mania of children which is studied in the chapter devoted to Beauraing, also asserted—with a certain amount of conviction, moreover—that they had witnessed a dance of the sun like that at Fatima. But we should note the differences: the sun did not zigzag from east to west, it did not rush towards the earth; it made "little jumps"; the "prodigy" lasted hardly a few seconds. It should also be noticed—and this is perhaps the most important factor—that everyone, acquainted with what happened at Fatima, was expecting this miracle. It was an obvious case of suggestion. Anyone who gazes at the sun (with phenomena in mind) would normally see it move. There are well authenticated disturbances of this sort, which occur, not in the sun, but in the retina.

At the Cova da Iria, on the contrary, there was nothing to indicate that the great miracle was to be a solar phenomenon. We can recall the scene: Lucia, following with her eyes the gesture made by the vision, looked at the sun and called on the spectators to follow her example. Who heard her at first and did as she told them? Only her immediate neighbors; the rest, all the rest, in that enormous crowd, if they also looked at the sun at that moment, did so because they noticed something. Furthermore, not only was there no suggestion that the sun would dance, but even the idea of the sun in association with the miracle could not have occurred to people's minds after the torrential rain. We can leave out of account the excited few who claimed they had seen Our Lady; their vision very likely was no more than an illusion like that of children who see the "man in the moon." Also, after all manifestations of this kind, there are always some who must go one better than their neighbors. The dance of the sun has absolutely no appearance of being a confused phenomenon described by each witness in his own way. It lasted for ten minutes, began and came to an end abruptly: after the ten minutes were over, though the crowd continued to gaze at the sun, they noticed nothing abnormal. The dance was divided into several movements—several steps—clearly defined and quite distinct. The miracle might well have been suspect if for some of the crowd the dance had continued, if each individual had seen something different or, I may add, if the crowd had made an exhibition of itself. But there was not the slightest sign of nervous disorder, fainting or collective hysteria. Photographs were taken; they show us, in every direction, peasants crowded together, tidily dressed or in their Sunday suits, gazing at the sky with their hands held to their eyes. Their faces show merely intense amazement. A child is pointing to the sky. A woman, gazing, open-mouthed, shows the fear in her heart. They were simple folk, but they were not escaped patients from the madhouse.

October 13, 1917, concluded with a veritable triumph for the three children of Aljustrel. Their parents only retrieved them in the evening. It may well be thought that the Marto and Dos Santos families were more than a little overwhelmed by an event all the consequences of which they did not yet foresee.

V

Francisco died on April 4, 1919, in his parents' house, a victim to the epidemic of Spanish influenza that was devastating Europe. He had been to confession and Communion the day before.

He never made any mystery about the nearness of his end. After the day of the great miracle, in obedience to Our Lady's wish, the Martos at last made up their minds to send their children to school. Lucia, also, had prevailed upon her mother to let her go. Francisco frequently remarked to Lucia, "What's the use of my learning to read, since I'm going to heaven so soon?"

His illness lasted five long months, with periods of improvement followed by relapses. Francisco said the rosary in bed with great fervor. For several consecutive days he managed to get up and make his way to the Cova da Iria. Neighbors meeting him as he went would greet him

"So you're better again, Francisco!"

"No," came his invariable reply.

Following the custom of the country, his godmother had promised to offer his weight in corn at Our Lady's altar in order to obtain his cure. Francisco dissuaded her.

"It's quite useless," he said. "I am going to die and no one can do anything about it."

On April 4th at six in the morning he called his mother. "Look at the lovely light," he exclaimed. The next moment he sighed, "I can't see it any more!" and smiled. His head fell back on the pillow.

Jacinta died on February 20, 1920, at half-past ten in the evening at the Dona Stefania hospital in Lisbon.

At the beginning of 1918 she was found to be suffering from a disease of the chest. In February, 1919, the doctor at Fatima diagnosed purulent pleurisy. He sent her to the hospital at Ourém where she remained for two months. When she returned to Aljustrel her state was so much worse that, her biographers tell us, "the fluid was so abundant that she had only to bend over to make it run out into a glass." Like Francisco, Jacinta was resigned to her approaching end. She passed her time in prayer, asking Our Lady for favors—among others, that the great war foretold to occur during the next pontificate should not affect Portugal. Lucia, who was her confidante at her bedside, attests that in her illness she was favored on several occasions with a vision of Our Lady.

On January 11, 1920, a Lisbon doctor, Dr. Enrico Lisboa, on his way through Fatima, asked for and was granted an interview with the little visionary. He it was who suggested the Dona Stefania hospital. Olimpia Marto hesitated at first, but finally took the doctor's advice. On February 2nd, the Monday after Septuagesima Sunday, Jacinta was admitted to the hospital and given bed no. 7 in the children's section. On Tuesday, February 10th, the chief surgeon, Dr. Castro Freire, assisted by Dr. Elvas removed two ribs under a local anesthetic.[16] This operation was not to

---

[16] A general anesthetic could not be used on account of the child's weak condition.

save Francisco's sister who, forty-one days later, followed her brother to the grave.

There are witnesses to the fact that, after lying for three and a half days in the sacristy of the Church of the Holy Angels, Jacinta's body gave off a fragrant perfume which amazed those who were there.

Fifteen years later, on September 12, 1935, the child's remains were transferred to Fatima. The coffin was opened. The body was incorrupt.

Francisco was dead, Jacinta was dead. Lucia remained.

VI

One of the secrets of the second apparition (June 13, 1917), as we have seen, had leaked out; this was the secret which formed part of Our Lady's message to Lucia: "Jacinta and Francisco I shall come to take soon, but you will have to remain longer on earth." Believers took the death of the two little visionaries as supplementary proof. Freethinkers, for their part, accused the Church of causing their death: "Their parents let them die out of religious prejudice on the orders of the priests. And as long as Lucia remains alive there is a risk that the 'miracle' of the Cova da Iria may be shown up by her as a fraud. Lucia, in her turn, will have to go; only then can the Church be free from anxiety."

On June 15, 1920, it began to be rumored that this had happened; Lucia had completely disappeared. The sub-prefect opened an inquiry. Maria Rosa dos Santos refused to answer.

In point of fact Lucia had been summoned to Leiria by the bishop. This prelate, recently appointed by the Holy See and charged with the special mission of investigating Fatima and its religious implications, had decided to move this thirteen-year-old girl from the village where she had become the object of an increasingly fanatical and questionable curiosity. Lucia and her parents had agreed. She had then been given into the care of the Sisters of St. Dorothea who had received her at their hostel (*asilo*) at Vilar. Vilar is a suburb of Porto. Her departure was shrouded in the greatest secrecy, and she had promised to mention it to no one nor to reveal her identity to her future companions.

Under the name of Maria dos Dores, Lucia dos Santos remained four years at Vilar; we learn from the chronicle of the house that, like Bernadette Soubirous with the Sisters of Charity, she was exposed to the distrust and even the persecution of the superior of the establishment, who had no belief in the miracles of the Cova. At the end of these four years Lucia, who had already frequently expressed a wish to take the veil, left to make her novitiate at the Spanish branch house of the Sisters of St. Dorothea, at Tuy in Galicia. She spent three more years there before being clothed in the black habit of the Order, on October 2, 1926.

On October 30, 1928, Lucia dos Santos, now known as Sister Maria of the Sorrows, took her first vows. She was twenty-one. On this occasion Bishop da Silva of Leiria at last decided to break the silence. Until now, not only had Lucia remained in the cloister, kept apart from the curiosity of the public and, in effect, hidden from all eyes, but she had been kept, also, in complete ignorance of all that had happened at Fatima for the past eleven years. Events of considerable importance had occurred there which had resulted in recognition of the miracles and the institution of a pilgrimage, events which, to cut a long story short, had, as we shall see, established Fatima. Lucia knew nothing of all this; her mother had been asked not even to mention it in her letters. On one occasion only—was it mere chance or a nun's indirect method of apprising Lucia of the truth?—the visionary found on her chair a card of Our Lady of the Cova with a form of prayer on the back. She gazed at it for a long time and tears sprang to her eyes.

"Ah!" she exclaimed, "I was sure of it!"

However carefully the secret was kept it was inevitable that some rumor of the truth should get about sooner or later. In Portugal it was whispered that Lucia was still alive, in Spain, in a convent in Galicia or Asturia. All the same, Bishop da Silva's official announcement came as a thunderclap. The country heard that Lucia had become a nun and had been sent, directly after her profession, to the institution of Our Lady of the Seven Sorrows at Pontevedra. It can be surmised that the bishop wished to test Lucia's modesty and humility, for the superior at Pontevedra was no other than the former superior at Vilar who, as we know, denied the miracle of Fatima and made no bones about asserting in public that the "little savage" had never been visited by Our Lady.

Thus Lucia, like Bernadette—the analogies between Lourdes and Fatima require emphasizing continually—fulfilled her destiny as the chosen one of God. And as these lines are written she is still fulfilling it. But unlike Bernadette, she has not retired into complete silence. At the request of Bishop da Silva she has spoken and has revealed some of the secrets of the Cova (which have been inserted here in the account of the apparitions); in the last place, she has revealed the first secret of all which was jealously guarded by the three children. Abruptly the Christian world received this astonishing announcement: *the apparition of May 13, 1917 was not the first.*

"No, it was not the first," Lucia said. "The marvels of Fatima did not begin on May 13, 1917, but a year earlier, on a day in the spring of 1916. I cannot say exactly what day it was, for I did not then understand the calendar and had not learned to count the days and the months. And this first 'miracle' did not occur at the Cova da Iria like the others, but in a place *Chousa Velha* (the old garden), at the bottom of the hill Cabeço. It was to this place that at that period Francisco, Jacinta, and I used to take our sheep to graze."

The revelations which follow have been fully approved by the Church; Cardinal Cerejeira, Patriarch of Lisbon, has mentioned them with approval at least twice: in a sermon preached at the Pontifical Mass at the Cova (May 13, 1942) and in the preface he contributed to the biography of Jacinta (October, 1942). Father da Fonseca, from whom many of the details for this section have been taken, does not hesitate to mention them in his book published at the Vatican itself.

The exact date, then, is unknown. On that day the three children took shelter from drizzling rain in a cleft in the rock called the "hole of Cabeço." They said their rosary there and played at knucklebone with the pebbles. Suddenly they saw a supernatural apparition approaching them. It was a white figure 'coming to them along the first rays of the returning sun. The apparition began to speak: "Fear nothing," it said. "I am the Angel of Peace. Pray with me."

The angel bowed down to the ground and said three times, the children repeating his words:

"My God, I believe, I adore, I hope, and I love You. I ask forgiveness for those who do not believe, nor hope, for those who do not love You."

The apparition vanished. It was to appear again two months later.[17] "What are you doing there?" the angel said to them this time. "Pray! pray much! The Sacred Hearts of Jesus and Mary have designs of mercy on you. Offer prayers and sacrifices continually to the Lord!"

LUCIA (*growing bolder*): "How shall we make sacrifices?"

THE ANGEL: "You can, if you wish to, make sacrifices of everything. Offer them to the Lord in reparation for all the sins by which He is offended—in supplication for the conversion of your country. I am its Guardian Angel, the Angel of Portugal. Above all, accept and bear with submission the sufferings that the Lord will send you."

The third apparition occurred two months later. This time the little shepherds saw a chalice in the Angel's hands. A host seemed to be suspended above it and drops of blood fell from it into the chalice. The Angel knelt down while the chalice remained suspended in the air. He spoke to the children and made them say after him three times:

"Most Holy Trinity, Father, Son, and Holy Spirit, I adore You profoundly and I offer You the most precious Body and Blood, Soul and Divinity of Our Lord Jesus Christ, present in all the tabernacles of the world, in reparation for the outrages by which He is offended. By the infinite merits of His Sacred Heart and by the intercession of the Immaculate Heart of Mary I ask of You the conversion of poor sinners."

Having said these words the Angel gave Communion to the

[17] Lucia added, "It was in July or August. In any case it was very hot. All the peasants were at their siesta."

three children and left them. They felt an extraordinary weakness: a strange feeling of physical prostration came upon them and affected them like an indescribable ecstasy. When they came to themselves they decided to return home and once more say nothing about this extraordinary vision.[18]

Lucia, therefore, gradually revealed the secrets to ecclesiastical authority together with the prayers that Our Lady taught her; it may be mentioned that the Church observes a somewhat cautious attitude with regard to some of them. It seems clear, too, that there are no grounds for coming to the conclusion that all is finished, and for writing off Fatima as something which happened in the past. For who knows that Lucia will not be privileged with further favors? In her convent cell she confines herself, for the time being, to prayer and to complying with the requests of the Patriarch of Lisbon by writing out one by one the revelations received by her which she has not before divulged. The greater part of these revelations—that are not yet known to the public—would seem to constitute actually a body of evidence for Jacinta's canonization process. We must wait in patience.

It now remains to set down, as quickly as possible, the course of events at Fatima after 1917, with particular emphasis on the miraculous occurrences that have been recorded there.

A few dates will help to give the picture. They are the landmarks in the history of Fatima as a place of pilgrimage and a religious center. January 17, 1918: re-establishment of the diocese of Leiria; May 15, 1920: nomination of Bishop José Alves Correia da Silva to the see; March, 1921: purchase of the site at the Cova da Iria by the diocese; October 13, 1921: authorization for

18 One of the secrets of Fatima foretold, as has been recorded, a sign in the sky in the form of "a great and unknown light illuminating the night." Lucia thought she recognized this sign in the aurora borealis of January 25, 1938, between 9 P.M. and 11 P.M. It was recorded by nearly all the European observatories: those of Austria, Germany, Switzerland, Italy, Poland, Greece, etc. In France it was particularly noticeable in districts of the Alps and in Brittany where people concluded that a second world war was at hand. The descriptions we possess of this atmospheric phenomenon mention a "blood-red glow" and "a red rainbow." One of my friends, Monsieur G.D. of Vannes, gave me a similar description, emphasizing particularly the terrible impression that this inexplicable aurora had made on him.

L.

the celebration of the first Mass at the Cova; November 17, 1921: a spring begins to flow on the site of the apparitions; [19] May 3, 1922: episcopal ordinance prescribing a canonical inquiry; October 13, 1922: foundation of the bulletin *Voz de Fatima;* June 14, 1924: approbation of a confraternity of brancardiers and helpers; April 14, 1929: final draft of the thirty-one chapters of the canonical inquiry; lastly, on October 13, 1930: the episcopal decision approving the apparitions and giving official authorization to the cult of Our Lady of Fatima.[20]

On February 18, 1934, was founded the Pious Union of the Crusaders of Fatima, and canonically established on April 28th. On May 13, 1928 the archbishop of Evora blessed the first stone of the basilica; the building was finished during the second world war. On January 15, 1929, Bishop Domingos Frutuoso of Portalegra, who until then had been opposed to the cult of Fatima, reconsidered the matter after a visit to Pius XI, and, declaring that he had no desire to be "more papal than the Pope," blessed statues of Our Lady of Fatima which he now allowed to be introduced into his diocese; on March 23, 1931 he officially consecrated the seminarists of Portalegra to Our Lady of Fatima.

He was the last of the ecclesiastical opponents of Fatima. On May 13, 1931, fourteen years to the day after the first apparition of Our Lady, three hundred thousand pilgrims packed into the

[19] A second spring emerged in 1927, five yards away from the first.

[20] The following is part of the text of this approbation:
"Dear Diocesans: We desire to delay no longer and think it unnecessary to do so. For the reasons we have given and for others omitted for the sake of brevity, and humbly invoking the Holy Spirit, trusting in the protection of the most Holy Mother, having heard the reverend Consultors of our diocese, . . . we have decided as follows: (1) To declare worthy of credence the visions with which the children were favored at the Cova da Iria in the parish of Fatima in our diocese on the 13th of the months from May to October, 1917; (2) To authorize officially the cult of Our Lady of Fatima. It remains for us, dearly beloved children in Our Lord, to warn you that if the grace that the most Holy Virgin has granted is for us a great source of joy, our obligation is the greater to respond to her goodness. Several years' experience shows clearly that, as the Psalmist says, 'The eyes of the Lord are open and His ears attentive to prayers in this place.' But by the purity of our prayer, by our keeping the commandments of God, our observance of the laws of the Church, by respect and submission to the directions of the Apostolic See we must show ourselves to be entirely Catholic."   JOSE ALVES

Cova to give thanks. Thereafter sanctuaries of Our Lady of Fatima multiplied throughout the world, from Portugal to Oceania. Our Lady of Fatima is now the patroness of Portugal, and the Cova has become a new Lourdes where hundreds upon thousands of the faithful come to implore graces for the soul and cures for the body.

A medical verification bureau has been founded after the pattern of that of Lourdes. This bureau recorded, between May and December, 1937 (the latest statistics published), 14,735 medical examinations; it has recognized upward of eight hundred cases of supra-normal cures. Among them, to quote the most important, are: instantaneous reduction of a fracture (Dr. Acacio da Silva Rebeiro, March, 1926), cure of total paralysis (Emilia da Jesus Marquès, May, 1929), cerebrospinal meningitis (Jeanin Sanctes da Costa, November, 1924), meningitis (Michael Veirea da Souza, May, 1928), acute sinusitis (Natalia dos Santos, May 13, 1928), and a pyloric ulcer (Gloria Forreira da Rocha Malheiro, on the same day). And, of course, as Canon Barthas and the *Voz de Fatima* both point out, a long series of moral cures were the accompaniment of these physical cures. In accordance with the plan adopted in this book which is concerned only with physical manifestations of the supernatural they are merely mentioned without examples being given.

One last word: Portugal—it seems scarcely necessary to say—has evolved politically in a Christian direction. The presence of Senhor Salazar at pilgrimages to Fatima is sufficient warrant of the reconciliation of Church and State. The Young Christian Worker movement, of considerable importance in the country, is dedicated to Our Lady of the Rosary. There is every reason to believe that the "triumph of the Cova" is not unconnected with this change of heart which has restored to Portugal its position as a bastion of Catholicism on the very tip of Europe—an ocean-bound Switzerland, as it were, preserved from the two last wars, a civil one and a foreign one, in accordance with the heartfelt prayer of little Jacinta on her deathbed.

· 3 ·

Therese Neumann
A Twentieth-Century Commentator
of the Passion

I

SEPTEMBER 14, 1224, is an important date in the history of Christianity, for as that day dawned there took place an event which was to occasion fierce discussion and make no small stir down the centuries. Its hero was a man of forty-four who had devoted the last half of his life to the praise of God in heaven and Poverty on earth. Because he despised and tormented his body he was granted an increase of suffering which was also an accession of joy beyond expression.

There is nothing to be added, perhaps, to what has already been said or written about the miracle of Alvernia; who indeed could do justice to that event and compare it with those seen in our day? The seven centuries that separate us from St. Francis of Assisi would form a gulf between us and him only if there were no documentary evidence, or if man's reaction to miracles had developed with the years. Few graces have been as public and as palpable as those received by St. Francis, and history proves that the same causes still operate in the same way; the world of the thirteenth century reacted just as would our own. To this may be added a specific and, if I may venture to say so, sensational factor: the novelty of the stigmata. The Christian world was lost in astonishment.

For the first time a human creature had identified himself with Christ. The whole thing seemed excessive and even sacrilegious. That a martyr should witness the crumbling of his prison walls, or the extinction of the fire beneath his stake, that he should walk headless among the crowd—in the face of such phenomena the faithful were ready to bow in reverence, seeing in them the intervention of a superior Being whose Essence was preserved distinct. But Francis had implored an infinitely closer union with the power of the Most High: "My Lord, my Saviour, grant me to feel in my soul and in my very body that bitter pain which You suffered. And in my heart grant me to feel that immense love which caused You to endure Your sufferings." We know how this prayer was heard. Time and space were no more. There appeared, flying through the air, borne on six wings, a gigantic seraph with the face of Christ, His extended arms nailed to a shining cross. In a flash Francis felt the five wounds so keenly that he fainted. When he came to himself the Seraph had disappeared but the five wounds remained imprinted upon his flesh.

That is the story of what happened to Francis. And, I repeat, we must not think that seven centuries ago this account was accepted entirely uncritically by a blindly credulous populace. While it can be admitted that thirteenth-century Italians evinced a more developed religious sense than the average man of the twentieth century, still, as an explanation, a miracle was hardly more satisfactory to them than to us. These men and women asked themselves just the same questions as we do nowadays when Konnersreuth, for instance, is mentioned instead of Alvernia. And, first and foremost, is he to whom the miracle happened sincere? That is the primary and essential question. In this particular case there could be no doubt of it. For twenty-two years Francis of Assisi had furnished untold proofs of exceptional, almost superhuman piety. The son of a rich cloth merchant, the boon companion in all sorts of carousals and gay parties, he had been suddenly roused up by his faith to kiss a leper, clothe himself in rags, and feed off ashes; toward the end of his days he would not have destroyed all hope of salvation for a mere imposture. No one obeyed the commands of Christ better than he did, turning his back on all human affairs; no one followed so faithfully as he in the footsteps of his Master.

He could be accused of pride in asking for the stigmata. But was the feeling which he experienced pride or lucidity—was it not like that which, six hundred and seventy years later, Thérèse Martin expressed on her deathbed when she declared, "I am a saint," and "Churches will be built in my honor"? Then, too, fraud in the case of the stigmata will not stand up to a careful examination. Francis's stigmata did not disappear with the seraphic vision on that day or the day after. He kept them until his death, that is, for two years; two years during which he was never left alone, nor even only with his brothers in religion, Angelo, Ruffino, and Masseo. His health grew worse and his sight dim; he was taken to San Damiano, then to Rieti for treatment of his trachoma by specialists; thence to Siena where other doctors studied the effects of the climate on his constitution. During these two years his was the usual lot of patients: he went from his bed to the operating room and from the operating room back to his bed. Finally, he was brought back to Assisi where the public could gaze upon him at leisure and a last group of doctors consider his case. Their examination must have included his miraculous markings. A description of them has come down to us; it is extraordinarily precise. Francis bore the mark not only of the wound but also of the nail, or rather a scab of dried blood in the form of a flat-headed nail; between the nail and the macerated flesh was a gaping hole large enough to allow the insertion of a finger. These stigmata were perhaps the most clearly marked that have ever been known. It should be added that bearing them he composed the well-known "Praise of Creatures," called also "The Canticle of the Sun" which is considered to be the first poem in the Italian language.

The stir caused by this miracle was, we repeat, exceptional, and it was to obtain an extraordinary heritage. For, curiously enough, and in spite of the difficulties of imitation, it gave rise to many impostures. These must be viewed as manifestations of pride, making unworthy subjects seek identification with Christ; certain hysterical phenomena are by no means unconnected with this outgrowth of stigmata. In any case henceforward it should be borne carefully in mind that any imputation of hysteria must be entirely ruled out in the case of Francis, and for a very excellent reason: the sanctity of his life—even in the ordinary sense of the words— is ground for material certainty. Seven centuries later our attention is claimed by another occurrence which implies nothing less than Christ's manifest presence in a human dwelling place.

II

Therese Neumann was born at Konnersreuth on the night of Good Friday–Holy Saturday, April 9, 1898. The village of Konnersreuth is situated near the little town of Waldsassen on the borders of the Upper Palatinate. It is one of those clusters of peasant dwellings, undistinguishable from thousands of others like it, of practically no historical or geographical importance. The countryside shows neither the untamed beauty of Lourdes nor the rugged but sun-basked wildness of Fatima. The canton of Konnersreuth is deeply Catholic; in their beribboned hats itinerant sellers of gaudily colored holy pictures scour the district: their wares include crucifixion scenes and Our Lady pointing to her sword-pierced, rose-crowned heart with, beneath, an inscription in Gothic letters.

Already in 1898, Therese's father, Ferdinand Neumann, and his wife Anne had the reputation in Konnersreuth of being fairly comfortably off, hard-working and of unblemished character. Ferdinand Neumann was a tailor by trade and, in addition, cultivated a small plot which provided him with fruit and vegetables throughout the year. The couple's piety was well known, and the fact that Therese was born at Eastertide seemed to them a special blessing from heaven. Births followed each other year by year until there were ten children to grace this Christian home; the father's plot of land was extended, but there was no change in the family's fundamental attitude to life: hard work, careful economy, scrupulous acknowledgment that they owed all to Providence.

All the biographers of Therese agree about her childhood. Apart from a few mild childish illnesses she was a sturdy and merry little girl who, we are told, cheered up those who were gloomy. (The village grocer was fond of her and often had her with him at the counter; she used to call out to the customers and wag her small finger at those who did not buy enough.) At school Therese was neither at the top nor the bottom. She was of normal intelligence. From the age of seven she attended the Sunday school catechism classes, and when she had learned to write used to note down in exercise books her childish thoughts and her artless aspirations to God, the Blessed Virgin, and the saints. She had a subscription to *Rosenhain,* a monthly magazine produced by the Salesians at Munich, and came to know *The Story of a Soul* by St. Therese of Lisieux. She used to make the Way of the Cross with a little girl of her own age, and when this companion died, at the age of fifteen, her loss caused a profound affective shock which gradually led Therese to a firm determination to scorn the world and become a missionary Sister in Africa.

Thus a future servant of God was growing up at Konnersreuth; she became a healthy, sturdy girl and shared in the work of the village and the fields. It is universally acknowledged that she was well-balanced, unimaginative, and by no means nervous; her only little weakness was to feel giddy if she climbed on a chair and a strange dislike for long-haired animals.

Soon the charm of youth was seen on her face; Therese was exceedingly attractive. Two suitors appeared and one of them asked her to meet him at dusk. Therese kept the appointment armed with a whip with which she laid about the over-forward suitor, and, as a final deterrent, informed him of her intention of becoming a nun. She had told her father a little before this, and he had done nothing to dissuade her. Then war broke out and Ferdinand Neumann was called up. He asked his daughter to postpone her entry until he came back and Therese agreed, but it was understood that when peace returned she would take the veil.

On the morning of Sunday, March 10, 1918, Therese was getting ready for the half-past seven Mass, at which she was to go to Communion, when shouts of "Fire! Fire!" rang through the village. A farm house was alight. It was a fire of no great importance and was caused by someone's carelessness; but this was March, 1918, a time when there were few men about and those who had not already fallen at the front were engaged in a hopeless war which was to last for some months still. As everywhere else in Germany— and in France too—the women of Konnersreuth had taken their place as responsible guardians of the home. The shout of "Fire! Fire!" brought them all quickly on the scene, together with a few old or disabled men. The women made a chain of buckets and fought the consuming flames with all their strength. Courageously, Therese Neumann had taken her stand at the head of the chain. She was very soon bathed in sweat and freezing water. Suddenly she cried out and dropped the bucket. She had just felt a sharp pain in her back and, simultaneously, experienced a feeling of extreme weakness; as she could not bend down or move her arms she returned home and went to bed at once, feeling extreme nausea; soon afterwards she was wracked by a dry cough.

The following days show us Therese Neumann contending with illness, trying without success to understand its cause, and reproached by her family—her father was home on leave—who ascribed her inaction to laziness. "Get up, lazybones! Cheer up!" Everyone was at her. They made her get up, and go down to the cellar for a supply of seed potatoes. Therese fell down the cellar steps and fainted. With great difficulty her sister Odile brought her round only to discover that now her eyes were causing trouble. "It seems as if my eyes were starting out of my head." She went back to bed and thenceforward was a victim to a humiliating weakness which, from modesty, she concealed from her relatives. Within a week her mood had changed. Her character was soured and her family, beginning to find her unbearable, decided finally that she should have treatment. About this, the least that can be said is that they might have thought of it before.

On April 23rd Therese Neumann was admitted to the Waldsassen hospital. Why was she sent to the hospital? Because the Neumann family, although fairly comfortably placed, found this the most economical solution. Therese was rated as an agricultural worker, and came under the social legislation then in force; she was entitled to free hospital treatment, and received, in addition, a daily allowance for illness. Moreover, she would receive more expert treatment in the hospital. Dr. Goebel, a well-known practitioner, took charge of her case. Unfortunately, from the very first day Therese conceived a strong dislike for him and did not tell him all her symptoms, confining herself to mention of the pain in her back. She said nothing of the convulsive fits and bodily spasms which wracked her every night. From the nurses, as from her parents, she apparently concealed her stomach and intestinal troubles. To cut a long story short, when she had had seven weeks of complete rest, more or less reluctantly, Dr. Goebel signed her exeat.

Therese's state now quickly deteriorated. Fainting fits followed in rapid succession. All work was impossible. Anne Neumann, in great distress, called in another practitioner, Dr. Burkhardt. To him we owe the first real diagnosis of the young woman's case and so can follow, almost day by day, the progress of her illness.

Dr. Burkhardt, an intelligent and informed country doctor, first diagnosed a characteristic pleurisy. He warned Therese, who questioned him about the probable course of her illness, that she would have to undergo a long period of complete rest and that very probably she would be unable to become a nun. Therese burst into tears. Her symptoms became suddenly worse. Her convulsive fits occurred henceforth every day; the slightest want of caution could bring them on, sometimes merely a light touch on some part of the body, as, for example, when she laid a finger on her back in hooking up her bodice. Her head was thrown back, her clenched hands beat the air and once again she lost consciousness. Her weakness affected the whole body. Eager as she was to go to church she was almost always obliged to turn back; on the way she could no longer recognize her neighbors. On October 22nd occurred a particularly acute crisis, and Anne Neumann, convinced that her daughter was going to die, sent for the parish priest, Father Naber, to give her Extreme Unction.

At this period of her life, practically speaking, Therese could live only lying down and in dreadful pain. The skin of her back and legs lost all sensitivity; she did not feel the injections that were given her. She gradually lost her sight. Therese was now blind. She could not speak; her jaws and lips were spasmodically clenched so tightly as almost to cause suffocation; to make her take a little food it was necessary to hold her nose. On occasion her convulsive fits threw her out of bed, and her now sightless eyes with pupils dilated rolled in their sockets and frightened the children whom curiosity had drawn to her bedside. What now remained to her in this living death? Hearing? That too left her in its turn. Lastly, one day when her jaw and lips resumed their normal position it was noticed that, as a crowning horror, Therese was now struck dumb.

Toward the end of 1919 Therese began to spit blood. All agreed that the end was now near. On February 27, 1920, the Neumann family received a notice from the agricultural section of the Sickness Insurance Office. Therese's disability was assessed at one hundred per cent and she was granted a pension fixed at fifty marks a month. This notification was a mere administrative formality, and would not be quoted here save for the fact that its conclusions are based on the latest diagnosis at that date. The document lays down, in fact, that the patient, Therese Neumann, living with her parents at Konnersreuth, originally an agricultural worker, has been suffering since March 10, 1918, from functional disorders of all kinds, among others blindness and paralysis, the result of grave hysteria. For the first time in black and white the word *hysteria* appears in connection with Therese Neumann.

III

At the beginning of 1923 anyone at Konnersreuth who inquired after Therese Neumann would have been edified by the unanimity of the answers and the earnest compassion of his informants. The fact that Therese was still alive was no longer ground for astonishment; for the last four years her death had been expected from day to day, but it had to be acknowledged that some vital thread kept her still alive; all agreed that, everything considered, death would be a blessing for her. These simple folk knew nothing, of course, of the typical symptoms of hysteria, and Therese's illness seemed inexplicable to them. Generally speaking they shared Anne Neumann's opinion: the doctors had been unable to cure her daughter because they could find no proper remedy for the "stitch in her back." In any case, obviously no one expected her to get better although there was some talk of partially recovered hearing. In this connection it was remarked that Therese had begun to hear again and to speak a little on the day that Anne, bending over her poor child, had let drop a tear on her face.

What can be learned of one in a living death? Apparently Therese was resigned to her illness. On April 25, 1923, she had a vomiting attack which was, we are told, more copious than the others: she brought up blood transformed into hematin under the action of the gastric juices. Meanwhile the Neumanns had acted as, in similar circumstances, all peasants act: they had called in a country "healer," one Heinzl, who had procured a herbal tea for them. As they had run out of this mixture Ferdinand Neumann decided to go and fetch a fresh supply. On April 29, 1923—a Sunday—after kissing his daughter he set out. It was six o'clock in the morning. At half-past six Therese who had fallen asleep woke up with a start. With mingled joy and wonder she found that she could make out the objects in her room. She called her mother and sisters—and could see them. She had a copy of *Rosenhain* brought in. She read the first article devoted to the religious event of the day, Sunday, April 29, 1923: the beatification of Therese of the Child Jesus at St. Peter's in Rome.

Anne Neumann hurried off to Father Naber and told him of her daughter's cure. A few days later Father Naber received a long communication from the Carmelite Fathers at Ratisbon: they had learned of the extraordinary event and now asked his opinion whether Therese's cure could be ascribed to a favor of her blessed namesake; if it could, obviously, they would submit it as evidence at the future canonization proceedings. The parish priest of Konnersreuth questioned Therese and was told that the evening before her cure she had offered a special prayer to Blessed Therese. But she had not asked for a cure. Father Naber answered that in his opinion there was no question of a miracle.

Two years passed by, two years during which Therese's state

grew neither better nor worse, and the canonization process of Therese of Lisieux was brought to its conclusion. On May 17, 1925, Therese of Lisieux was enrolled among the saints of the Catholic Church. On that day, at three o'clock in the afternoon, just as Ferdinand Neumann was getting ready to go to church for a Sunday service a loud cry from his daughter sent him running to her bedside. Therese seemed to be in ecstasy; she was looking fixedly at the wall and was radiant with joy. To her father's question, "What's happened? Do you want your medicine?" she replied in a hollow voice, "The parish priest, the parish priest . . ." At the very moment Father Naber entered the room Therese was supporting herself by holding on to her bed; suddenly she stood upright and began to walk. Her paralysis had disappeared.

Therese's account: "Suddenly a light appeared above my bed. It was a very bright light and it did me good. I heard a voice which asked me, 'Would you like to be cured?' I answered, 'Both are good, to live or die, and the good God knows it better than I do.' The voice asked me, 'Wouldn't you be glad if you could walk a little?' Then, 'Try, try, I am going to help you.' I then felt myself as it were taken by the right hand and I sat up. The voice went on, 'You will have more to suffer, in spite of the doctors. But fear nothing. It is only through suffering that you can realize your desires and your vocation as a victim. *Far more souls have been saved through suffering than by the finest sermons.*' And the voice concluded: 'Now you will be able to walk.' "

Father Naber was startled. A sentence in Therese's account (it is italicized here) was an exact reproduction of a saying of St. Therese of Lisieux in her sixth letter to missionaries. He asked Therese if she had read it anywhere. She answered in the negative.

From this day onward Therese began to get up again and to walk leaning on a stick or holding on to the furniture; she was slightly lame. She appeared in public on the feast of Corpus Christi, and was able eventually to undertake some of the housework. But now occurred a further phenomenon which caused astonishment to all about her; she could no longer tolerate solid food and often refused even all liquid food, stating with a smile that she felt no need of eating at all.

On September 30, 1925, the anniversary of the death of St. Therese of Lisieux, there was a further vision. This is Therese's account of it: "The bright light returned and the same voice said to me, 'Resl,[1] it is God's will that the marks of your illness should disappear. In return you will undergo still greater sufferings. Urge men to believe in God. Obey your confessor and tell him everything. You must die to yourself continually and increasingly. All your life keep your childlike simplicity.' Then the voice ceased and the light disappeared and I perceived that I could walk without help. I walked to the church and only experienced slight fatigue. It was scarcely necessary for me to pause as I went up the steps."

That was the third "miraculous" occurrence; the fourth did not lag far behind. On November 7th Therese Neumann felt a sharp pain which Dr. Seidl—who on Dr. Burkhardt's death had taken his place—attributed to an acute and exceptionally serious appendicitis. An emergency operation was necessary. While preparations were being made to move Therese she was twisting and turning on her bed and crying out continually, but she had the strength to utter a prayer to her new patron and a relic of the saint was applied to her. The pain ceased at once. This is Therese's account of the experience: "I saw a white hand stretched out towards me and heard the voice once more, 'You will have no need of an operation. Get up and go to church and thank God.' And again it added, 'You must die to yourself continually and increasingly. All your life keep your childlike simplicity.'"

The following night, at about midnight, Therese evacuated a certain quantity of purulent matter together with a shred of skin about four inches long. Resorption of the appendicitis had occurred.

At this point in our story we may well be allowed to pause. All that has so far been related is witnessed to by a great number of people, among them Therese's parents, her neighbors, Father Naber, Sister Registrude; in any case so far as is possible it seems to be established that up to this time no fraud can be imputed either to the witnesses or to Therese Neumann. From now onward the village of Konnersreuth and district was divided into two camps

[1] A South German diminutive of Therese—*Translator.*

with the skeptics in the majority. Therese's near relatives, of course, were the most inclined to believe in a miraculous intervention; Father Naber was beginning to come round to their view. Dr. Seidl answered all inquiries evasively, "Mediation of St. Therese? Well, I suppose it might be." He quoted also Dr. Burkhardt who before he died remarked of Therese Neumann, "This girl is blessed with rare vigor. What a pity that such energy should be made fruitless by suffering!"

If this were the end of the "Neumann case"—a sad, a tragic story even, with a happy ending—we should be concerned only with the connection between Therese and her heavenly patron. The whole question would be reduced to that put by the Carmelites of Ratisbon. The Church would merely have to give judgment whether this additional favor could or could not be attributed to St. Therese of Lisieux. And there can be no doubt that the question would be far from simple. Father Naber's first considered opinion does not stand up to serious examination from the religious standpoint. The assertion that Therese was not miraculously cured because she did not request it reveals its inherent weakness. For it is precisely when a cure or some other personal advantage is asked for that the favor of a miracle is often refused. At Lourdes, for example, instances abound, and cures may be witnessed that have been requested not by the sick themselves, who have sometimes gone to the grotto with no faith at all, but by others. The "coincidence" of Therese Neumann's successive cures in close connection with the beatification, the canonization, or the mere anniversary of St. Therese is not conclusive evidence of their reality. If the possibility of suggestion is admitted, it is obvious that the devout Therese Neumann, with her special devotion to the saint, could not fail to be susceptible to suggestion on those days. Two points for discussion with regard to her illness deserve bearing in mind at this juncture. In the first place, it is by no means uncommon for a doctor to be mistaken over the diagnosis of appendicitis and, in the second, Therese Neumann's certified illness was grave hysteria: one of the fundamental characteristics of hysteria is the possible sudden disappearance of disabilities and morbid symptoms.

Thus the issue to be decided turns largely on the fact that in Therese Neumann's case, unlike certain cases observed at Lourdes, there is no formal contradiction of the laws of nature any more than in the "ordinary extraordinary" cures of Marguerite or Blanche (of the Salpétrière asylum) for which no suggestion of a miraculous cure has ever been put forward. On the contrary, what arrests attention particularly, over and above any supernatural intervention, is in fact Resl's character, her deep, genuine piety (as one of her biographers puts it). Even were the Church to challenge the fact of intervention having taken place, there is nothing—up to this point—in Therese Neumann's deeds or words but what is very pure, edifying, and extremely orthodox. Therese Neumann is no Nicole Tavernier, no Rose Tamisier; even in her earliest childhood she was in a totally different category from Fernande Voisin who experienced visions of Our Lady on a Sunday evening after spending her afternoon at the Beauraing cinema which was showing *The Mystery of the Yellow Room*. And the message which she passed on from St. Therese of Lisieux is closely allied to the teaching of her "Little Way" for reaching heaven.

But these considerations, I repeat, apply only to this stage of the narrative. It is easy to imagine Therese Neumann, cured of her infirmities and carrying out her dearest wish, bearing the Word of God to remote countries as a missionary Sister; but her stupendous adventure had only just begun. Not merely Konnersreuth but the whole world looked on amazed as a new Therese Neumann took the stage in a dazzling pageant of the supernatural.

IV

At the beginning of Lent, 1926, to the surprise of her parents and all the villagers of Konnersreuth, Therese Neumann experienced a sudden recurrence of illness. It began with a sharp attack of influenza, followed by an abscess in the right ear. Then, unaccountably, blood began to ooze from her eyelids.

During the night of Thursday to Friday (March 4–5) Therese

had another vision. And this time it was no mere bright light nor yet a hand stretched out to her; its content was of deep, rich imagery. She saw Christ Himself with His disciples in the Garden of Olives. There is this first detail to be recorded: the Saviour's disciples were not lying down as they are usually represented but were sitting on stones. At the same instant Therese felt an agonizing pain near her heart. She put her hand to her breast. Blood was trickling down. Once more a tremendous weakness overcame her; she was to say later that the vision had made her numb.

On the night of Thursday to Friday (March 11–12) occurred two further visions: the Garden of Olives and the scourging of Christ. The wound in her side began to bleed again and, on the following Friday, when Christ appeared to her carrying His cross, going up to Calvary, Therese noticed an open wound on the back of her left hand. On Good Friday, April 2, 1926, the entire Passion of Christ passed before Therese's astonished gaze. Her sufferings were terrible. Her feet and hands bore the stigmata. When she returned to her normal state, at least so far as the visions were concerned, Therese made a confidante of one of her sisters who informed their parents. Once again they sought out the priest. Father Naber examined the stigmata: he could observe round, bleeding wounds as if a knife had dug into the flesh and cut discs out of it. These stigmata remained until April 17th in spite of the dressings and ointments applied to them. From this time onward, every year during Holy Week stigmata and visions reappeared, while Therese's state grew worse until her condition was stabilized, so to say, as one of continuing disability and pain. Finally, Therese, who by this time no longer took any solid food, began gradually to refuse all liquids and to fast completely for periods of several weeks and even several months.

The Neumann case could now no longer be confined to Konnersreuth and its district. The whole world had learned that on the borders of the Upper Palatinate there was living—but for how long?—a human creature in touch with the Unknown. The newspapers of the world mentioned Therese Neumann and began to publish photographs of her house, her parents, photographs of herself with her oval, deathly pale face, her cheeks lined with a trickle

M

of blood. The most astonishing rumors were afloat and, even more astonishingly, found confirmation at Konnersreuth. It was learned that St. Therese had again spoken to the stigmatic (she had said to her, "Our Saviour is pleased with you. You are not going to die, you will help with the salvation of souls."); that Resl's visions had enlarged in scope to an astonishing degree and now included the Passion, the life of Christ, the apostles, and the saints; that wonders were piling up, were, it might be said, jostling one on top of another: prophecies, the gift of foreseeing the future, and revealing the past of others, of discerning authentic from false relics, of knowing the saved and the damned, the gift of tongues, not to mention the fast, unique in history, which neither weakened Therese nor even caused her to lose weight. All these phenomena were observed, noted down daily, hourly, by the villagers and soon by a whole crowd of priests and doctors, believers and skeptics, who had flocked from all parts eager to clear up or to publish abroad the "mystery of Konnersreuth."

From this time onward occurred sensational conversions like those of the Protestant Gerlich or the socialist leader Benno Karpeles. A group of religious and laymen was set up with the object of studying the Neumann case; and this group, which adopted the name of the Konnersreuth Circle (*Konnersreuth Kreis*), soon aroused enthusiasm in some quarters, offset by the disparagement in others. A prelate of the Catholic Church, Bishop Schrembs of Cleveland, arrived one day from the other side of the world; he sat by Therese's bedside, was present while certain phenomena, later to become quite usual, took place, and set out again declaring that for the first time in his life he had experienced the nearness of the supernatural.

The opposing view was represented by doctors, men of learning, and priests, who were filled with doubt on the matter or refused to believe; they put question upon question, set traps for Therese and, having left her house, disagreed with each other's conclusions, exchanged arguments and pamphlets, and produced great tomes reaching diametrically opposite conclusions.

In the midst of all this commotion Therese remained calm and unflurried; her family instinctively adopted a course which it was to preserve unchanged in the future. What mattered principally to Ferdinand and Anne Neumann was to safeguard the dignity of their family home and their daughter's good name. Catherine Emmerich's sister had surrendered her to the curiosity of the public and a veritable inquisition; Therese's parents asserted that their rights over their daughter were unimpaired, whether she were the subject of miracles or not, and that her primary duty was to obey them. Gradually the members of the Konnersreuth Circle came to assume similar rights. The Church and the diocese of Ratisbon had far less authority.

We must anticipate the sequel. For the moment, in Dom Aloïs Mager's phrase, we are faced with "a fact and a problem." Therese Neumann is primarily an "ecstatic." She is completely engrossed in the visions which accompany her stigmata and hemorrhages. Following these visions there comes a kind of secondary state, differing from the first, during which Therese is apparently granted, and is simultaneously under the influence of, supernatural powers. Briefly then, there are three successive states. First, the usual state which is normal save for the stigmata and the fast; then the state of higher ecstasy (visions, voices); thirdly, the state of "exalted rest." The sufferings and weakness occasioned by her ecstasies would be enough to lay low any modern constitution in a very short time; yet directly after her agonies and what has been called her mystical death, Therese Neumann is once more in perfect health with pink complexion and smiling face. So it must be admitted that from her ecstasies, and, it might be asserted, from her ecstasies alone, she draws some element of strength, some restorative property.

We must pause here to notice a certain originality about Therese Neumann's visions. This phenomenon merits more extended study than the others and forms the justification for the title given to this section of the book: Therese Neumann's visions are indeed in this twentieth century a veritable eyewitness account of the Passion.

V

On the Thursday and Friday of Passion Week, 1929, Archbishop Kaspar of Prague was "witness" of forty of Therese Neumann's visions. She has disclosed the following information about them:

"I neither see nor hear nor feel anything of my exterior surroundings. My parish priest has tried to talk to me during a vision, but I did not react in the slightest. When the vision begins I always see Our Saviour suddenly, just like a flash of lightning. Each separate event absorbs me so completely that I cannot imagine that there is anything to follow, or that I have already seen it in a vision on another occasion, or that long ago I learned about the chief facts in sacred history. It is not pictures that I see but events. I see Our Saviour and the others just as clearly and easily as what is going on in the street. I am incapable of thinking; it is just this or that event that I desire to see. However, I do not choose the subject of my visions myself according to my dispositions, as is done in formal meditation. The outstanding episodes force themselves on my attention of themselves. I have no time for the distractions of curiosity. . . . Even if I had been alive and present there two thousand years ago I could not have seen things more clearly . . . *To me it is just as if everything I see and contemplate was taking place before me, right in front of me for the first time.*"

The originality of Therese Neumann's visions will be recognized at once. Everything occurs as if a reporter—a radio commentator shall we say—with no fear of being blamed for bad taste, told the public exactly what he saw at the very moment it happened, heedless of what came before or was to follow. And this "commentary" deals simply with the judgment and death of Christ. Therese Neumann "guesses" the identity of the Saviour and mentions Him by name. But no one else. All the other actors in the Passion are characters that she is unacquainted with and does not identify at the time. She even confines herself completely to what she sees and witnessing, for example, Judas' kiss takes the traitor for a loyal friend. On the other hand St. Peter seems to her to be merely a rough fellow who cuts off someone's ear—she classes him with the undesirable characters. In short she sees the Passion in an entirely new light, just as a scribe of those days, lost among the crowd, might have witnessed it. Lastly, but by no means of the least importance, certain details of her visions, always repeated in exactly the same way, complete the facts as they are recorded in the Gospels and sacred history and sometimes are contrary to them. This appears clearly in connection with the Crown of Thorns, the nailing to the Cross, and the shape of the Cross itself.

Therese Neumann's visions of the Passion give so moving, so touching an impression that they deserve a long quotation. There follows here, then, the Passion of Our Lord Jesus Christ as it is seen by Therese Neumann. All comment would be superfluous. It produces a very real impression of being actually present at the greatest event in history.

"The first thing that I always see is Christ on the Mount of Olives. I see Him with three disciples. He is very restless. In a short time He falls to His knees and soon afterwards rises, joins His hands, and on several occasions looks up to heaven. In this prayer and in the whole struggle and agony of Jesus I can clearly make out three stages, for I see the Agony in the Garden in three visions. It is during the second prayer that Jesus is at the cruelest stage of His conflict. I see little red drops begin to appear on His face and then all at once the blood begins to trickle down.

"The third time Jesus seems to be looking at a cloud. It is a real cloud. I do not know what special meaning this cloud has for Jesus; it is very low and near, quite clear but not shining. There is no light or fire in it.

". . . The soldiers who arrest Jesus wear something stiff on their shoulders and breasts. Their clothes are short and come down to their knees. On the under edge of their clothes some of them have gold braid.

"A little time afterward I see Him undressed to be scourged and I witness the terrible scourging itself. The column to which the Saviour is tied is quite high. He is tied by His hands and in such a way that His body is stretched considerably, but His feet are on the ground. He is struck very hard by two men simultaneously. His torturers are changed three times, so that altogether He is scourged by six men. . . . They begin on His back, then He is turned around and the front of His body is scourged. The stripping off of His garments causes Him very keen suffering.

"At the many blows weals form in the skin, then it is torn and the blood runs down; the whole body is disfigured and stained red with blood and wounds. When the soldiers have had their fill of cruelty they untie the Saviour. He collapses to the ground. It is pitiful to see . . .

"All at once I see the crowning with thorns: it takes place in a colonnade, out of doors, the sky can be seen. Fresh from the scourging the Saviour is now led beneath the arches; He has not been given back His clothes and is wrapped in only a long, sleeveless cloak. He is escorted by the soldiers who arrested Him. The Saviour is made to sit upon a stone projecting from the wall; I cannot imagine what other purpose this stone serves.

"The crown of thorns is already prepared. It is placed on our good Saviour like a cap, so it is not just a simple wreath as our pictures show. The blood runs down all over His face which, from the cruel treatment He has received, portrays His terrible pain. Then His torturers put into the Saviour's hand a kind of stick with a natural knob at the top, like a head of Indian corn such as I saw at Tockenfeld, but smaller.

"Then they amuse themselves by kneeling to Him, jeering at Him. They spit in His face and burst out laughing at their prisoner's helplessness. The Saviour frequently opens His mouth as if in need of air or because He is thirsty. Then one of the torturers spits right into His mouth. . . ."

"*The Way of the Cross.* Round the Saviour's waist is a leather belt. Ropes are tied to it and He is controlled and led along by them. Now He is pulled forward. He is wearing a long, reddish brown robe which comes down to His ankles, but no cloak.

"Every Friday I see the meeting between Jesus and His mother.[2]

[2] It should be borne in mind that all the characters in the Passion except Jesus are only identified by Therese Neumann after her visions. At the time she sees *a man, a woman, an old man,* etc.

Jesus speaks to her, but it lasts a very short time. They hardly do more than exchange a few words, like a greeting. His mother wears a large greyish blue cloak which is placed over her head like a veil, but made of thicker material than our veils. Mary is always accompanied by several women and St. John. St. John is younger than the Saviour; he has long hair but no beard. The meeting between Jesus and His mother is soon brought to an end by the crowd behind them pushing its way up. Jesus falls under this pressure. His mother does not see Him collapse. His fall causes a slight pause while the leaders look about them. Then Simon of Cyrene arrives on the scene. They reckon on Simon, who has so far taken no part at all, allowing himself to be coerced more easily into giving this ignominious assistance than the others who are full of hate for Jesus. Simon, who arrived with three young men, was not in the procession. I saw him coming down a side road. He wanted to refuse; he makes difficulties but has to give in. Later on, however, he feels pity for Jesus.

"The cross borne by Jesus is not like our crosses. In fact it is not a cross at all, but pieces of wood to make one. It consists of two beams—or three. Later on, when it is put together, it is in the shape of a Y.

"The veil that Veronica offers to Jesus on His way to Calvary is taken from her left shoulder. Jesus presses it to His face, but does not actually wipe it. Is this because to do so with all His injuries would hurt Him or because the handsome veil might be caught in the thorns of His crown? I don't know. When Veronica receives back the veil I notice on it stains of the blood of Jesus. She hides the veil under her clothes.

"*The Crucifixion.* As He approaches the place of execution Jesus falls again. I do not see the cross being got ready because during this time Jesus is taken aside. As He waits for them to come for Him, Jesus is lost in prayer. His hands are not joined and He frequently twists them about; often He looks up to heaven or bows His head towards the earth.

"When Jesus is nailed to the cross the great crowd does not seem to prevent my seeing. On the contrary I witness this fearful sight very clearly.

"Right at the beginning the soldiers offer the Saviour something to drink. But He does not do so. They cannot take off His long robe while the crown of thorns is on His head. They remove that. But it is by no means easy because it is attached to His head by several thorns. Afterward they put it on Him again. Once more blood flows down over His whole face. As Jesus is being undressed the sight of the deep wound on His left shoulder made by carrying the cross causes me especial sorrow.

"The same men who led the Saviour to Calvary carry out the Crucifixion. They have a yellowish brown complexion and appear to be almost savages. The Saviour is nailed to the cross while it is laid out on the ground. First He has to sit on the cross then to lie out along it. Ropes are wound round His hands to keep them in place. The right hand is nailed first. When it comes to nailing the left His executioners have to pause. They are unable to make the nail go in straightaway. I think it is because the holes for the nails have been bored ready in the wood, and they find that they have been placed too far apart. One of them pulls hard on the rope attached to the left arm while another kneels on Jesus' chest to keep His body in the middle. Finally the nail is placed on the left hand and driven through it; it penetrates into the wood. Directly they begin to nail a limb blood flows out of the wound. When with sharp hammer blows the nails are driven through these living hands, the sound of it goes right through me.

"When the hands have been nailed, groaning the Saviour draws up His two feet, for He is wracked with pain. To nail the feet ropes are attached to them and they are forced downwards. They are first bound then one nail is driven through both. When all is ready the cross is raised and Our Lord hangs there in the sight of all.

"I have no time to pay special attention to the behavior of the crowd while the cross is raised. I cannot even say if Our Lord looks especially at His Mother . . . The mother of God's face is pale yellow as if she were feeling ill. The cross on which Jesus hangs is very low. I can hear Him speaking from the cross, but I don't understand the language He uses. It is not Latin. The inscription over His head is in three lines of different sorts of writing. When Jesus' side is pierced by the lance I notice that it is thrust violently into the right side opposite the heart. The point of the lance comes out on the other side but is only just visible. I do not see the two thieves.

"Behind Jesus I see very many houses. What to me is most noticeable about these houses is that they have neither roof nor ridge. They look as if they had been cut off flat; I do not understand it. It is very strange.

"Shortly after the Crucifixion it grows increasingly darker. Our Lord gets weaker and weaker. He opens His mouth and His tongue hangs out for some time, then He says something. A soldier has placed a kind of sponge on the end of a stick—it is not very long— and dips it into a bowl which is near and holds the sponge up to Jesus' mouth. I don't see if Jesus drinks. Our Lord cannot hold up His head; the crown of thorns prevents His doing so, and for the whole time up to the present He has been unable to lay it against the cross. His body is beginning to turn blue all over. His eyes seem to sink back into their sockets, His face and nose grow pinched, His complexion pale, almost ashen. After a moment or so, Jesus suddenly raises His head as far as He can as if He were gathering all His strength together and cries out to heaven with a loud voice. Then He bows His head, His knees slip sideways. Our dear Lord collapses on the cross. He is dead. Slowly His head falls forward on to His breast."

That is Therese Neumann's vision. In connection with the crown of thorns it is worth noting perhaps that the visionary Gemma Galgani also saw it as a cap. It should be added that Therese does not merely see, but to some extent, mimes the scenes of the Passion; at different moments she suddenly sits up on her bed and stretches out her hands towards the spectacle before her. Nor is she backward in giving expression to the feelings aroused in her.

For Therese behaves just as if she were a living witness in those days. But unlike an impartial commentator she takes sides. She is caught up in the drama enacted before her eyes. She is for Christ.

She takes an indirect part in the action. Seeing one of the soldiers kick Christ's clothes to one side after His scourging, she shouts out, "I'll box your ears!" When the crowd insults and jeers at Jesus, "The scoundrels," she exclaims, "they've not had anything to drink yet and they're drunk already!" She abuses Simon of Cyrene because he does not try hard enough in helping Christ carry the cross—he is old and lets the weight fall on Jesus. As for the second thief (whom she saw finally after she had experienced her visions for several years), his blasphemies send her off into a regular tantrum. She jumps about on her bed as if she were going to hit him. On another occasion as she saw the Last Supper she said out loud that one of the apostles looked quite stupid. An hour later Father Naber took her to task for using that word. "Well," she replied, "he's a good fellow, but a stupid good fellow."

Her ignorance of history—and even of any acquired knowledge: during visions of scenes from the lives of the saints or Church history, for the time being she is entirely unable to give names or titles to the different characters, recognizing their rank merely by the style of their dress and calling a bishop, "an important priest," and the pope, "a very important priest"—involves her inevitably in frequent mistakes. Pilate ("who has no hair on his head or around his mouth") seems to her throughout the "narrative" to be kindly; Judas, as we have seen already, "was very fond of Our Lord." And on one occasion even, as she saw again the arrival at the place of execution, Therese imagined that Christ was going to be set free. She quivered as if she was hearing some entirely unhoped-for outcome and cried out in transports of joy (it was probably the time when Jesus is left on one side while the cross is being put together). Sometimes when she comes to herself Therese expresses wonder at finding herself in her room again. "What's this?" she asks. "I thought I was on a mountain and here I am in bed." She notices her stigmata and her astonishment increases. "Who's been bleeding?" Sometimes she is worried: "What day of the week is it? How long have I been asleep? Why didn't you wake me up?" And, on occasion, she merely yawns, stretches herself and noticing the people standing round her remarks, "What a crowd! What's going on?" Then too she makes rather odd remarks that sometimes, in spite of the gravity of the occasion, provoke laughter. One day Father Naber even said to her, "You're very silly today, Resl!" "Silly yourself" was the reply.

Therese speaks languages that she does not know. She repeats words she has "heard" during her visions which are recognized as Hebrew or Aramaic. When she was asked for some sort of analysis of all the moral suffering to which she has obviously given expression, she merely replies, "I am sorry for all the harm that has just been done to Jesus," or "They have just been very wicked to Our Lord." It is very noticeable that there is no variation from one occasion to another, and the change in her features after her "awakening" is so rapid that one has the impression of being present when a peasant woman wakes after a good night's sleep, preparing to get up and go on with her work. But Resl has not gone back to work in the fields, and her hands nowadays are occupied in light household tasks; generally speaking knitting seems to be her only secular occupation.

Her conversation is at once simple and profound. A Dominican came to talk to her about Faith and Grace, and the conversation was rapidly turning into a theological discussion when Therese abruptly made reply, "Why do you put it all in such a complicated way?" and went on to state the problem so clearly and movingly that the friar was filled with admiration. There is no doubt that Therese possesses the gift of touching hearts, and it often takes on the appearance of being supernatural.

Some people indeed find her visions less convincing than the phenomena which come after them during the state of "exalted rest." The news of Konnersreuth which is carried in a local Sunday newspaper is full of lists and descriptions. There is, so to say, almost too much to choose from. Therese has insight into men's spiritual condition, reveals past events and the secrets of persons unknown to her. She can expose apostate priests, and discomfited one who was introduced to her as an artist. She can give "news" of the dead. She can discern authentic from false relics and divine the presence of the former; when Archbishop Kaspar entered her room, quite spontaneously she kissed the foot of his pectoral cross at the spot where the relics were enshrined. She manifests a painful reaction if relics are applied to her, to her back for example, or when she is asleep. She foretells the "time table" of her visions and her stigmata. Lastly, she has the power of suffering in another's place. Her body will be covered with sores for some days and then these sores disappear leaving generally a pinkish mark; at this stage Therese indicates the sick person in whose place she was suffering. She has even been known to take on herself not only wounds and illnesses but also vices; on at least three occasions, without, of course, in the slightest degree taking to drink, she exhaled all around her an offensive smell of beer and alcohol.

Her fast would be sufficient to make hers a sensational case. But from the religious point of view something of far greater importance occurred which was to cause considerable disquiet among the stigmatist's onlookers. The starting point of this event was a mere ordinary sentence uttered by Resl.

On that evening Father Naber had spoken to Therese when she was in her third state, that is, of "exalted rest." He saw her lips move and distinctly heard the words, "You can't speak to Resl now, she is asleep." A little later her lips moved again, giving orders in clear, authoritative tones. On the following days similar orders were given in the same way. "Tomorrow a man will arrive (a detailed description followed) whom you must allow to come to her. Today, in the afternoon, she will begin to suffer at four o'clock." Unlike Therese's usual way of talking these sentences were spoken in the third person in good literary German. When she came to herself Therese had absolutely no idea that she had uttered them.

What especially struck the priest—and after him all those who happened to hear these orders—was the tone with which they were given which was in evident contrast to Therese's usual tone of voice. The question that then arose was so disturbing that the devout were brought up short before it as at the edge of a precipice. Was it possible that someone else was speaking through Therese's mouth? Could it be that the voice was the voice of God? The miracle—if it was one—was something quite unknown hitherto. The visionary was questioned. She answered, "My self—

or what you call by this name—is at that time very near to God, in close union with Our dear Lord." And so the list of mysteries of Konnersreuth has one more added to it.

Yet if crowds of the curious came from all quarters of the globe, and minds which could hardly be called credulous accepted the reality of the miracles of Konnersreuth, accessions to the number of skeptics continued to augment the ranks of the opposition. And from this moment those who denied any supernatural superven-tion, especially those among them for whom the Neumann case from the beginning of the visions had amounted to nothing else than a gigantic swindle, increasingly controverted every asser-tion.

VI

On Thursday, March 22, 1928, six persons, all reliable witnesses, called on Therese Neumann to be present during her visions of the Passion and note down hour by hour the various external manifestations expected to occur. These six witnesses were Bishop Buchberger of Ratisbon, his auxiliary Bishop Kierl, Professor Killermann, Professor Hilgenreiner, Professor Stöckl and, lastly, Professor Martini, head of the University Clinic of Bonn, who was entrusted with the actual drawing up of the report.

The Martini report is an essential document in the Konners-reuth case. It is difficult to say whether the author is to be com-mended more for his accuracy, the exactness of the terms he uses, or the clarity of his conclusions; but there is a further element to be added. It is in the Martini report that an accusation of fraud against Therese Neumann and her parents is raised for the first time with any appearance of justification.

It would be outside the scope of this book to quote the report in full so it must be confined to an accurate summary. At 11:45 P.M. the commission was ushered into Therese's room, though not without encountering some opposition from her parents. Her father's offended attitude should be mentioned. At 11:45 P.M. the Passion began. Therese's eyes bled or, at least, were full of blood

though the origin of the blood could not be detected. Therese's
face was radiant and Father Naber, who was also present, assumed
that she was seeing angels. Then she called out to the Saviour and
was seized with a fit of coughing. At last she spoke. She mentioned
the moon which she could see lighting up the Garden of Olives—
just a crescent with a broken end. Professor Killermann intervened at this point to inform those present, who were unaware
of it, that in the East the moon does not appear in that way, like
an upright sickle, but horizontally like a canoe. Consequently
Therese was either mistaken or lying.

At midnight it was noticed that her wounds were not bleeding.
At 12:15 A.M. and 12:45 A.M. Therese called out some words in an
unknown language: "*magera, gallaba*." Father Naber continued to
explain the Passion which was being enacted for Therese alone.
At the end of the episode of the Mount of Olives, Therese pulled
up the end of the coverlet hiding half her head. "Behind the coverlet she moves her arms about." At 1:15 A.M. Therese cried out
"*mahad*," and it was observed that her left hand was covered with
a little blood.

At 1:25 A.M. Therese again pulled up her coverlet, and as she
moved in doing so Professor Killermann noticed that the wound
at the heart was bleeding. Professor Martini bent over to look at
it and concluded that the blood came from her hands moving
over her chest. Therese's parents intervened at this point; Therese
herself continued to toss about wildly under the clothes. At 1:30
A.M. "a trickle of blood flows towards the wrist."

At 1:50 A.M. Therese was lying on her back in a restful attitude.
In her state of "exalted rest" she spoke, and greeted, among others,
Bishop Buchberger, telling him that Our Lord had forewarned
her of his visit. She appeared unaware of the auxiliary bishop's
presence. Quite suddenly she mentioned Socrates and quoted his
well-known aphorism: "All I know is that I know nothing." It was
noticed that the blood on her left hand had gradually dried.

2:30 A.M. Therese requested those present to go home.

3:05 A.M. She ordered them to leave the room for the sake of
decency. They thought that she wished to pass water and complied.
They remained outside for five minutes and when they returned

found that the wound in her left hand was bleeding again and that also her face was marked with "fresh, moist blood."

At 3:30 A.M. the blood had dried again as, of course, it should have done. The commission, foreseeing that no more was likely to happen, decided unanimously to withdraw.

On March 23rd at 8:25 A.M. Professor Martini went back to Therese's bedside. His notes run: "Much blood on the left hand. The face is covered with it. Her headcloth is soaked with blood." At 9:30 A.M. Therese started tossing about again beneath the bedclothes and complained of the heat. As during the night, the coverlet was pulled up and stretched vertically. At 9:35 A.M. Bishop Buchberger returned and reported to Professor Martini that when he looked in at 8:15 A.M. "the headcloth was still quite clean." At 11:10 A.M. Professor Killermann took Therese's pulse; it was normal. At 11:30 A.M. the stigmatist's parents again ordered those present to leave the room, ostensibly because of the heat and the vitiated air. All obeyed except Professors Killermann and Hilgenreiner who refused. But at noon Therese's mother lost her temper and turned them out. They remained outside for an hour and when they went back found that "Therese's hands and face were again covered with fresh blood." In the afternoon, finally, the commission noted that no blood was flowing. When Professor Martini requested permission to make an auscultative examination of Therese, with the bedclothes removed for this purpose, Ferdinand Neumann refused categorically. Thereupon the commission decided that their "experiment" was finished.

It was obvious what their findings would be. They never actually witnessed blood flowing. Bleeding took place only when they were absent. The whole party was sent out of the house, on the pretence of bad air, when they had merely asked that one of them might be allowed to stay. They received the impression that the whole thing was staged. Their "diagnosis," consequently, was almost bound to follow the lines that it did: *State of grave hysteria* (agreeing with the original diagnosis) accompanied by all the intrinsic symptoms of the disease, *habitual fraud included.*

These conclusions, of course, refer only to the phenomena of stigmatization. But it is impossible not to view them in relation with certain facts already mentioned, for instance Therese's refusal to allow herself to be examined by several doctors, some of whom had traveled from a great distance, her excuse being that they were "men of learning" and that science, in her view, could do nothing for her. (Her father turned the doctors away, shouting, "Only the Saviour can cure her.") The Church and medicine joined forces in an endeavor to persuade Therese to go to a clinic for a period, even for only a month, and the Ratisbon hospital was ready to receive her. But once more she refused. To the gentle advice given her by some priests that God Himself desired the truth to be known, her refusal was equally categoric. "I will go," she declared, "only if my father consents." Of course Ferdinand Neumann persisted in his refusal.

It must be admitted that none of it is very clear—or else it is only too clear. Even Father Naber, by his opposition to the visit of certain specialists, has been blamed by doctors and religious. The following reflection is not my own but comes from a priest well informed about the facts of Konnersreuth: he has no hesitation in recalling in this connection certain frauds, recorded by history, where a desire to convert unbelievers, to make manifest the glory of God, caused weak souls to stoop to trickery—a sin less venial, certainly, than they imagined.

VII

Extraordinary as the phenomena of Konnersreuth seem to be, the theologian finds in them no great matter for wonder. For his principal qualities are scholarship and great prudence. He treats ecstatic phenomena with extreme reserve because he knows very well the power of imagination over human beings and the almost stupendous suggestions that it can provoke.

The power of suggestion merely on its human level with no supernatural intervention was experienced in masterly fashion by a great saint who also caused others to experience it. Moreover he laid down rules for it. Reference to St. Ignatius of Loyola and his *Spiritual Exercises* falls naturally into place here. So that his novices should control their imagination and learn to distinguish good from evil, he decided to put their fully developed senses into operation. It is true to say that sanctity is primarily a method; St. Ignatius's method evinces not only an extraordinary determination but a thorough knowledge of man's physical and mental make-up, exceptional for his times.

St. Ignatius begins by requiring his novices to imagine hell as actually present. Their eyes must see the infernal region with its tortures and the souls of the damned, their ears should hear the cries and moaning, and their sense of touch should feel the infernal fire. Filled thus with fear and seeing his own damnation as actually possible the novice is then made to represent to himself the chief events of the life of Christ. "He sees the road to Nazareth and can say whether it is flat or hilly, straight or winding; he can taste the bread and fish that Jesus distributes to the people; he notices the smell of the oil brought by the sinful woman. This 'composition of place' is an essential element. The novice must imagine to himself the road leading from the hill of Sion down to the valley of Josaphat and the garden, its length, breadth, and exact position. *He suffers with Christ*, experiences the scourging, all his tortures, and his crucifixion." The very severity of the method admits no exceptions. "The fifth point," writes St. Ignatius in one place, "is an exclamation of wonder accompanied by a tremendous effect on the soul." A rule and a fixed time—four weeks—produce a complete discipline of the will.

All this, it bears repeating, is entirely outside any element of the supernatural; we are concerned here with what are merely exercises. But these exercises proved particularly effective with Ignatius's first companions. It may well be imagined that exercises of this sort would produce a certain transference when, instead of a fully determined soldier of Christ, they are carried out by a simple country girl dominated not by her will but by the most baffling physical phenomena in existence on which science, in the absence, perhaps, of a clear understanding of its effects and causes, has bestowed the name of hysteria.

There is a very great difference between the "supernatural"

phenomena experienced by Therese Neumann and Teresa of Avila. We have already seen how, even after seven centuries, we are compelled to believe in the stigmata of St. Francis of Assisi. Here were no mere effusions of blood from some doubtful source —like those produced by Rose Tamisier,[3] who in the absence of witnesses caused a representation of Christ to bleed—but real, deep, permanent wounds that could be observed for two years *de visu* and *de tactu*. St. Francis Xavier's *charismata* (when on the day of his death he preached in Tamil, Malay, Basque, and Japanese) are not to be compared with Resl's "Aramaic." That to some extent Therese Neumann possesses the gift of tongues by no means presupposes a formal divine intervention. Consideration of the well-known case of the Brazilian medium Carlos Mirabelli should serve to show the truth of this statement.

Carlos Mirabelli when in a trance could speak and write in thirteen languages: Czech, Bulgarian, Hebrew, Dutch, Persian, Latin, Portuguese, Greek, Syriac, Italian, Chinese, Russian, and French. He then passed through a state of ecstasy followed by one of listlessness not entirely dissimilar to that experienced by Therese Neumann—with the addition of an irregular pulse. Does Therese's fast make us pause? Those who oppose the preternatural hypothesis about Konnersreuth quote in this connection another case, that of Mollie Francher of Brooklyn. She possessed the same power of going without food under the influence of a generalized organic state. Neither Carlos Mirabelli nor Mollie Francher have been studied from the supernatural point of view, for their general conduct rules it out entirely. It is certain that on moral grounds and for piety a clear distinction should be made between Therese Neumann and these two mediums; but when that is done, and her critics have not failed to do so, the comparison remains valid none the less on the material, physical level.

Down the centuries innumerable visions have occurred. Connected with the case of Therese Neumann is that of a priest to whom the stigmatist of Konnersreuth had "disclosed" the miraculous origin of the apparitions of Limpias. Having made the pilgrimage, the good priest in his turn saw the face of Christ appear

[3] See Chapter 6.

on the walls of this Spanish church, though as is known, the Church did not recognize this miracle. The sincerity of the visionary was not in question—the distinguished poet Max Jacob, too, was sincere when, towards the end of his life, from his devout retreat in the country, he announced that he had been privileged with a similar apparition "between the wall of his room and the bed." And it must be admitted that Therese Neumann has been questioned very often about the reality of apparently miraculous happenings—a little too often sometimes, and without sufficient reflection. She has been asked, for example, to give her opinion about the case of Marie Goebel of Bickendorf and that of Claire Moes of Luxemburg. They were both stigmatics. In a state of "exalted rest" Therese answered unhesitatingly that these two cases were supernatural. A medical and religious investigation came to a contrary conclusion. Thus Therese was mistaken. At this juncture one of the members of the Konnersreuth Circle replied, simply, that Therese was too good-natured not to give pleasure to the inhabitants of Bickendorf and Luxemburg who greatly esteemed their stigmatists. Such a reply needs no commentary.

Then there are the voices she hears. One of the participants in the controversy about Konnersreuth has adduced evidence of Therese's penitents "guided by a voice from the Beyond." But that is nothing else than mere suggestion analogous to the phenomena that are produced at table-turning seances—and in this case there is not even any open discussion. But what value is to be given to Therese's claim, for example, that her guardian angel whispers in her ear and commands her to send away doctors and photographers?

What about her gift of recognizing relics? But Therese has frequently been mistaken (within two days it has happened that she has asserted the same relic was authentic and false). The following incident should be noted: Miss Isenkrahe, daughter of the author of a treatise on experimental psychology, wished to submit certain objects for Therese to discern which of them had been blessed. This occurred after several years of controversy, at a time when this "gift" of hers was particularly called in question. Father Naber, present on this occasion, opposed the experiment's taking place.

About Therese's power of telling the saved from the damned, science, of course, does not concern itself. But the Church has something to say about it—and she has done so, choosing for the purpose certain outstanding instances. Among *false miracles* one of the most obvious is that of Mirebeau. A certain priest, Father Vachère, claimed that he had in his possession a representation of the Sacred Heart which shed blood. Almost immediately the claim was found to be completely false. Called on to retract and do penance, Father Vachère refused, was excommunicated by Pius X, and then died unabsolved. Now the "Sacred Heart of Mirebeau" was brought to Therese Neumann by a certain councilor Böller of Gladbach. The picture was applied to Therese's heart and she acknowledged it as authentic. To the question, "Where is Father Vachère now?" Therese answered, "In heaven, with the dear Saviour." Shortly afterward Therese went one better—if I may venture to put it thus. An unidentified relic was submitted to her; "St. Marcel, lay Brother" she pronounced. But such a saint is not to be found in the official list. It is quite usual for Therese to predict heaven for some woman of the village, a notorious sinner, lately dead. Of course that is no proof one way or the other, for the ways of Providence are impenetrable.

We come to the "teaching" of Konnersreuth. The advocates of a supernatural interpretation make much of this, and it must indeed be recognized that Therese manifests a certain "wisdom": she is never heard to say anything contrary to the moral teaching of the Gospel. But this "teaching" . . . in reality teaches nothing at all. It merely repeats, extremely aptly perhaps, the lessons of the catechism and the many pious books read by Therese when she was preparing to be a nun. This point, which crops up in the following sections of this book, requires emphasis: miracles do not occur without reason; they have a purpose. To put it in plain language, they contribute something new. At Konnersreuth there is nothing new. Resl's remarks may possibly edify those present, but neither more nor less than their own spiritual books.

"In olden days there was not so much *poverty*. Things would be better if men would praise God more. Even a little flower which gives us joy may be a motive for thanking God and giving Him glory. Our Lord allows sufferings to punish certain sinners and to try the faithfulness of His friends. We have all the same God. Our Lord died for all. There is only one heaven." One of Therese's biographers tells us that at these words her hearers were "deeply touched." Indeed, they well might be before such simple faith. Yet there is a great difference between these words uttered by Therese as she sits in bed receiving her visitors and the homely sermons of the Curé d'Ars. To put it plainly, it sounds exactly like a lesson learned with care, or the repetition of what she heard in church the day before. When, three years after the definition of the dogma, Bernadette received the message from Our Lady "I am the Immaculate Conception," its religious importance cannot be denied. But Konnersreuth has no important message for Christianity.

Therese Neumann has been greatly blamed for her ill-regulated gestures and homely, even unrefined, exclamations when she is in ecstasy. Such an accusation can scarcely be held as valid if we recall the example of St. Catherine of Siena who mimed the whole drama of the Passion, or St. Mary Magdalen of Pazzi who wandered through the entire monastery following out the stages of the Passion and even danced "to give vent to the inexpressible joy of her holy exultation." St. Philip Neri was so excited that the whole altar shook when he said Mass; he, too, seemed to dance with joy after the consecration. In connection with the fact that Therese speaks *in persona Christi* (though this is questioned by many advocates of a supernatural hypothesis as against those who, a trifle prematurely, have entirely accepted the "oracle of Konnersreuth"), the earlier case of Ursula Benincasa should not be forgotten. "One day," we are informed by Imbert-Goubeyre, quoted by Father Lavaud, during the lengthy and arduous investigation she underwent in Rome, Ursula Benincasa, after Communion in Cardinal San Severino's chapel, fell into an ecstasy which lasted several hours. When the ecstasy was over the Cardinal, with considerable ceremony, submitted her to exorcism in the presence of a large congregation. When he addressed her with these words, "I command you in the name of the Father and of the Son and of the Holy Ghost, to tell me who you are—*tu quis es . . .*" Ursula at that instant raising herself from the ground stood upright, and her face glowing and fearful to look upon declared with great dignity, "I am He who Is—*Ego sum qui sum.*"

But the Church can produce other and more serious objections to a supernatural explanation of the events of Konnersreuth. She can quote St. Paul who wrote, "And the spirits of the prophets are subject to the prophets" (I Cor. xiv, 32); or St. Thomas in his commentary on that very quotation, "The prophets declare what they have seen in complete self-possession, *ex proprio sensu,* and not in a disordered mental condition like soothsayers"; or Cajetan, "Ecstatics, who proclaim their visions to all and sundry, are not prophets." Lastly, not quite so distinguished an authority perhaps, but one nearer to our own time, Dom Aloïs Mager informs us, "Anyone who knows the psychological states of the mystical life will find that Therese's states during, between, and after her ecstasies are not real mystical states. The fundamental phenomenon of the mystical life is infused contemplation which is a state wherein the soul is raised to an activity which is, so to say, proper to pure spirits . . . She (Therese) speaks in a childish manner, cannot count consecutively,[4] does not recognize persons or events. There is no doubt that her condition strongly resembles an hypnotic state." [5]

St. Teresa of Avila has already been referred to. Her visions may be mentioned in comparison with those of Therese Neumann, but first of all they must be "placed" in their special period. Now it is a very common mistake to imagine that Spaniards in the sixteenth century were more credulous concerning miracles than Germans or Frenchmen of the twentieth; credulity has nothing to do with deep religious conviction. The latter believes that miracles occur but confronted with one will inquire into its merits; credulity on the other hand passes quite easily from magazine descriptions of fakirs and their phenomena to apparitions of

---

[4] Therese in ecstasy does not say the number *three,* for example, but *one and one and one.*

[5] *Études Carmélitaines,* April, 1933.

the divine. In comparison with Therese, her namesake of Avila's situation seems poor indeed. Consider Resl's entourage. From the time of the first "supernatural" phenomena she was surrounded by a whole host of people, all a prey to their curiosity but predominantly sympathetic to her; almost immediately a Circle was formed composed of men of importance like Father Naber, Canon Naab, Father Fahsel, Dr. Gerlich, Herr von Lama, and Dr. Witt. This Circle publishes a weekly bulletin, as well as books and pamphlets, and is in touch with newspapers and secular and religious publications all over the world. The stigmatist fears no threat of violence—the worst that can happen to her is that she might be neglected and left alone. Teresa of Avila's circumstances were far different—probably, because she lived in "an age of faith." She was a nun who was already at variance with her own Order, and at that period, it can be asserted, was in revolt against it, a woman all alone, an object of hate and persecution. Not only her reputation, her very life was at stake. "To the Inquisition with her!" howled her fellow townsmen of Avila. Some demanded that she be sent to the stake, at the very least to the dungeon. The Dominicans of San Tomas, among whom rested the bones of Torquemada, were called in to oppose her.

Teresa of Avila was no tranquil, sheltered invalid on her bed of suffering, admitting or refusing visitors at will. She stood out, upright, she bore up nobly, she did combat inch by inch for the reality of her ecstasies. Father Balthazar Alvarez, whose severity of character was notorious, was sent to examine her; the sought-for condemnation was expected at his hands. He questioned her at length, referred to the Fathers and to St. Thomas, and after scrupulous consideration gave it as his opinion that Teresa was in the way of truth. For what reason? Precisely because, from the religious standpoint, she stood revealed as the exact opposite to Therese Neumann. We quote what she said of her own visions: "It is not a vision perceived by the senses, I saw no form. I saw nothing with my bodily eyes but I felt His presence by my side. I heard no words. The Lord communicated His thought to me by other means. But it was far clearer than if it had been said with words. Truth, the very essence of truth! O! what a difference between hearing words and understanding the Truth in that blinding flash."

Hypnosis, hallucination, catalepsy, somnambulism, all kinds of hysterical phenomena. . . . It is not our purpose to plunge the reader into this medical labyrinth of the "case of Therese Neumann" which has caused much ink to flow and will cause still more to do so. But it is important to note that medical opinion agrees with that of those priests who have been able to view the case as a whole. Like the rest of the world, Konnersreuth has experienced the war. The stigmatist remains the object of a discussion which is at present more or less retrospective; as long ago as 1933 Father Bruno de Jésus Marie wrote, "Of this I am certain: Therese Neumann's states, as I have found them everywhere reported, have no place in the classic psychology of St. Teresa and St. John of the Cross. From the medical point of view, her case calls for great caution."

Cardinal van Roey, archbishop of Malines, declares, "I desire to state that the Church attaches the utmost importance to medical opinion, even when it is contrary . . ." As a conclusion to this study it will be of advantage, I believe, to quote the opinion of a Catholic doctor whose extensive knowledge of physical phenomena such as are observed in Therese Neumann is incontestable. In the preface to a book by his colleague Dr. B. de Poray-Madeyski, Dr. Jean Lhermitte, Professor *agrégé* of the Paris Faculty of Medicine, writes these lines:

"Most of the distinctive phenomena in the life of the stigmatist of Konnersreuth are of a hysterical nature and must not be considered therefore as supernatural or miraculous. On the other hand it must be carefully borne in mind that hysteria does not develop into fraud or mythomania, that there is no direct intervention of the will in the genesis and persistence of symptoms. . . . We are concerned precisely with a particular psycho-neurosis which leaves the intellectual faculties intact and, in the case of Therese Neumann, casts no slur on her moral being, personal dignity, sincerity, or piety. The fact that the stigmatist has been affected by hysteria is not necessarily a barrier to her being favored with impulses, a certain fervor of devotion, and authentic mystical gifts. But we must beware of mistaking for charismatic and mystical experience those phenomena that a painstaking study completely justifies our including as part of a psychoneurosis."

It could not be put better, nor more humanely. The rest belongs to the unknown. And, as Hamlet says, "There are more things in heaven and earth, than are dreamt of in our philosophy."

· 4 ·

Catherine Emmerich
"Narrator" of the Gospels

I

IT has always seemed to me that to write a life of Jesus is to give proof of a certain vanity, for as everything is to be found in the Gospels the Christian is in possession of the basic, fundamental book which does not lend itself very well to paraphrase. But there is at least one "Life of Jesus" to which this reproach does not apply. It, too, is an "inspired" book, and in the most extraordinary fashion; to read it is to be immersed in unfathomable depths of speculation and wonder.

We have studied the case of Therese Neumann who sees—or thinks she sees—the Passion enacted before her very eyes. But is the stigmatist of Konnersreuth indeed present at the drama of Calvary? Whatever the current opinion about this in a hundred years' time, it is to be noted that upward of a century before Resl's experience another stigmatist was favored with the marvelous privilege, and in this case the Church has acknowledged the fact. The book in question is the extraordinary account of the visions of Anne Catherine Emmerich which has come down to us through her faithful friend and amanuensis, the poet Clemens Brentano.

Like Therese Neumann, Anne Catherine Emmerich was a German; she was born in Westphalia at Flamske, a hamlet which even in those days—1774—formed a kind of outer suburb of the town of Coesfeld. Her parents, again like Therese's, were hardworking peasants, though a trifle more devout and better prepared, it seems, for the intrusion of the marvelous into their humdrum lives. We may gather this perhaps from a small scrap of evidence which belongs to 1784, when Anne Catherine was just ten years old. Some rumor of the wonderful tales that his daughter was telling to the other village children came to farmer Emmerich's ears. He summoned his daughter, took her on his knees and demanded to hear one of those tales himself. He expected, possibly, some fairy story and was considerably surprised when his small daughter began to tell him about Abraham and Jacob, in substance what she had heard from the village priest during the sacred history lesson, but in language so vivid and with so strong an illusion of reality and so great a wealth of detail that the whole of this Old Testament episode, from being buried beneath the deadening effect of conventional phrases, shook off the dust of ages, and suddenly came to life in an extraordinarily vivid narrative, as if the events it portrayed had taken place the day before in Westphalia with the neighbors as its principal characters. Honest Emmerich, more worried than he cared to admit, asked his daughter who had told her all that. Without a moment's hesitation the little girl replied, "I saw it." Her father was upset to the point of tears. He could not believe Anne Catherine's answer, yet all the same he felt that there was something inexplicable in the whole circumstance and that it would be better, perhaps, not to pursue it any further.

All the witnesses are in complete agreement about Anne Catherine's piety. It was quite uncommon to see a little girl so regular in churchgoing, so adverse to untruthfulness, vanity, and all the shortcomings of childhood. But the visions which Catherine asserted she was privileged to experience at so early an age were something outside the scope of ordinary graces, although at the outset Catherine's attitude gave the impression that she herself was inclined to be vague about distinctions between the ordinary and the extraordinary. It became usual at the catechism lessons to question her first, before all her classmates, and her answers amazed the priest. "Where did you learn that?" he would ask. "Those are matters which are taught only to grown-ups." "No one taught me," replied the little girl. "I saw it." And she too wondered at it and tried to make herself believe that it had been mentioned in previous lessons. But gradually a certain disquiet took hold of her; instinctively she understood that her visions required of her still greater piety. While she was quite young, it was observed that she avoided the games and pastimes of her age, practiced self-mortification, and spent hours in prayer. She used to get up during the night to pray, and during the day would fall to her knees whenever the idea came to her, on the spur of the moment, just where she was, even on a snow-covered road or a stony path. When she went to church she was accustomed to walk by herself, apart from the rest, to avoid the distraction of conversation. At length, at the age of fifteen, the sound of a convent bell in Coesfeld ringing the Angelus one evening served to make her realize that she was being drawn by an irresistible vocation to the religious life. On account of her poverty and her parents' grief, it was only with great difficulty that she could put her plan into execution, and she was twenty-eight (1802) when she was received as a novice by the Augustinian nuns at Dulmen, and then only by a special favor: a novice whose family was in better circumstances provided her with the necessary dowry.

Catherine Emmerich remained only a few years in the cloister; the Augustinian convent was suppressed by the new king of Westphalia, Jerome Bonaparte. We need not dwell on the great disturbances which affected the whole country and resulted in the return of the nun to her own home. Henceforward the visionary remained there bedridden through an illness that no doctor could diagnose and still less cure, though it deserves to be emphasized at this point that it manifested none of the symptoms of hysteria. Anne Catherine was entirely dominated by one of her sisters, a most uncharitable woman who tyrannized over her and quite outrageously exposed her to the curiosity of all and sundry. The story of her visions had already traveled all over Germany and Europe; priests and doctors besieged the humble dwelling; there was endless discussion over this strange case, though skeptics, of course, all proclaimed it a mere case of fraud.

When discussion was at its height, Clement Brentano appeared on the scene. He was introduced to Catherine, on whom a short time previously the stigmata had appeared, by two "sponsors," Father Overberg, her confessor, and Bishop Sailer of Ratisbon. The interview between the poet and the visionary is now famous. Anne Catherine announced that she had seen beforehand "the man who was to be given her to write down her visions," [1] and Clement Brentano left this account of the interview: "Gaily she held out to me her hands marked with the stigmata; so far as I could see there was no sign of excitement or strain, but she gave an impression of unaffected playfulness and there was often a sort of innocent mischievousness about her. All that she says is brief, to the point, with no thrusting forward of herself but full of charity, depth and life. She lives amid the most unintelligent and troublesome entourage imaginable, made up of simple and decent but rather coarse people, disagreeable visitors, and an extremely unpleasant sister. Catherine is continually at death's door, nursed by rough and awkward hands . . . abandoned by all and ill-treated like Cinderella, she is yet always affectionate and gentle."

From that day Clement Brentano never left Anne Catherine. Seated by her bedside, he listened to the account of her visions and took notes which he set down in plain, correct language, taking infinite pains all the while to add nothing, not even the slightest embellishment, on his own account. He merely allowed himself occasionally to add in the margin certain considerations showing his astonishment, or sometimes even his doubts. Volume on volume was completed as Brentano "recopied" the whole of the Old Testament as portrayed in Catherine's visions; then came the New Testament, followed by the history of the Church. A summa was growing under his hand, a paraphrase of the divine Summa; these thousands of pages beginning with the story of the prophets concluded with the final triumph of the New Jerusalem. Sometimes Brentano threw down his pen in a state of mind bordering on terror.

In 1823 Catherine Emmerich's sufferings increased to such an extent that all about her—her secretary included—predicted her approaching death. Her visions developed and were now terri-

[1] Joseph-Alvare Duley, *Visions d'Anne-Catherine Emmerich* (Paris: Téqui).

fying and overwhelming, as if all the evil and sin of the whole world was displayed for her to see and comprehend. The year ended as the stigmatist experienced great physical and moral suf-·fering; she prayed earnestly for the pardon of sinners and besought the privilege of taking their crimes upon herself. On February 9, 1824, Catherine Emmerich having gasped three times "Lord, help me! Come, Lord Jesus, come!" breathed her last. She had insisted on an extremely simple funeral—"a pauper's funeral"—but it was not in her power to make it take place unnoticed. Thousands accompanied the coffin in a triumphal procession to the cemetery. A devout Dutchman had offered to buy for four thousand florins the coffin in which the stigmatist's body lay; it was rumored that the grave had been violated and the body stolen; the inhabitants of Flamske and Coesfeld demanded the opening of the grave. It was effected, and the body, bearing the stigmata, was found incorrupt.

Catherine Emmerich never made any mystery about her visions or the way in which they occurred. The following is her account of the first she ever experienced:

"One day (I must have been then about five or six) I was trying to meditate on the first article of the Creed—'I believe in God, the Father Almighty.' Pictures of the Creation appeared before the eyes of my soul.[2] The fall of the angels, the creation of earth and paradise, of Adam and Eve, and their disobedience were all shown to me. I fancied that everyone could see these things just like our ordinary surroundings.

"On another occasion when I was at school, quite artlessly I recounted details about the Resurrection which we had not been taught. I did so with entire assurance since, as I believed, these details were known to all. The other children were astounded and then began to make fun of me and even told the master about me; he strictly forbade me to indulge in such daydreams." Later on, Catherine seemed to feel the need to make her meaning quite clear: "My visions did not cease," she declared. "I was like a child who sees beautiful pictures and voices his thoughts about each of them, without any great effort to discover what this or that one

[2] They were, therefore, "interior visions" like those described by St. Teresa.

represents. I used to think of my visions as *my picture book* and I considered them quietly in my soul, saying to myself that all was for the greatest glory of God."

Time went on, Catherine was growing up and was soon to experience other favors. She shall again speak for herself: "In 1798, in my twenty-fourth year, I was kneeling before a crucifix in the Jesuit chapel at Coesfeld; I was praying as fervently as I could when suddenly I saw my heavenly Bridegroom in the form of a young man, all surrounded with brilliant light, come forth from the tabernacle. In His left hand He held a crown of flowers and in His right, a crown of thorns; He asked me to choose between them. I asked for the crown of thorns and He Himself placed it on my head; I thereupon pressed it firmly to my forehead. He disappeared and at once I felt sharp pains all round my head." Thus were the stigmata heralded.[3]

The supernatural had seized hold of Catherine Emmerich. That is not just a manner of speaking, for according to her own statements the supernatural assumed effective outward form in the shape of her guardian angel who would suddenly appear by her side, take her hand, and lead her out of the house. He transported her over the whole world, opening houses to her, and pointing out those in their agony, sinners, and all those standing in need of one last prayer; he caused her to visit battlefields where she helped the dying; and in the last place, took her to the East and let her be present at the scenes which she afterward described as if the Old and New Testaments—the comparison is somewhat distasteful perhaps, but it is the nearest there is—were a film run through for her benefit alone after many centuries of silence.

The parallel between Catherine Emmerich and Therese Neumann is not a little disconcerting: Catherine, just like Therese at a later date, if the latter is to be believed, had the strange power of assuming several existences, of donning, so to say, successive personalities, especially of those who were in danger of

[3] It should be added that some years earlier Catherine asserted that she had been granted an extraordinary grace, though it did not, of course, occur again: according to her account, after spending some time in intercessory prayer, she was transported to the prison of the martyr queen, Marie Antoinette.

hell. She was continually the cause of considerable astonishment both to her relations and the witnesses of her "torments" who, of course, thought that they were present at her own struggle with the devil. Dr. Resener, who treated her during the last years of her life, was, as may well be imagined, one of the first to make this mistake. He was dumbfounded and not a little frightened when he diagnosed in Catherine one after another the most deadly diseases. They appeared suddenly and at an already incurable stage, in a few hours they reached their climax and produced a state bordering on death, and then disappeared in the twinkling of an eye as they had come. As an instance may be mentioned an acute attack of pulmonary tuberculosis of which Catherine was the "victim"; and while this attack lasted the visionary was observed to be literally possessed with fury, insulting all within reach, and blasphemy pouring from her mouth; then finally she became quite peaceful, asked pardon for her sins and—there is no other word—*died* in an atmosphere of merciful forgiveness. A few moments later Catherine, smiling with her usual serenity restored, related that a woman who had greatly grieved Our Lord was now in heaven.

Creation is love. It must therefore be admitted that certain chosen creatures are capable of such great love that they can bear the sins of the world: that "huge stone" that Catherine one day mentioned and whose weight drew from her a groan. When her stigmata appeared for the first time she tried unsuccessfully to hide them. This happened on December 29, 1812. Catherine "in contemplation" saw the Passion of Our Lord enacted before her. Suddenly Christ appeared to her very much as He had to St. Francis, "crucified, with His five wounds shining like suns." Simultaneously she had the sensation of three blood-red rays, like arrows, directed upon her; she felt the piercing of her feet, hands, and side. Blood flowed immediately from the wounds. Bruises appeared all over her body; Catherine experienced the parched mouth, the terribly painful contracted tongue, and the fearful thirst of Our Saviour on the Cross. From that day onward the miracle was repeated every Thursday, and before witnesses; the blood flowed on Friday mornings from seven until midday. It may be readily supposed that these witnesses were not sparing with their comments. They were by no means confined to believers or the simply credulous: Catherine's house was open to all and was visited by atheistic doctors and army surgeons who tried without result to make the wounds heal. There is even a story that one day when there was an enormous crowd at the door, two French officers boldly jumped in at the window, but noticing round Catherine's head "a strange light which looked like a halo" they took fright and, muttering some excuse, made themselves scarce.

The manifestation of the supernatural at Coesfeld deserves a fair-sized volume to itself, but as I intend to confine myself principally to more recent miracles, readers are referred to works on the subject already in existence. Nevertheless it seemed of interest to add, by way of appendix to Therese Neumann's extraordinary contemporary adventure, this short summary of the characteristic elements of Catherine Emmerich's visions. For, as I have already mentioned, her "inspired book" exists and is by no means the least important record of the miracles of the last century.

II

Therese Neumann we described as in some sort a commentator or reporter on the Passion; keeping to the same sort of comparison Catherine Emmerich may be called the narrator of the Gospels. The narrator's function, it will be remembered, is to shed light on, to comment on, and to amplify for the audience an action or a plot as it is being played. Catherine Emmerich's role is very similar.

All readers of her *Visions*, as transcribed by Clement Brentano, have been struck by the extraordinarily lifelike and authentically truthful impression they produce. And I could tell of Catholics, who through these visions have rediscovered the Gospels as if the sacred text furnished merely an outline, a kind of divine, preliminary sketch: after all, God may very possibly have made use of Catherine in this way. *All her visions undoubtedly bear the* *stamp of strict historical accuracy,*⁴ but that is hardly enough. Put quite plainly this "inspired book" has that quality of credibility that is essential if a document is to win respect.

Catherine does not merely describe her visions; she seems to take us by the hand and urge us to witness the drama. There is never the slightest breath of unorthodoxy, but at every line some typical detail, some authentic touch seems to take us beyond time and bring us near to the greatest drama of all time, so that without effort we can believe it as actually taking place, and at every moment encounter the play of those feelings and passions which are to be found in everyday life. The life of Christ is made so modern that the Pharisees who are portrayed, for instance, might well be compared with certain entirely contemporary political factions; the crowd which continually surrounds the divine Miracle Worker, imploring His teaching—and especially, miracles and still more miracles—is that same crowd which we all know so well, and time and again have seen gather and run riot. That Jew of the first century might be the man in the street of our own day. He has not changed. His appetites, and desires, ill-temper and obtuseness are everlasting.

Continually we encounter in Catherine's visions men who might be our contemporaries, incredulous, vain and changeable, who, in common parlance, "can't be kidded." So when Christ mentions His Father, "Your father!" they exclaim. "We knew your father! Why, there's so-and-so and that other fellow who have spoken to him, who lived next door to him. Your father, you say? He was only a poor carpenter! What are you trying to pretend he was? And what's all this about his vineyard? Don't make us laugh. Why, he never owned a vineyard, and you, you're only a poor workingman's son. You've got ideas in your head and want to rise above your station." If the majority spoke in that tone, there were others who listened to the Word and were won over. A young man came forward and asked to follow the prophet and be one of His disciples. Jesus called on him to give up his fortune and his parents. At the youth's rather ungracious refusal the crowd began to jeer: "There you are, he volunteered and you

⁴ Clement Brentano.

don't want him. Was he a bit too brainy for you? You'd rather have ordinary fishermen and idiots around you, wouldn't you?"

Jesus turning the traders out of the temple. In the Gospels this is certainly a profoundly moving and edifying passage; but Anne Catherine's visions arouse an indefinable feeling of reality and urgency when they portray Christ suiting the action to the words, seizing a table laden with merchandise for sale and pushing it out of the holy place; among the crowd some appear uneasy and even moved to indignation; others show their approval. And that great multitude listening to the Sermon on the Mount, seeing night drawing on and beginning to feel the pangs of hunger— how clearly the scene is depicted. Of course we knew that they must have felt hungry, the Gospels tell us so, just as we were aware that the miracle of the loaves and fishes was about to take place. But how very real the scene is made for us when we read that a child begins to cry, other children follow suit, their mothers endeavor to pacify them and then cry out themselves, "We too are hungry! It is time to eat." A wave of discontent runs through the crowd, there is a continual murmur from among them sitting there haphazard on the ground just like an open-air meeting in which little pockets of discussion break out from time to time.

We may well pause to consider the miracles. Anne Catherine describes them with great accuracy and in unrivaled detail. When in childhood some good priest spoke of the miracles of the Messiah we saw them perhaps as a simple gesture, a sign, a word which was spoken, which lingered in the memory—"Arise!" "See!" "Hear!" But Catherine shows us the scene in full detail. Christ draws near to the man sick of the palsy, takes his arm, holds it up a moment and massages it—it is the only description—with his fingers. Gradually He brings life back into that flesh, into those muscles; He rubs the wrist and then the hand. Next, He lets go the arm and the paralyzed man perceives that he is cured. But frequently the cure is not effective at once.[5] The progress of the disease is first arrested and convalescence ensues, lasting a few days; sometimes even, the dying man whom Jesus has restored to

[5] As at Lourdes. See Chapter 1.

health returns to life with difficulty. With His own hands Jesus puts before him the bread and water which will help him regain his strength. On every page we can find people coming in crowds, bearing their sick on stretchers to the doors of the synagogues or waiting with them in the street. Singing and praying they throng at the Saviour's heels. On one occasion the Pharisees—like some modern enemies of religion—endeavored to provoke a bogus miracle so that they might catch Christ redhanded. They went so far as to have brought to Him the embalmed body of a man three days dead. "He is sick," they said, "he sleeps; you must cure him!" Jesus made a sign: the body of the "sick man" burst open showing the worms and the decay within.

The miracle of the loaves and fishes could hardly be described in detail by a reader of the Gospels. Did the loaves appear as they were brought round and distributed to the crowd, who immediately fell on them and ate them up? On the contrary, according to Anne Catherine, Jesus took only one of the loaves and broke it into small pieces; and from each morsel, each crumb, there sprang a whole loaf. The fishes, too, were first cut into slices and Jesu divided these slices into small portions which became as man dried fish. The symbolism of all this is obvious. Indeed Ann Catherine teaches in her visions or, rather, re-emphasizes the ele mentary truth that miracles are primarily symbolic; [6] they are not gratuitous phenomena and still less are they performed with the sole purpose of causing amazement among men or gaining their adherence. The many miracles Christ publicly performed did not prevent the Jews from condemning Him to death and nailing Him to the Cross.

Miracles were not always successful in convincing even the apostles. Our Lord's disciples appear in a very human light. And how those visions of Catherine Emmerich's bear the stamp of truth in their every line when they show us, for example, St. Peter's differences with his fellows, his anxieties, and continual complaints—"What about my work which is still not done?"

[6] Jesus walked on the water not to amaze His disciples (rather were they frightened) but to symbolize the abiding presence of the Divine over the stormy waves of the world.

"Why did I leave all to follow this prophet? After all I'm hardly the sort of fellow for him."

Matthew (known previously as Levi) believed in the teaching of the Messiah; but when he saw Him coming towards his house—he was a tax collector and at that moment his office was full of visitors arguing about their taxes and squabbling as men do even now with any income tax official—he was afraid and sorely tempted to sneak out and disappear.

But, apart from Christ, one figure stands out more clearly than the rest in Catherine Emmerich's visions; the portrait of Mary Magdalen, the sinner, is unforgettable. We can see her, before she was touched by grace, as she comes on the scene, tall, well-made, decked in fair linen and lace so fine that it can be worn but once, and with roses in her hair; a band of admirers comes with her, young dandies who joke and jeer because she desires to hear the Messiah preach. They imagine it is a passing whim. The sermon takes place in the open air, so they put up a tent for the courtesan and place cushions beneath her feet. And how those ever-present Pharisees gloat in all their obtuse narrow-mindedness when Mary faints at the sound of the Master's words.

These little authentic touches are joined, in Catherine Emmerich's visions, to revelations of an almost divine beauty. Sometimes they are moving (as the death of Joseph, carried off before Christ began His public ministry because the Passion would have been too painful for him to witness), and sometimes awe-inspiring (as the character of Mary the Silent whose only appearance is on her deathbed where she slowly expires holding Christ's hand in her own); occasionally they are even extravagant (as Salome's dance and Herod's great fear). There is the unforgettable incident when Jesus eluded His earthly parents to confer with the doctors, and Mary's fright as she searched everywhere for her son. Catherine Emmerich has certainly given us a unique record of these events, or rather, as a heavenly interpreter has passed it on to us. Clement Brentano's words can be quoted with approval: "It is a great religious epic, enacted between heaven and earth. It is like an immense sea flowing out from some mysterious spring to bathe the earth with its waves in which are reflected all the beauties of the waterside and the accumulated wealth of centuries. But these pure pellucid waters enable the eye to penetrate to the very depths, there to discover, among all sorts of marvels, the inmost properties and secret of things."

"These things must be told," Catherine's guardian angel informed her, "for no one has yet received nor ever will, a favor as great as yours."

5

Authentic Miracles and Doubtful Miracles
The Beauraing "Epidemic"

"SHE was dazzling light. . . ."

This expression of Lucia dos Santos, on being asked to describe the "Lady," deserves comparison with certain well-known passages in which the greatest mystics have expressed their union with the Unknowable. It is the *light without sun,* mentioned by Rolland de Renéville [1] quoting Baudelaire's wonderful verse:

> *Nul astre d'ailleurs, nul vestiges*
> *De soleil, même au bas du ciel*
> *Pour illuminer ces prodiges*
> *Qui brillaient d'un feu personnel.*

Those crowds of Fatima, nonparticipants in the miraculous contemplation, who were not among the chosen ones, had need of the sun; it was indeed an instrument of the miraculous. But mystical light is from within. From beyond time Marie de Valence echoes Lucia dos Santos and Bernadette. She says, "What I saw was something without shape or figure and yet it was infinitely beautiful and pleasing to the sight. It was colorless and yet it had the charm of all colors. What I saw was not a light like that of the day and yet it emitted a wonderful brightness from which came all light, both corporal and spiritual."

Teresa of Avila adds her authoritative description; she stands alone above all the mystics, taking as it were the solo part in their great concert:

[1] *L'Experience Poétique* (Paris: Gallimard). He quotes also the passages from Marie de Valence and Teresa of Avila which are here reproduced.

"It was a brightness which did not dazzle, a whiteness of great softness, an infused radiance, delighting the eye but in no wise tiring it. The light which helps to make manifest this divine beauty is not of this earth. The brightness of the sun seems so dull beside this brightness, this radiance shown to the eye of the soul, that there is no further desire to open the eyes.

"There is as much difference between these two kinds of brightness as between clear water flowing over quartz, sparkling in the sun, and turgid water flowing, beneath a cloudy sky, over an earthy surface. But no such sun is to be seen nor does the light in question resemble the light of the sun. No, the light I am speaking of seems natural and it is the other which appears artificial. This light knows no night, it is so beautiful that the most intelligent person in the whole world never, by the efforts of a lifetime even, could imagine it as it is."

Were Our Lady's visionaries, Bernadette Soubirous and Lucia dos Santos, really mystics, "little sisters" to St. Teresa of Avila and St. John of the Cross? An answer to this question will emerge later, but it provokes also consideration of the judgment of the Church about miracles and, more accurately, to use the proper term in spite of its unpleasant modern sound, the tests by means of which the Church separates the wheat from the chaff, the authentic miracle from the questionable or "fabricated" miracle. A further example has been chosen to illustrate this part of the book. The reader must now come down from the mystic heights where the extracts, quoted above, have led him; and before returning there turn his steps to the vulgar plains where he will encounter one of the most equivocal manifestations of the supernatural in the twentieth century.

For consideration here we have chosen Beauraing and its veritable "epidemic of miracles," still fresh in men's minds, and particularly that side of it represented by the case of the five alleged visionaries: Fernande, Gilberte and Albert Voisin, Andrée and Gilberte Degeimbre. What follows might be called "Beauraing, or childish fiction detected and unmasked."

I

Certain side issues require mentioning in connection with the mysterious events of Beauraing, but they will be emphasized no more than is absolutely necessary for a clear presentation of the subject. As always, a few lines about the district constitute the best introduction to the subject.

Beauraing is a village situated on the edge of the Walloon territory of Belgium and on the borders of the Ardenne and the Famenne. Up to 1932 there was nothing to provoke the thought that even temporarily it would ever make the headlines in the press. Its population was made up partly of rural and partly of factory workers. In any case, the district and the whole neighborhood held absolutely no interest for the tourist. The point needs mentioning, as a common objection raised by opponents of the supernatural is that miracles, or so they assert, occur only in "suitable" neighborhoods or near them. In answer to another common argument it can be stated that in 1932, that is, when the "apparitions" took place, there were in Beauraing about an equal number of Catholics and freethinkers, the latter being readers of the socialist newspaper *La Dernière Heure* which numbered some fifty subscribers in the village. There were two dance halls and a cinema; the latter, as we shall see, was not entirely unconnected with the events which are here described.

During the few years between 1932 and the second World War, Beauraing was the scene of an absolute epidemic of miracles, or rather of visionary phenomena. Here only the original manifestations will be dealt with, that is, those with which the children named above were alleged to be favored. All the rest—the sequel of apparitions and hallucinations, etc.—seems hardly worth serious study. Since 1932 many facts unknown at the time have more or less cautiously been brought to the notice of the public. A political movement, Degrelle's "Rexism," took a special interest in Beauraing and chose it as the jumping-off place for its propaganda. The archbishop of Malines, supporting Van Zeeland against Degrelle in an electoral contest that has remained famous, pointed out emphatically and very properly that the Church could not tolerate anyone daring to make use of her for their own ends. It has been asserted that Degrelle purchased land at Beauraing. His money was spent (and his shame incurred) to no purpose.

The five children of Beauraing who figure in this story belonged to the Voisin and the Degeimbre families, both of local origin. The children's ages were as follows: Fernande Voisin, born on June 21, 1917, was fifteen and a half at the time of the apparitions; her sister Gilberte Voisin, born on June 20, 1919, was thirteen and a half; her brother Albert Voisin, born on November 3, 1921, eleven. Andrée Degeimbre, born on April 19, 1918, was fourteen and her sister Gilberte, born on August 13, 1923, was nine.

The two families had lived in Beauraing for the past two generations. They were friends but not related, contrary to what has been written about them; the error arose perhaps through an association of ideas with the Marto and Dos Santos families at Fatima. Neither household appears to have been particularly edifying from the religious point of view. Monsieur Voisin worked on the railway and was an active socialist; his wife had opened a small shop in the village. They were married in church and sent their children to the catechism classes, gave themselves out as Catholics but did not practice their religion. The Degeimbre family had lost their father; he had been a subscriber to *La Dernière Heure* and, on his own showing, a socialist, though it appears he was not a very active one. At the time of the "apparitions" the widow Degeimbre enjoyed the reputation of being loud-mouthed; possibly all it meant was that she had acquired the habit, not unusual in a woman left on her own and burdened with a family to rear, of speaking somewhat forcefully. Still, the Degeimbre family can unquestionably be classified as indifferent to religion: their attitude can be depicted by the phrase, "There may be some truth in all that, in any case it does no one any harm."

Of course, these few short particulars furnish no evidence

either way about the nature of the phenomena under investigation, nor do they raise the slightest imputation against the honesty of the two families. When Pathé-Nathan, the newsreel firm, offered the Voisins several thousand francs for permission to film the little "visionaries," the father and mother refused point blank. Nor is there the slightest evidence that they ever accepted any kind of present. Those facts require recording. We can now consider the course of events.

The five children of Beauraing claimed that between November 29, 1932, and January 3, 1933, they had been favored with thirty-three apparitions of the Blessed Virgin. The "apparitions" may be broken up as follows:

November 29, 1932 (Tuesday): At half-past six in the evening Fernande and Alberte Voisin, together with Andrée and Gilberte Degeimbre, rang the bell at the door of the village convent school. They had come to fetch their sister Gilberte Voisin. Albert shouted out suddenly, "I see a light." His sister and their two companions turned round and noticed "a white form which moves over by the grotto at the side of the road."

"Who's there?" cried Albert. Then he added, "It's a man." Fernande joined her hands. "It's the Blessed Virgin," she said. The convent gate opened and an out sister appeared holding little Gilberte by the hand. Albert said to her, "Sister, the statue in the grotto moved." The nun did not trouble to answer and shut the door behind her.[2] The five children ran back to the village keeping their eyes half shut because they were afraid.

November 30th: The children were at the same place at the same time and noticed, as before, a moving white form. The same out sister opened the door and found them in the same state as the day before.

"Sister," said Albert, "there's someone walking about there."

"Well," replied the nun, "I expect it's Sister X."

"Oh, no, Sister," rejoined Albert, "or else she's in her dressing gown!"

---

[2] She said afterward to the other nuns, "The children waiting at the door muttered something and *laughed* when they saw me. Is anything wrong with me? Were they trying to play a joke on me?"

The out sister laughed and shut the door. As on the previous evening the children ran home in a panic.

December 1st: The same thing happened. When they reached home the children asked their parents to go with them to the "haunted spot." Madame Degeimbre agreed on condition that the youngest girls, the two Gilbertes, stay at home. Arriving at the convent, Fernande and Albert Voisin and Andrée Degeimbre knelt down and said a prayer. Andrée Degeimbre exclaimed to her mother, "Don't move forward, mother, the Blessed Virgin's there and you'll step on her."

December 2nd: Albert Voisin went to Communion that morning. In the evening his father went himself to fetch his daughter Gilberte. On his return the children, accompanied by their parents and some neighbors and a few curious persons, went to the site of the "apparitions." Hardly had they arrived there than the children threw themselves on their knees, as though struck by lightning, and said a Hail Mary. They declared that the vision had appeared.

ALBERT: "Are you the Immaculate Virgin?"

The vision replied with an affirmative nod of the head.

ALBERT: "What do you want?"

THE VISION: "Be very good."

ALBERT: "I promise that we'll be very good."

The children said a Hail Mary and returned home.

They came back again at nine o'clock that evening. Once more they fell to their knees, recited a Hail Mary and declared that the vision had returned.

THE VISION: "Will you really be very good?"

ANDRÉE VOISIN (*in a loud voice*): "Yes, yes, we will!"

The vision vanished. After a short time the children and the spectators started off home again. One of the spectators, Omer Marischal, turned on a flash light and with it searched the grotto and bushes near by. Albert noticed him. He ran back shouting, "There she is again," and fell to his knees. He then hurried back to the others. "I saw her again all by myself," he declared, "and she looked at me and smiled."

December 3rd: It was the day before the regional elections.

Monsieur Voisin, the father, went to a socialist meeting. It lasted longer than was expected; his wife and children came in for the end of the meeting and the Voisin children heard the conclusion of the electoral speeches and then went home for supper.

December 4th: The children went back to the grotto accompanied on this occasion by two chronic invalids: Eugène Havenne, aged thirty, born blind, Andrée and Gilberte Degeimbre's uncle, and little Joseph Degoudenne, aged eight, who was paralyzed. They all knelt down, recited a Hail Mary, then Albert spoke again.

ALBERT: "Holy Virgin, we beseech you to cure, please, Monsieur Havenne and little Joseph. Tell us on what day we must return here."

THE VISION: "The day of the Immaculate Conception."

ALBERT: "Thank you, holy Virgin. I asked you for these cures, but you will only make them if you wish to grant us a favor."

FERNANDE (*this was the first time that she questioned the vision*): "Must we have a chapel built here for you?"

THE VISION: "Yes."

The vision then disappeared. An hour later Albert returned at the request of the parents of a little girl, one Paulette Dereppe, who was paralyzed. He put the same question and received the same answer concerning the day they should return there.

That evening the local doctor, Dr. Maistriaux, was present for the first time. This practitioner, who a few days later was to come out very strongly on the side of the "miracle," on this occasion noted the fact that the sick of the district, having heard of events at Beauraing, had postponed their surgical operations in the hope of a miraculous cure. The date of December 8th was mentioned: it was rumored that a miracle would occur then.

December 5th: Prayers. The vision occurred almost instantaneously.

ALBERT: "If you wish to grant favors, work all the miracles you can by daylight."

The vision made no answer. Albert insisted. Still the vision kept silence. The children began to cry.

ALBERT: "But when will you work them?"

THE VISION: "In the evening."

ALBERT: "Very well, then, we'll come back in the evening."

It was then 6:30 P.M. At 8:30 P.M. exactly the children were back again. They knelt down, said a Hail Mary; the vision appeared.

December 6th: In the morning Albert was questioned by his schoolmaster. This was the first interrogation of any seriousness that he had undergone. He declared that the Blessed Virgin wore a white dress; that possibly she had a blue sash, but that he could see hardly anything but a blue glow; she had no rosary, he said, but kept her hands joined and still. To the question "What is the color of her eyes?" the boy answered, "Blue." At this his mother, who was present at the interview, gasped. "But you didn't tell me that!" she exclaimed. The boy went into greater detail: her dress was draped, her feet rested on a cloud of smoke, etc. Her face, he said, was "luminous."

"What do you mean 'luminous'?"

"It looks as if she had an electric bulb inside."

The master returned to his former question: "Are you quite sure that the Blessed Virgin is not holding a rosary?"

"Yes, there is no rosary."

8 P.M. Directly on arrival they knelt down, said a Hail Mary and the vision appeared. The same question was put concerning the day they should come back; the same answer was given. Albert stood up and declared, "It's quite true, she has a rosary over her right arm."

The blind child, Joseph Degoudenne, said that he had seen "the head." He then put a question, "What must I do to be cured?" but the Blessed Virgin did not answer.

December 7th: They knelt and said the Hail Mary as before. The vision appeared for only a moment and said nothing.

December 8th: It was on this day, it was said, that Our Lady of Beauraing was going to work a miracle. From 5 P.M. onward upward of ten thousand persons could be counted at the site of the "apparitions."

Several doctors were present in the crowd, including Drs. Lurquin, Goethals, de Greef, and Rouvroy, and, of course, Dr. Maistriaux; they had obtained permission to go close to the "vision-aries" and even to undertake some experiments when the children were in ecstasy.

The long-expected miracle did not occur. In vain the two sick persons, Monsieur Havenne and the little boy Degoudenne, in moving tones besought the Blessed Virgin for their cure amid the crowd of greatly affected spectators, among whom several women were sobbing. But nothing happened, save that the children declared that they had seen the Blessed Virgin. But she did not speak and disappeared fairly quickly. At the request of the crowd the children said the rosary. Still nothing happened.

But this evening, the occasion of such great disappointment, was not entirely without result. For the doctors performed certain experiments in public. They were as follows:

1. *Experiments by Dr. Maistriaux:* Going up to Albert Voisin while he was in "ecstasy," he unexpectedly seized hold of his wrist. The boy looked at him, showing he had felt the contact. Tactile sensibility, therefore, was still maintained. Dr. Maistriaux then went close to little Gilberte Voisin; he noted that she was sobbing, the tears running down her face. He questioned her point blank: "Why are you crying?" The child sobbed out, "Because she is so beautiful!" thus demonstrating that there was no suppression of hearing.

2. *Experiments by Dr. Lurquin:* Placing a lighted match near Gilberte Voisin's left hand he kept it there until it had more than half burned out. This was witnessed by Dr. de Greef who noted, "The flame licked the back of the hand." The child showed no reaction. The experiment was repeated with Gilberte Degeimbre with the same result. Dr. Lurquin tried his experiment a third time, choosing for his subject the sick child, Paulette Dereppe, who was not a visionary. The child drew back and cried out.

Dr. Lurquin called on a witness willing to help, chosen from the crowd. He gave him a tap or two on the hands and face with a penknife. The man felt pain and some faint marks appeared. The doctor then repeated the experiment on Gilberte Voisin: no reaction followed and no marks were to be observed.

With regard to the first experiment on Gilberte Degeimbre

there was a conflict of evidence between the doctor and another witness, the Beauraing chemist, who tried the experiment himself and observed "a movement of withdrawal of the hand"; he added, however, that no sign of erythema appeared.

Joint experiments conducted by Drs. Lurquin, de Greef, Goethals, and Rouvroy: Beams of electric light were directed into the eyes of the visionaries while they were in a state of ecstasy. Normal reflex of the pupil was observed, but none of the eyelid. It may be remarked that the first reflex is involuntary but not the second. Finally, Dr. de Greef proposed to try, as a last resort, pricking with Franck's needle and a burn with a cigarette end. Dr. Lurquin refused categorically; he feared the reaction of the crowd.[3] "They're only children, after all," concluded Dr. Maistriaux; and he asked his colleagues not to continue their experiments. In any case, the ecstasy was now over.

December 9th, 10th, 11th, and 12th: The rosary was said but no vision occurred.

December 13th: After a wait of three minutes the "vision" appeared. Four of the five children knelt down. Fernande Voisin did so ten seconds after the others. "I was disentangling my rosary," she declared afterward in answer to a question. The spectators noticed that the children's voices grew simultaneously softer; it was the exact moment, they asserted, when the vision vanished.

December 14th: When the children had been there for two minutes, Fernande cried out, "Look carefully!" and after a short interval all five knelt down together. Dr. Saint-Viteux, who was present, wondered why, for during the past few "apparitions" Fernande Voisin had always been the first to begin; he communicated his suspicions to one or two others. That "look carefully" might have been a signal.

December 15th and 16th: Rosary, no vision.

December 17th: About two thousand spectators took up their position before the grotto. As they left their homes the children called attention to the fact that they had their rosaries with them.

[3] "You must be mad," he exclaimed to his colleague. "Do you want them to set on us? (In my experiments) I had *no intention of hurting or burning them*" (Professor de Greef, *Les faits mystérieux de Beauraing*).

On arrival at the grotto they stood there restlessly looking about to right and left; Albert joined his hands for a moment; Gilberte Voisin bent over Andrée Degeimbre and pointed to the glow made by a car headlight; Andrée shook her head and nudged her. Then Andrée knelt down and gave out the beginning of the Hail Mary. The others followed suit almost at once.[4]

ANDRÉE: "At the request of the clergy we ask you what you want."

THE VISION: "A chapel."

ALBERT, ANDRÉE, FERNANDE: "Yes, we'll have it built."

Gilberte Degeimbre did not join in with the others. She began to mumble and tremble; "Yes, yes!" she exclaimed, and suddenly burst into tears. A surprising scene, to say the least, then took place: Andrée Degeimbre slapped her on the back. In spite of that the child continued to cry and groan. Andrée Degeimbre tried to speak but her sister's cries prevented her. Dr. Maistriaux leaned over to the child and asked her, "Why are you crying?" "It's because I'm so terribly happy," she sobbed.

Monsieur Gaston Robert, one of the spectators, and author of a book about Beauraing, acknowledged that at this moment the idea that it was all a fraud first came to his mind. The general hubbub increased. Gilberte Degeimbre was hiccuping. Her sister spoke to her, got up, and explained to the crowd, "We can't hear ourselves." In the end Gilberte gradually grew calmer. She seemed exhausted and on the verge of fainting. Little Albert Voisin seemed to have kept quite calm and so he was the first to be questioned.

"What did the Blessed Virgin say to you?"

"She said a chapel was to be built."

"But look, that's impossible," said Dr. Maistriaux. "She used a sentence, try to remember what it was."

"Yes, she used a sentence which meant that a chapel was to be built. But I don't remember the exact words, I was too excited."

GILBERTE VOISIN: "She said nothing except merely 'A chapel,' and then she disappeared, opening her arms wide as usual."

DR. DE GREEF: "But this morning I asked you if you saw the

[4] "Within four- or five-fifths of a second" (Dr. de Greef).

P

rosary hanging down when she opened her arms and you answered me, 'She does not open her arms.' "

FERNANDE VOISIN: "Today she did not open her arms. She kept her hands joined."

ANDRÉE DEGEIMBRE: "She vanished as usual, opening her arms wide."

December 18th: No vision.

December 19th: A vision occurred. The children said thirty-nine Hail Mary's very quickly. One of the spectators noted that they pronounced the opening words rather carelessly.

December 20th: The vision occurred after the twenty-ninth Hail Mary, after a wait of seventeen minutes.

December 21st: A vision occurred. The children asked once again, "Who are you?" The answer was, "I am the Immaculate Virgin."

December 22nd: Precautions were taken. The grotto was lit up and, in addition, the children were separated by witnesses, with no material possibility of communicating with each other. A vision occurred: Andrée, Fernande, and the two Gilbertes knelt down together, Albert shortly afterward.

December 23rd: The same precautions were taken. Albert was again slightly late in kneeling down. Fernande Voisin asked the apparition, "Why do you come here?" and received the answer, "So that people will come on pilgrimage." This question had been suggested—and to her alone—by Dr. Maistriaux. *She alone* heard the answer.

December 24th: The children knelt down "with extraordinary cohesion," repeating thus, though scattered among their witnesses and unable to communicate with each other, the collective movement which at the first apparitions had so amazed the crowd of onlookers.

GILBERTE VOISIN: "As you are the Immaculate Virgin may we hope that you will soon do something?"

ANDRÉE DEGEIMBRE: "If you are the Immaculate Virgin, will you soon give some proof of it?"

Only Albert Voisin claimed to have heard the answer, "Yes." On that occasion the doctors present were, generally speaking, hostile to the visionaries; on the other hand, numerous sick persons in the crowd lit candles and implored their cure.

December 25th: Christmas Day. Nothing.

December 26th: Nothing.

December 27th: An apparition occurred at 9:45 P.M. in the nuns' garden, after the crowd of spectators had left.

December 28th: The crowd was less numerous, scarcely two thousand. A vision occurred, and announced, "It will soon be my last appearance."

December 29th: In the morning Dr. Maistriaux had pamphlets distributed in which there was mention of a "golden heart." That evening Fernande Voisin noticed that the Blessed Virgin, opening her arms, displayed a golden heart. That same evening the doctors, who were becoming increasingly hostile, asked a question on the spot requesting the children to put it to the vision. This question was, "And what must we do now?" The great advantage of this question thus unexpectedly requested is obvious; if the children, kept apart during their "ecstasy" and afterward questioned separately, gave the same answer it would increase the credibility of the supernatural phenomena. But the doctors waited in vain for the children to comply with their request. They remained silent. "I was going to speak when the Blessed Virgin vanished," Fernande Voisin declared.

December 30th: A vision occurred. Andrée, Fernande, and both Gilbertes saw the golden heart.[5]

December 31st: A vision occurred. This time Albert saw the golden heart. Two new doctors, Dejace and Van Gehuchten, were present; they made some interesting observations: firstly, that the "visionaries," who were separated from one another, all gazed at the same spot; secondly, that Gilberte and her sister were the first to go into ecstasy. Andrée Degeimbre led the Hail Marys in a very loud voice. The children spoke of two additional apparitions at 9:45 P.M. and 10:10 P.M.

January 1st: A vision occurred. The following peculiarities were observed: (1) A witness of the former apparitions had, in Fernande's presence, expressed his astonishment that the Blessed

[5] "We saw it at last today" (Andrée).

Virgin now spoke to her alone. This evening Fernande declared, "I saw her lips move as if she wished to speak, but I did not listen because I don't want to be the only one to hear." As Dr. de Greef points out, it is rather difficult to imagine the Blessed Virgin working a miracle in order to appear to Fernande and that she should refuse to listen to her. (2) Another witness notes that before their arrival at the grotto there was some consultation in a low voice between the children and Monsieur Voisin. They nudged each other when anyone was seen to be listening to them. (3) Fernande Voisin declared, "Then, too, I couldn't hear the Blessed Virgin because people were making too much noise." It must have been a peculiar sort of ecstasy. (4) Questioning of the children was brought to an abrupt end by Dr. Maistriaux.

January 2nd: Fernande said, "Today the Blessed Virgin told me, 'Tomorrow I shall speak to each one of you in private.'"

January 3rd: The last "apparition." It was also the most sensational and the most pathetic of them all. Its heroine, if she may so be called, was Fernande Voisin. To begin with, she knelt down a little after the others. Unlike her companions, she experienced no vision, and when she rose to her feet her face showed signs of grievous disappointment. The other children mingled with the crowd; Fernande, alone, remained motionless before the grotto as if she still awaited some last sign. At one moment some of the spectators cried, "A ball of fire!" but it was only a photographer's flash. Suddenly Fernande fell to the ground as if struck down. "Yes, yes!" she exclaimed, prostrating herself with hands joined and overcome with a terrible fit of sobbing. The attack lasted some minutes. Fernande had a rapt look. On their return home all the children were crying.

ANDRÉE DEGEIMBRE: "The Blessed Virgin said, 'I am the Mother of God, the Queen of Heaven, pray always. Farewell.'"

GILBERTE VOISIN (*upset and sobbing*): "The Blessed Virgin told me a secret and said, 'I will convert all sinners. Farewell.'"

ALBERT VOISIN: "She told me a secret and said, 'Farewell.'"

GILBERTE DEGEIMBRE: "A secret and 'Farewell.'"

FERNANDE VOISIN: "I saw and heard nothing the first time. The second time the Blessed Virgin said to me, 'Do you love my Son?'"

'Yes,' I answered. 'Do you love me?' I answered, 'Yes.' 'Very well, then, sacrifice yourself for me.' "

A WITNESS: "What do you understand by sacrifice?"

FERNANDE VOISIN: "To become a nun."

A WITNESS (*to Andrée Degeimbre*): "Do you believe the Blessed Virgin will come back again?"

ANDRÉE DEGEIMBRE: "I hope so. When she said farewell she had a queer look on her face."

A final piece of evidence must be added: Gilberte Degeimbre only spoke of a secret confided to her after the four others (and after a full half hour during which she was questioned apart from the others and did not mention this . . . trifling matter). "I, too, have a secret," she finally told the investigators.

A few days after these events and in spite of the pastor-dean of Beauraing's refusal to give an opinion about the "supernatural occurrences," or to implicate the Church, a novena of thanksgiving was announced. The hotelkeepers of Beauraing forecast the arrival of forty thousand pilgrims from all parts of Belgium. There were between seven and eight thousand the first day, four thousand the second. Business at Beauraing was on the downgrade.

II

If the technique of the detective story could be applied to the investigation of Beauraing, the detective's first care would be to study the children before and after the apparitions; he would pay particular attention to the behavior of each, and dwell less on their points of resemblance than on the physical and moral qualities which differentiate them. The children of Beauraing were not a single entity like those of Fatima.

This imaginary detective would first consider Fernande Voisin; she was by far the most developed, the most intelligent, and, it may be added, the prettiest. She was rather short, dark, and bright-eyed. It was common knowledge that she was fond of reading novels (her mother had been obliged to forbid them for she was ruining her eyes), "penny dreadfuls" for preference and love stories. She was also fond of the cinema and went there nearly every Sunday. Thus it was that she saw in succession before and during the "apparitions" the following films: *The Fallen Rose*, *The Miracle of the Wolves*, *The Mystery of the Yellow Room*,[6] *The Perfume of the Lady in Black*, *Congress Dances*, *The Road to Paradise*, and *The Woman of My Dreams*. At school she was an average pupil, more or less up to standard; sometimes she gave her parents to understand that she was first in class which was untrue. It was also common knowledge that she had a "boy friend." Her parents did not mind and the village hardly concerned itself with the matter.

Her sister Gilberte was a fairly intelligent girl, inclined to be sly, apt to vary her attitude according to the person to whom she was speaking. Dr. de Greef notes, "She speaks unctuously of the visions and winks at her mother at the same time . . . scarcely ever looks one straight in the face." She too was very pretty. She was reputed to be mischievous and secretive.

Her brother Albert was rated at school as average in his studies and excellent in conduct. "A model schoolboy, quiet . . . truthful, well-behaved, with no bad qualities. Was never any trouble." There is just one slight shadow over the picture; on his way home from school, as a joke, he would ring the front doorbells as he passed. Not a very grievous fault and one with which the present writer would be the last to be annoyed.

Then there are the two Degeimbre children. The younger, Gilberte, a charming fair-haired girl, of whom also we are told that she was quiet in class but rang doorbells on her way home, gave evidence of average intelligence, but did not seem particularly sweet-tempered. The superior of the convent, who told her that she was not to come and pray at the grotto, received the answer, "May God punish you, Reverend Mother." And to the nun's reply, "We'll summon the police," she cried, "I'm not afraid of the police." Her mother told the investigators who called on her that

---

[6] The five children often went to the cinema together in the charge of Fernande Voisin, but it is to be noted that she alone saw *The Mystery of the Yellow Room*. Cf. below.

her daughter had no secrets from her and that she was absolutely incapable of the slightest secretiveness; upon which one of the investigators informed Madame Degeimbre that her daughter kept a private diary—a fact of which the mother knew nothing. Too much importance should not be attached to this detail.

And, last but not least, Andrée Degeimbre. She was a tall girl of rather unpleasing appearance, with an underhung jaw and straight hair, who could not in any case be accused of vanity. She was hardly of average intelligence; rather was she backward in class, failed in the simplest intelligence tests, and showed no higher level of intellect than her small sister. Puberty had brought no mental development with it. She was sullen and preferred the work of the fields to any other form because, she said, "there one is alone." She, too, was a tireless ringer of doorbells; she even added a refinement to this pastime by investigating the contents of the letter boxes, and was caught doing so on more than one occasion. But, on account of her mental deficiency, there was a general unwillingness to punish her. When the rumor of the apparitions began to make the rounds at Beauraing, the village schoolmistress exclaimed, "It's a pity that Andrée Degeimbre has anything to do with it! For if anyone in this affair is suffering from hallucinations it's she. If Andrée were not mixed up in it, it wouldn't be too hard to believe in this miracle."

There is a still more interesting fact to be added. Backward as she was Andrée Degeimbre had invented a better game than bell ringing or investigating letter boxes. It consisted in frightening others, and preferably she played at this with Albert Voisin: she would tell fearful tales which gave him nightmares. She tried this game on other children at Beauraing, but their parents were obliged to intervene. A last characteristic should be known: Andrée was quite as vindictive as her sister. One of the doctors who was present at the "apparitions," Dr. Saint-Viteux, was involved in a motor accident. "Serves him right," Andrée told her cronies, "he didn't believe in our visions." To those who expressed astonishment at this attitude, she added, "Of course it's unfortunate that it should happen to him, but it's God's punishment on him, and so it must be a good thing." But what is important for our purpose is the game of frightening others and the fearful tales. After this preliminary portrait of the children we can go on to further elements of the inquiry.

In investigating this case of supernatural manifestations a detective would not fail to have noticed the fact that Fernande Voisin went frequently to the cinema. It was indeed her favorite Sunday pastime and, it may be noted in passing, the fact of the apparitions did not keep her from it. On December 11th, the crowd waited outside the cinema for the "visionary" to come out so that they might escort her to the grotto. (On the same day Fernande had been to the hairdresser for a permanent wave.) There is nothing particularly wicked in all this, of course, but what are we to make of one of the early "descriptions" of the Lady? "It was all very beautiful, just like *The Perfume of the Lady in Black*." The cinema and visions were her two principal preoccupations. *The Miracle of the Wolves* and *The Fallen Rose* were other film stories which she saw just a month before the apparitions.

Fernande's recent reading at this time provides a further disconcerting element in the case. Perhaps her taste in reading had developed or else *The Miracle of the Wolves* or *The Fallen Rose* had edified her, and turned her to more devotional books; at all events, just before the "apparitions" Fernande gave up her usual mental fare—*The Sullied Maiden,* and *Driven Out on Her Wedding Night*—for a little booklet about Fatima, bearing on its cover a picture of Our Lady of the Rosary. This booklet—I have a copy —narrates the chief facts of the miracle of the Cova da Iria; it is significant that in it appears the statement that the Marto and Dos Santos children saw the vision at the same time and fell on their knees simultaneously. On the other hand, it is true that the expression "thunderstruck" used by the Beauraing children does not appear there, but the pastor-dean of Beauraing states that in that same year, 1932, he had preached a sermon on Bernadette Soubirous and quoted at length her words and her cry of "Penance! Penance!" And the booklet about Fatima naturally mentions the conversion of sinners asked for by the Lady. Referring to the message of the "Lady" of Beauraing we find that she is alleged to have said, "Pray for the conversion of sinners." Finally, there is hardly need to mention the "secrets." There was a secret at Lourdes, there were secrets at Fatima—Beauraing, obviously, needed its own.

What did the Blessed Virgin say to the Voisin and Degeimbre children? She said, "I am the Immaculate Virgin." At Beauraing, at the request of the spectators, the children sang the Lourdes hymn, "Immaculate Mary." It was begun, almost instinctively, *but before the Blessed Virgin spoke.* Her words, when she did speak, seem to have been suggested by the hymn.

She said, "I am the Mother of God, the Queen of Heaven." The children of Beauraing learned their catechism out of *The Small Catechism of the Diocese of Namur.* In part one, page 9, we find:

"Q. Is she to be honored?

"R. Yes, as Mother of God and Queen of Heaven."

She said, "I desire people to come here on pilgrimage," and what happened? On December 10th the mayor of Beauraing was talking of a future pilgrimage from which he foresaw, no doubt, all sorts of material advantages for his village. On the same day a real estate agency put up plots of land for sale ("exceptionally good investment") and found buyers at once; men with an eye to future business to be done in Beauraing booked rooms in the hotels. On December 19th a devout man of the district invited Fernande for a drive in his car in order to question her about the visions. Before he could get out even the first question Fernande gave vent to her feelings on the subject—"And what do you think of Beauraing now? It was about time that something happened to help us through this slump. But wait another fortnight and you'll see the crowds there'll be!" Her host had obtained information, but hardly what he hoped and expected. He made no further attempt to question her.

Mention has been made of the grotto before which the children knelt. It was, purely and simply, a grotto near the convent, and, what is more to the point, a Lourdes grotto, a not very beautiful reproduction of that of Massabielle such as may be found not infrequently in convent gardens or chapels. A statue of Bernadette at prayer had been placed there. But there was none of Our Lady; there was, however, a statue of Our Lady of Lourdes at

Beauraing, a luminous one too (one of those mass-produced pilgrimage souvenirs). What is particularly interesting is its location. All comment, indeed, is needless, for it was to be found in Fernande Voisin's bedroom. In other words, every night of her childhood, before the occurrence of the apparitions, when she went to bed and put out her light in the darkness she could see this statue of Our Lady shine out with its phosphorescent glow. And she acknowledged the fact without difficulty, "I was frightened of it," she remarked, "and I said to mother, 'Take it away!' I was afraid of it. . . ."

A miracle occurs with stupefying suddenness, it strikes like lightning; it seems to happen quite unexpectedly to little children who may be unprepared for it, like Lucia dos Santos who was hesitant and seemed to delay in carrying out Our Lady's orders when she told her to learn to read. The Voisin and Degeimbre children cannot be blamed, therefore, for behavior which seems hardly to tally with the great experience they suddenly underwent. But if we venture to set their behavior beside Bernadette's, for instance, how very much greater in every way does she emerge from the comparison. When the apparitions began Fernande Voisin merely remarked with a toss of the head, "It's curious, strange, queer almost!" But not for long were her reactions so very simple. A few days later the druggist at Beauraing expressed his concern for her.

"My poor child," he remarked, "you must be worn out."

"Oh, that's nothing," was the reply, "do me good to lose a little weight."

On December 11th, after that famous cinema performance—the film was *The Woman of My Dreams*—when she saw the crowd waiting for her, she exclaimed, "Where are the others? Come along then. I didn't enjoy myself as much as usual." Five days later she remarked, "I'm getting a bit tired of all this business!" When Albert was being questioned on December 15th and telling the investigators that he had seen the Blessed Virgin—"I saw her twice when the girls didn't"—Fernande laughed, shrugged her shoulders, winked and nudged Gilberte Degeimbre. She could hardly stifle her laughter. The crowd that went with her to the "apparitions" looked sometimes as if it were going to trample on her, "Come on, let me through," cried Fernande, "I'm the visionary. If you go on like that I shan't go to the grotto, nor will the others, and you'll have come here all for nothing."

Albert Voisin evidently derived a certain feeling of importance from his "visions." As was probably noticed, on December 2nd, he was favored with a vision all to himself; [7] during the following "apparition" a doctor who was present came to the conclusion that he had seen nothing at all; but that did not prevent his outdoing the girls in boasting about his "visions." When Albert Voisin said "the girls," there was a certain tone of superiority in his voice; he liked to show off in front of them. Thus one day he took two little village girls to the grotto, told them to look, fell to his knees and cried out, "I see her!" Before the "apparitions" he did not go to Mass very often and after they occurred he went no more frequently. He was not, in fact, greatly enamored of priests. On January 1st an old, white-haired country priest in a cassock green with age knocked timidly at the door and asked for him. Albert was furious, set about the priest with his fists and feet and threw him out. "Priests," he remarked, "are like everyone else; they're liars like the rest." We saw how he went to a socialist meeting with his father. No special inference need be deduced from this detail; the socialist ideal is not necessarily opposed to the faith. But it so happened that the regional elections at Beauraing, as often happens in the provinces, were fought largely on the religious question; the speaker at the meeting did not fail to hold up the local religious traditions (miracles, pilgrimages, etc.) to scorn.

"I'm in the *Patriote*," exclaimed Albert proudly, holding up the newspaper which published his photograph. He showed it to "the girls" straight away. Finally, on January 1st—after ill-treating the old priest—Albert went to the grotto with such obvious ill will that all present were struck by it. A moment before the "vision" he yawned, brushed down his clothes with the flat of his hand, did not say the rosary but gossiped with Degoudenne, the little invalid. An hour afterward, when taken to task for his conduct, "I've had enough of this," he exclaimed; and two days later, "I was sure

[7] "There she is again!"

the Blessed Virgin would not come back," or in other words, "Now I can do what I like."

"That boy wanted a good smacking," remarked a spectator. The behavior of Gilberte Voisin, and Andrée and Gilberte Degeimbre was no better than Albert's. Andrée, a rougher type, was also more natural, indeed it might well be said that she was simple-minded. She was observed to be not a little worried—or feigning it—when the villagers suggested her eventually becoming a nun. This suggestion, it should be noticed, came from the crowd even before Fernande Voisin put the question to the "vision." Fernande was herself questioned about this subject before January 3rd. Mentioning Bernadette Soubirous' and Lucia dos Santos' both becoming nuns, Fernande remarked in a puzzled tone, "Will 'she,' I wonder, ask me to be one too?" Andrée, hearing the word "nun," did not hide her own preference: "I'd much rather look after my cows," she admitted. And when she examined her photograph in the *Patriote* (illustrated Sunday edition) just for once she showed some trace of vanity. "Oh, I'm not as good-looking as that. They ought to have shaded it a bit." Nor was she particularly concerned about the "visions." As she was being urged to move a little faster towards the grotto, one evening of the "apparitions" when she was dawdling along, she replied nonchalantly, "Don't worry, the Blessed Virgin will come when we get there. She'll wait for us all right." At first she liked recounting her "visions" to a circle of spectators. On one occasion her mother called her. She stamped her foot and called back, "But I like it *here*." No doubt it was much better fun than the frightening stories. But another, somewhat touching remark of hers should not be forgotten: "I'm sorry I ever said anything; I should have been happy alone." Her cherished solitude still haunted Andrée Degeimbre.

At this point of the inquiry our imaginary detective might well find himself with a smile on his lips; he would probably classify the various titbits of evidence disclosed in the last page or two as anecdotes—unless like Fernande Voisin, he merely shrugged his shoulders at her brother's bragging and announced his conclusion that it was an obvious case of fraudulent imitation of miraculous phenomena. And there he would be wrong. Not of course in his conclusions—the reader, it is to be hoped, will have formed the same ideas after these few pages—but in his haste to shut up his notebook and put up his pen and leave Beauraing by the first available train. For we are confronted with a crime, if the word is not too serious to be used of children, whose perpetrators have been unmasked; but we do not know how they carried it out nor how the idea came to them; though, as in a properly constructed detective story, we are in possession of all the elements for the reconstruction of this crime. By a method of simple deduction the blanks can all be filled. The case can be resumed, then, at the point where the detective left off.

There are no grounds for supposing that the fraudulent imitation of a miracle was premeditated, thought out a long time beforehand or even effective at the start. Right at the beginning this fact occurred: the Voisin and Degeimbre children, as they stood at the convent door, saw, or thought they saw, "a white form." The first reactions of those they told of their "vision" were, "It's a joke" (the out sister) and "Someone is playing a trick on you" (Madame Degeimbre). The latter view was at first current, for it so happened that these events occurred round about the time of St. Nicholas' day, a season when the young fellows of the Ardennes play practical jokes, like hiding themselves behind a bush to scare the passers-by. This view prevailed so extensively that for the first few days no one sought another—it was either that or a miracle—and Monsieur Omer Marischal with his flashlight was merely trying to discover some joker in the grass. It was indeed a pity that this light and so many others, including the strings of electric bulbs at the last "apparitions," were ever lighted, for there are mysteries whose explanation is to be found not in bright light but in shade and darkness. Beauraing is one of them. The first investigators were more sagacious and went to the place without their pocket flashlights; and thus several facts were established. In the first place, the convent path was not completely dark but continually traversed by gleams of light, those "silent, fleeting gleams" that were nothing else than the glow or the beams of car headlights on the nearby road to Pondrome. They were silent, for the road just there is straight and motorists need not sound their horns.

Secondly, these gleams threw shadows which traveled laterally. Thirdly, men on their way home, with lanterns in their hands, passed in either direction along two paths and the swinging of those lanterns at different heights from the ground, jointly and separately, made all sorts of crisscross patterns on the white railway embankment. Lastly, there is the "white form" to be found. But that too was there. A spectator noticed it, was startled and pointed to it. "There *is* someone there," she cried. A light was brought; the "white form" was the signpost put up there by the touring club. On November 29th it was a very dark night and the signpost appeared huge between the leafless branches of the trees. If further proof were required, it was available on December 17th. Just as the prayers before the "apparitions" were being said three Beauraing women cried out together, "Look, a light!" But it was still only the signpost.

The terrors of childhood are not always easily forgotten. Most people can remember something of the sort, like being sent by their parents every evening to shut the door of the hen house, and how fear of this task in the dark haunted their early years. There is some effort at courage; the child goes out into the garden, which looks ghostlike in the moonlight; every object, every detail of the landscape seems like some monster risen up out of the darkness—the well rope, a forgotten bucket, a white stone whose very existence had before passed unnoticed, all assume terrifying forms. If, for a crowning misfortune, the next-door neighbor for some reason is prowling in his garden with a dark lantern, why, he is a bogieman, the devil, straightaway, an object of almost mortal terror. Now at the outset the children of Beauraing did no more than acknowledge that they were afraid. "Who's there?" cried Albert in a voice which cracked with emotion. "It's a man," he added, expressing his need for reassurance and understanding. "A man," that was all the explanation required—a man would speak, would do no harm. But Fernande had already joined her hands. "It's the Blessed Virgin!" she exclaimed. To be sure, instinctively, automatically, in her mind's eye she saw the statue of Our Lady of Lourdes, shining in her phosphorescent mantle directly the light was put out—the object of her fear at home. But notice that Fernande added nothing to that remark. She did not assert in so many words, "That light, that white form is an apparition of the Blessed Virgin," but her thoughts ran, perhaps, on these lines, "It's just like the Blessed Virgin we have at home." But at once there followed this transposition. Albert remarked to the out sister, "Sister, the statue in the grotto moved." And that was the origin of the transformations of the touring club signpost.

All that was then required was a little light; it was indeed the moment to project an almost blinding light on the whole scene. Had it been done, the story would have ended there. But no light was provided, and the children returned home with heads lowered, still quite terrified. The laughter mentioned by the out sister is not important; what she took for laughter may have been a facial contraction due to fear, or perhaps, as she opened the door and by the simple fact of her presence freed them from their terrors, that hollow laughter to be observed always in those who have experienced fear or some strong emotion. No one more easily gives the impression of trying to be funny than someone who is afraid. It may be caused by the change from a state of fear to normality. Poor children, they trembled with fright and provoked laughter.

That they trembled with fright is not entirely accurate, or rather not all of them did so, for at least one of the five experienced at that moment an instant of joy, of supreme pleasure. One of the children said nothing, did not cry out, was in her element like a fish in water. Which one? Why the big girl with the underhung jaw, whom the people of Beauraing forbade their children to frequent, Andrée Degeimbre who played at frightening others.

She alone had kept calm. She alone quivered not with fright but with pleasure; she alone retained her self-control and, of the five, she was the most matter of fact, realizing full well that a signpost was nothing but a signpost and that there were no such things as bogiemen. From the evidence of that evening we ascertain that a quarter of an hour later the five children arrived at the Degeimbre home. Albert said to Madame Degeimbre, "We were frightened, very frightened." "What were you frightened of, you sillies?" inquired Madame Degeimbre. Albert said nothing, nor did Fernande. Then in the silence Andrée's voice boomed out suddenly:

"In my opinion it was the Blessed Virgin."

The whole thing is so childishly simple that there is hardly any need to insist further. All the way back Andrée Degeimbre's somewhat feeble but perverse mind was working ponderously. She could not help being disappointed; this game of frightening the others, which chance had unexpectedly provided, was far too short for her taste. She would have liked to go on with it and could not resign herself to letting it slip so easily. Thinking it over as she went along Fernande's cry occurred to her. The Blessed Virgin . . . of course, something out of the ordinary, a real marvel, wonderful material for future games. The Blessed Virgin, of course, is good and kind, but there is no denying that her sudden appearance would cause a certain feeling of fright in little country children. What child indeed would not be afraid of Santa Claus if he really saw him coming down the chimney? Fernande's exclamation did not, in fact, fall on deaf ears. At home unobtrusively, nonchalantly, but realizing full well what she meant to do, Andrée settled the future course of events. Thereupon the two families separated, supper and bed followed. That evening Madame Voisin went up to her son Albert's room to tuck him in; she discovered him peacefully asleep twenty minutes after going to bed.

At this point chance—the only element in all this fantastic adventure that smacked at all of the marvelous—came into play. Here were two girls, one of them (Fernande Voisin) was intellectually far superior to the other; both were eager for amusement but of quite different kinds. Since Fernande had seen *The Miracle of the Wolves* and *The Fallen Rose* at the cinema and had read the story of the little shepherds of Fatima, she thought of nothing but miraculous apparitions, crowds kneeling before a "visionary" and shouts of joy and blessing. To become in her turn a Bernadette Soubirous or Lucia dos Santos would be in some sort to be a star. That, she thought, might be quite as amusing as the cinema. This child, who indeed was no longer a child, for she had attained the age of fantasy and daydreams—the carnival age as Rose Tamisier's father called it—was offered by chance a more imposing falsehood for her own self-glory than she could ever have imagined. We may well believe that Fernande Voisin identified herself automatically with the heroine of books and films. Girls of our days generally fall victims to this spell. (The cinema is the opium of the people—and, in some sort, its hashish.) Thus this falsehood had already been practiced on herself, in secret, in the darkened cinema theaters, but she had never reached the point of even hoping to deceive others, let alone thousands of credulous, excited admirers. And now dull, rough Andrée Degeimbre was proffering both the opportunity and the means. That night she can hardly have slept as peacefully as her brother; more than once she must have glanced at the phosphorescent statue. She no longer feared it. Around this object of devotion she planned her whole scenario.

Fear and frightening games were all right for Andrée Degeimbre, who her whole life long would play at childish pastimes. It was just as silly as ringing doorbells. Fernande Voisin was no longer of an age for children's games. She was going to change to her own liking the theme her playmate had provided. Andrée gave her a piece of rough, badly cut material. Fernande would create from it a silken robe.

No one knows the precise moment at which the two girls agreed on the part to be played—or rather at what moment Fernande took command of operations and obliged her companion to play at the astounding game of miracles. I am inclined to believe that on the day after the first occurrence—Wednesday, November 30th, therefore—the scenario was not entirely worked out. For on that day nothing very remarkable occurred. But on the Thursday the children began to pray, and Andrée shouted to her mother, "Don't move forward, the Blessed Virgin's there, and you'll step on her!" And on Friday they fell on their knees "thunderstruck," and for the first time the Blessed Virgin spoke and asked them to "be very good." It may be remembered that Albert Voisin went to Communion that morning. It is quite possible that that Communion was already fixed—no one in telling the story of Beauraing raises the question—or perhaps Albert himself demanded it. All our knowledge of the boy points to the fact that he had little respect for sacred things.

The five children were now involved and took part in the affair with equal enthusiasm. How far each was sincere, if indeed there was any sincerity, is a difficult question. It would be wrong to deny the possibility at the outset. Children who give effect to, who are ridden by, their fantasies are like patients suffering from hysteria: they are more or less the victims of their own lies. The only difference is that the hysteric sinks deeper and deeper into his lies, as if penetrating farther and farther into a forest, whereas the normal child can retrace his steps in time and sooner or later find the way out. After a very short time the Beauraing children were hankering after this way out. Remarks like "I'm beginning to have enough of this," "If I'd known, I would not have spoken," and "I was sure the Blessed Virgin wouldn't come back any more" are clear indications. In the magic forest of their imagination these clever little Tom Thumbs remembered the white pebbles showing the trail back home and the return to reason. Nevertheless, I repeat, there is nothing to contradict the hypothesis of partial sincerity. It is probable that Andrée Degeimbre and Fernande Voisin acted a part before the two Gilbertes and especially before Andrée's sister. "It's the Blessed Virgin, of course! I tell you it is. And we shan't be the first either. What about Lourdes and Fatima? . . ." This was the moment for Fernande to display all her cunning. Her fantasy had come to life, just as seriously as the make-believe of a game of hopscotch, for example, with its heaven, its hell—as everyone knows, nothing is taken more seriously than hopscotch. One slip and all goes wrong. But Fernande felt sure that she had thought of everything. And right at the outset chance came to her aid. A game of the sort she was playing required the complicity of others; and at once it was there for her to use, the complicity of grown-ups.

The philosophy of Beauraing, the inner meaning behind the events that occurred there, reveals not a little about the relations between children and grown-ups. They seem to inhabit two different worlds with no communication between them. The child is naturally hostile to the adult. The child, like a patient, industrious, hard-working artisan, sketches out on the pavement his familiar signs, that algebra of unreality; a man passes by, head in air, his thoughts elsewhere, careless, and steps on the signs: the child, loathing on his face, leaps up.

"Don't walk there!" he cries. "It's not allowed."

Nonplused the man looks foolishly at his feet. He can see only a chalk sign, or perhaps nothing at all, like Andrée's mother. But to the child the terrible, mysterious thing is there, and the passer-by has just committed a crime. "Don't move forward, don't move forward! The Blessed Virgin's there, you'll step on her!" At this point one of two things occurs: either the man laughs shortly, shrugs his shoulders, and goes on his way heedless of treading the image underfoot; or else some feeling is awakened in him, mere curiosity, regret for his own childhood perhaps, or some obscure qualm based on superstition, and in this case he gives an understanding smile, bends down and gravely assents, "Ah yes! It's not allowed, of course. What was I thinking of?" The wisest course will be for him to let this smile suffice, to step round and go on his way with no more ado, putting the whole fantasy aside without intruding on it; a more foolish man, forgetting all his concerns of a moment before, his age, and position and claiming the right to join in the game, will borrow the child's chalk to make his own signs. And the child, at once delighted and suspicious, will let him do so. He will even be eager to explain it all, the words tumbling over one another—"here's my house, this is the devil here, and heaven's over there." And so are forged the links in the iron chain of complicity; from that moment onward the man becomes prisoner of the child, and he will not recover his freedom.

All our knowledge of Beauraing shows clearly the existence of such flagrant, uninterrupted, stubborn complicity; everything occurred just as if from the outset the adults were caught up in the game and to all intents and purposes became children again. The five little "visionaries" did not long remain the only ones to lie. Consciously or unconsciously everyone began telling lies with them and for this simple reason: the game was worth it. We need not consider the hotelkeepers, those with land to sell, or the hawkers, stocking up their trays and cases with pictures of the visionaries, of Our Lady of Beauraing, etc.—those tradesmen in the supernatural who spring up like mushrooms after the rain. Our concern is with the sincere believers who *wanted* a miracle, who desired it and called for it with all their strength but who, unlike the pastor-dean with the processes of canon law at his back, possessed no effective weapon against the perils of credulity. From the very first days all the credulous souls of the village, with Dr. Maistriaux at their head, interposed a barrier between the skeptics and the children. They, too, were caught up in the game. They had no hesitation in compromising position, career, and future. They crowded round the children not so much to question them as to protect them, and fencing them in with all kinds of safeguards made their position impregnable.

It was only with difficulty and after many attempts to prevent it that the separation of the children during their visions was at last obtained; the further elementary precaution of forbidding all communication between the children was never secured. And yet it would have been simple enough and called for no harsh measures; it would have caused the children no suffering to have put them in the care of different priests in the district during the day, or to have separated them among various families who would have been chosen for their kindness and religious convictions. Instead of that the little "visionaries" were allowed the mistaken privilege of being in touch with each other all the time and so were continually able to go over together the events of the previous evening and to rehearse those of the next without interference. The results of this state of affairs were what we should expect. It took just forty-eight hours for the "golden heart" to pass from Fernande's imagination into that of her companions. When Fernande gave the signal agreed between them—the recitation of the Hail Mary —the four others fell to their knees together but when one of the spectators noticed this signal, twenty-four hours later it was given by Andrée. Another fact to be noticed is Albert's behavior. Witnesses considered him the most distracted of all five "visionaries": he came to forget the signals, he knelt down at the wrong time, and stated on one occasion that he had seen the Blessed Virgin when the spectators nearest him were sure that he had seen nothing and told him so quite clearly; the next day, overcome by further distraction, he was more skillful and confessed that he had seen nothing. It is hard to resist the conclusion that he had received a dressing down from the others. The investigators caught the children in glaring contradiction about the exact spot at which the Blessed Virgin appeared; the next day the five "visionaries" edified the crowd by all looking toward the same spot. We need not consider all those conferences, those whispered discussions, those winks and nudges, in which Monsieur Voisin played a part as well; just one such demonstration ought to be enough to cast doubt on the whole affair.

There is this additional piece of evidence to be noticed in connection with the exact spot of the apparitions. On December 11th the investigators questioned Fernande Voisin and asked her where she saw the Blessed Virgin. Fernande answered, "In the air, above the railway embankment." The answer was recorded, and the investigators were going on to the next question when one of those present, provided with a photograph of the site that he had been careful to take and on which he had followed out the indications given, noticed suddenly that the railway embankment at that point was hidden by the branches of the trees. He voiced his difficulty aloud. But it made not a bit of difference. Fernande corrected her statement then and there and pointed out another place, at an angle of about thirty degrees from the first. It was only necessary, as we have seen, to interrogate the children apart for them not to know if the Blessed Virgin opened her hands or closed them. Actually, according to Fernande's scenario, she opened them as at Fatima. But if any doubt was cast on the matter, if the question was asked a second time, giving the impression that one of the children had contradicted herself, Fernande at once revised her own carefully prepared statement. It seems almost ungracious to insist further. Without the shield of grown-up complicity, especially of Dr. Maistriaux, who one day ordered off the investigators, the great falsehood of Beauraing would not have lasted more than four or five evenings.

It is incontestable that in the end this falsehood came to weigh heavily on the children. They realized full well that sooner or later the whole carefully constructed fabric would crumble to pieces. And also they were tired of it. Then, too, they experienced vague forebodings—if exposure came, would they not be punished, imprisoned? The time had come, they considered, to declare the era of the Blessed Virgin at Beauraing definitively closed. So they gave out her farewell message when nervous tension had reached its zenith, when confusion was at its culminating point. If the falsehood had been prolonged, possibly it would have been no longer falsehood: Fernande Voisin sobbing, breathless, on the point of fainting, was, on that last evening, at the very edge of the abyss; another step and she would have believed in her own game and given way entirely to hallucination. Andrée Degeimbre had every ground for satisfaction, those old terrors, the age-old superstitions had come back in full strength again. On that evening of January 3, 1933, Fernande was really frightened of being made to become a nun. But the way out was not long in occurring to her, and these wise little Tom Thumbs regained the high road in all tranquility. They were to live in the world, marry and have children—and one day perhaps they would laugh at their fantastic escapade.

They forsook a magic land into which they had made but a brief and lightning-like incursion, leaving, it seemed, no trace of their visit. Yet traces of it unfortunately remained and their cruel game opened this land to three at least who were never to find the way out; Eugène Havenne, the blind man, and the two paralyzed children, the little Degoudenne boy and Paulette Dereppe. For them the wondrous dream went on; in it they saw, they walked. And when morning came and the dream faded, in their great disillusion their tears were endless. No miracle occurred. Our Lady of Beauraing gave sight to no eyes, revived no limbs. Beauraing was just a place where children once played.

III

The Church, with her usual meticulous prudence in these matters, sent witnesses to the spot and called for reports; a dossier of the case, crammed with documents, plans, and photographs, was compiled. And yet there was no real need for her to unearth these material facts in order to discover that the children were lying.

The truth, as the Church possesses it, lies beyond the efforts of a Fernande Voisin to make fiction seem like reality, even with the help of such reference literature as the catechism and a pamphlet on Fatima and of pulpit accounts of the miracle of Lourdes. Fernande imagined that she could copy Lourdes and Fatima at her leisure: over-influenced by their outward appearances herself, she could offer but a pale, unconvincing reflection of these marvels. The picture as she presented it was like a well-arranged and properly exposed photograph, but it was only a negative. The Church alone was in possession of the reagent which would change the black to white, and the white to black, so as to reproduce the likeness.

Fernande was asked to *describe* the Blessed Virgin. Her answer was as follows:

"As we were praying, suddenly she stood before us, quite near to us. It was like turning on a switch. She was very beautiful, more beautiful than anything I have seen. We saw her very clearly, as if she were illuminated, but she did not light up her surroundings. Her eyes were blue. She did not move. Round her were golden rays like needles. When she spoke her voice was very clear. It was not a human voice. She disappeared, as she came; it was like a light being switched off."

This description should be compared with the passage from St. John of the Cross quoted by Father Bruno de Jésus-Marie [8] in reference to it.

"The sight," writes the Mystical Doctor, "perceives figures and persons of the other life, saints and good or bad angels, certain extraordinary lights and wonders. The hearing receives extraordinary words uttered by persons who are seen or unseen. . . . Although God may be the author of these extraordinary effects produced in the senses of the body, they should never be considered or accepted with security but should rather be shunned completely without seeking to examine whether they come from a good or evil source. Moreover, the more they are exterior and corporal, the less certain it is that they come from God.

[8] In the number of *Études Carmélitaines* devoted to Beauraing; it is from this source that the essential information about Beauraing given here has been obtained.

"Bodily sense is as ignorant of spiritual things as a beast of burden is of things of the mind, even more so. . . . All these corporal favors have no comparison with spiritual things . . . and, I add, the more these corporal manifestations are exterior, the less do they profit the soul."

In Fernande Voisin's description it is precisely the importance given to material details, the corporality of her vision, which is striking. Fernande resorts automatically to comparison with an electric switch, not realizing that by the very fact of doing so she is diminishing the light she describes; an electric light represents to her the very height of intense light. "She was very beautiful, more beautiful than anything I have seen"—what is that but a reminiscence of Lourdes? And "it was not a human voice" seems a faltering description in comparison with those of authentic utterances of true visions. It all gives the impression of a childish account, drawn up by an unpracticed hand, a miracle reduced to its crudest form. The four others, generally speaking, merely repeated the lesson they had learned. They made many serious mistakes and contradicted themselves on several occasions; at no time did any one of them, not even transiently, utter one sentence, one word which so much as came near the ring of truth to be discerned at Lourdes or Fatima. But the Church has many other reasons for not acknowledging Beauraing.

It is quite obvious that a characteristic of the visionary state is ecstasy, an ecstasy which comes nigh to alienation, loss of the faculties in the vision. This ecstasy the children of Beauraing, in spite of all their . . . good will, were unable to simulate. Bernadette at Massabielle, as she was described by the witnesses to her visions, should be recalled: they describe a little girl, her cheeks white, her features drawn, her lips tightly compressed together; her appearance was that of a death mask which both deformed and enhanced the beauty of her face. But the Voisin and Degeimbre children show nothing like this; their faces do not change. (Nor do they experience fatigue, save that caused by standing up and by the crowd pressing upon them.) On January 1st, Andrée Degeimbre declared that though she saw the Blessed Virgin's lips move she heard nothing. Why was this? "Because there was too much noise all around us." Her sister Gilberte also complained of the murmur of conversation and prayer and the hooting of cars on the road.

"That is," she added ingenuously, "I could hear the Blessed Virgin. Only I didn't understand what she said."

That the Church might be satisfied with that answer is incredible; it is theologically inadmissible that the Blessed Virgin should speak without making herself understood, for hers is an interior voice. In the same way, the Blessed Virgin appearing on earth and showing herself to her chosen ones could not allow her presence to suffer the interference of a third person, not a visionary. At the second Lourdes apparition Jeannette Abadie's fooling did not hide the Blessed Virgin from Bernadette; no one can screen the vision from the visionary. At Beauraing, on the contrary, when a spectator slipped his hand in front of Gilberte Degeimbre's eyes, instinctively the child pushed the hand away, exclaiming that she "was prevented from seeing." That same evening at the daily interrogation she realized, it is true, that her reflex action had been mistaken, that she had blundered badly. "I saw just the same," she said, and, giving herself away completely, "the Blessed Virgin appeared through the hand." But if Gilberte were telling the truth, she would not even have perceived the hand. The Blessed Virgin indeed chooses a place and a person, but directly the colloquy begins, materially the place ceases to exist. The vision is in the beholder.

Bernadette made this clear when to those who asked her "In which direction was the Blessed Virgin looking?" she replied, "She looked straight in front of her," and also when she was indignant with the sculptor for representing Our Lady with her eyes looking upward. For Our Lady is in heaven, in the infinite, and all round her is the infinite. Thus there was not ecstasy at Beauraing, nor any pre- or post-ecstatic state; there was nothing like that interior summons which impelled Bernadette to the grotto or that gradual return to life that was to be observed in her; she was thought to be in a faint or dead and then, very slowly, the color came back to her cheeks and she began to speak in her ordinary voice. For that, too, should not be forgotten. When Bernadette spoke to Our Lady her voice was quite unlike that which was known as hers, and was

familiar to her relatives and neighbors. The voices of the Beauraing children showed no more change than did their faces. The
point requires some emphasis. Certain witnesses claimed that a
change in voice occurred. They were wrong. Tied down to a definite statement they admitted finally that there was nothing extraordinary about the voice, but merely about the tone in which
the words were uttered. Quite simply, the children were shouting.

Fernande Voisin was well aware as a result of her reading that
Our Lady of Beauraing would not carry conviction with the crowd
if she, too, did not bring a message. The point deserves further
examination.

In the first place, what sort of notion could the Voisin and Degeimbre children have had, or expressed, of the reason for the
apparitions? In that form the question may appear futile; the
visionary has no concern with such matters. Nevertheless certain
investigators deemed it fruitful to use it as a psychological test;
prudently they waited several weeks, to enable the children to
steep themselves, so to say, in the supernatural and be inspired
by it.

"Why did the Blessed Virgin visit you?"

"Because she was pleased to do so," replied Fernande.

"You know, don't you?" was Albert's answer.

Andrée Degeimbre thought for a moment. "It was my dead father who sent her," she remarked.

On dogmatic grounds the Church is obliged to counter that
statement with a flat denial. Our Lady is not a dead man's mes-
senger. To hold such a view of the miraculous is to reduce it to its
lowest expression and to put it on a par with the phenomena of
table turning; the very idea smacks of sacrilege. Closer examination
will reveal what we can gather from the message.

"Be very good" is both childish and vague. ("You must learn to
read" was Our Lady of Fatima's more definite command.) Besides,
what would be the result of this good behavior? Their parents and
schoolmasters would be pleased. That, no doubt, is praiseworthy
in itself, but by no means lofty and has nothing much to do with
religion. It seems difficult to imagine that the Queen of Heaven
appeared on earth to request children to sit in school with their

arms folded, not to chatter in class with their little schoolfellows, and give up ringing doorbells. In this instance again, Fernande Voisin remembered Fatima perhaps and the look of kindly, motherly reproach turned on Francisco Marto; but Our Lady of the Rosary was not blaming him for bad behavior. She did not look reprovingly at him as if he were a little boy in school.

"Pray always" is, as Father Bruno points out, a Gospel counsel (Luke xviii, 1); but here again it is extremely vague and dreadfully conventional. "Convert sinners"—how, and by what means? The request for a chapel seems almost to be expected, but it was hardly enough to say merely "a chapel." At Lourdes Our Lady told Bernadette to go to the parish priest and acquaint him of her wish; at Fatima she gave directions about the money and to some extent arranged the details of the procession. But, contrary to what Fernande imagined, the construction of a chapel does not make a complete message. To whom, indeed, was it to be dedicated? Our Lady of Beauraing of course. But what does that mean?

This brings us to consideration of the gratuitous nature, the uselessness, of the message. This message serves no particular purpose. Our Lady at Lourdes did not say, "I am Our Lady of Lourdes," but "I am the Immaculate Conception." At Fatima she did not say, "I am Our Lady of Fatima," but "I am Our Lady of the Rosary." How, in fact, could the Blessed Virgin tie her name and her presence to one place on earth when she is everywhere, in human hearts and dwellings? If she chooses a place in which to appear, it is not only to possess another sanctuary there to which crowds will especially resort for prayer; it is to assert a point of dogma or the necessity of penance for very definite intentions, in order to avert the anger of heaven. When the news "broke" of "supernatural occurrences at Beauraing," many Christians in Belgium were thrilled: they recalled the prayers offered by Cardinal Mercier to Our Lady Mediatrix of all Graces and they hoped fervently that so she would name herself. But the "visionaries" confined themselves to the ordinary and the commonplace. Except for the conversion of sinners and the chapel, the message referred only to themselves. Its "high spot" was the direction to Fernande to become a nun.

It has probably been noticed by the reader that no such injunction was given by Our Lady either to Bernadette or Lucia dos Santos. This somewhat moving fact should be emphasized. The Queen of Heaven is in possession of an infinity of time and space; she reads the hearts of men; fifteen years beforehand, enjoining on Lucia to learn to read, she could see her in her nun's cell writing the account of her apparitions and coming at last to full realization of the deep reason behind this order from on high; and yet Our Lady never ordered her to take the veil, for to do so is a vocation and every vocation is from within. It necessitates a conflict in the soul, a simultaneous choice and refusal, and this conflict, this choice and refusal, is significant only if no outside person influences the decision. If one might venture to join two contradictory terms in the same phrase, it might be said that even the chosen ones of God are not exempt from the exercise of free will. Moreover, how can obedience to a peremptory order be a complete gift of oneself to God? The signs written in the heavens do not mark the boundaries of earthly existence, and as for Fernande's expression "sacrifice" the answer is simple enough: sacrifice for Bernadette or Lucia would have meant the obligation of remaining in the world.

These children of Beauraing hung on grimly to their position as leaders of the game; though the crowd thronged round them they did not consider it, subconsciously they ignored it. An existentialist would say that others did not exist for them. "Others" meant those vague, shadowy sinners to be converted, the common herd above whom they had so amazingly raised themselves. The sum total of all the sins of the world aroused no compassion in them. They showed not the slightest emotion, shed no tear, at mention of the damned—but at the idea of becoming a nun Fernande sobbed bitterly. The few tears that fell on Gilberte Degeimbre's plump pink cheeks were due solely to the nervous state she was in. Was Bernadette ever observed to bewail her lot, or lament because she was questioned, even in the Imperial Procurator's office? Only what was subordinate and personal seemed to upset the children of Beauraing. Our Lady's words are thus gradually given the appearance of futile recommendations intended solely for five little school children. "You will pass on my message to my people," said Our Lady at La Salette. The "people" of Beauraing are reduced to nothing but a microcosm, a "children's corner," even if the children had obeyed the message.

We come to the last rock on which the too flimsy craft finally foundered completely: divine locutions are substantial. They are, in the truest sense, not mere words, but food for the soul. They have the power of transforming the visionary, of "working" on him or her, to quote again the expression used by some priests about Bernadette: "a creature worked on by God." But nothing is more jejunely formal than these "recommendations" of Our Lady of Beauraing which become dead letters as soon as they are uttered. It has been stated that Madame Voisin was glad her children did not change after their experience: in fact they continued their ordinary manner of life, were badly behaved, short-tempered over trifles, and went on playing their innocent though rather unseemly practical jokes. On December 22nd, Gilberte Degeimbre somewhat timidly tried to edify the crowd; hypocritically, with eyes cast down, she accused herself of formerly having rung the doorbells in the village, bewailed this terrible sin, then smilingly acknowledged that for the last three weeks she had given up this pastime; unfortunately, ten minutes later, an investigator was able to prove to her that that very day she had been observed ringing doorbells. This little "saint" was nothing but a hypocrite. It could hardly be otherwise. In spite of all their efforts this game played by the children of Beauraing never reached the level they desired. Heaven and hell remained just squares chalked on the pavement. They thought that they could produce the illusion of a miracle, and so introduce into everyday life a sacred person; all they managed to do was to portray an out-and-out schoolmistress, a haughty severe figure, harping on good conduct, giving out the sort of moral lessons that are listened to with folded arms in class and forgotten the moment the bell rings for recreation.

"Many people," writes Alain, "retain in their memory, so they say, a picture of the Pantheon, and can recall it, it seems, easily enough. I would ask them kindly to give the number of pillars on the façade; not only are they unable to, but they cannot even try to do so. Now this action is simple enough when they have the Pantheon before their eyes. What then do they see when they imagine the Pantheon? Do they see anything at all?" [9]

That statement refers only to normal imagination which is within everyone's experience, but the same principles may be used, on a higher level, to distinguish visionary from imaginative concepts. Thus if the Imperial Procurator, instead of questioning Bernadette about her visions, had asked her simply to describe the policeman who had shown her into his office, the child would certainly have stammered out some description, mentioning perhaps his cocked hat, his saber and his shoulder belt; but she would surely have been unable to say how many buttons there were on his gaiters and, possibly, even whether he wore a mustache. This brings us to that frailty of human evidence which is the constant anxiety of the law courts and is the cause of miscarriages of justice. The magazine *Détective* (April, 1936) conducted an investigation on this subject with decisive results. Some trifling incident was arranged in public, and fifteen witnesses were questioned about it within the next twenty-four hours. All were positive and explicit, and all added contradictory, frequently absurd elements to their description of the scene at which they had been present; its main lines, though graven on their memories, were deformed as if seen through a distorting mirror. What then is the value of solicited evidence? A day does not pass without an accused person in some court complaining of it bitterly. It is a well-known fact that a child can be induced to say whatever the questioner wishes, provided the interrogation is to a certain degree "managed." The investigators at Beauraing were aware of this. They had to put a question in a certain way to obtain from the five visionaries the answer they desired. Now one of the characteristics of the authentic visionary state is, as has been mentioned already, precisely that accuracy of detail (white dress, blue sash, golden rose at the feet, etc.) which in ordinary life is beyond the powers of even the most careful observer. And these details are so firmly fixed in the mind that the

[9] Alain, *Système des Beaux-Arts*, quoted by J. P. Sartre in *L'Imaginaire*.

visionary never varies the description of them. The interrogation may turn this way and that, traps may be laid, and, as at Lourdes, the secretary recording the answers may be instructed to note down certain facts in a sense contrary to the witness's assertion, yet still the visionary remains quite positive, supplies a correction whenever it is required, points out the slightest mistake, clears up the smallest point of confusion. However well a lesson has been learned it cannot stand up to hostile investigation of that kind.

It must be admitted that the faculty exercised by a visionary excels the normal faculty of vision; it is knowledge, infused knowledge. A theological discussion would be out of place here; this book deals with history. But it is obvious that the accuracy and the assurance of the visionary are not qualities belonging to the individual as such; there is no psychological explanation for them: Bernadette Soubirous, the shepherdess, was not one of those prodigies who could remember any detail, a child with an extraordinary brain fitted to give performances on the music-hall stage. Her extraordinary power was a gift which she had received in full measure. A somewhat commonplace but striking comparison is that made by Armand Pierhal [10] in another connection: the modern electric clothes iron is *infused* with electricity, it is actuated by a power which is simultaneously interior and exterior to it. The visionary is endowed with a sublime faculty of knowledge and is in touch with the supernatural by other ways than those of the senses. It is not a sixth sense which may come into play on occasion; it is union with Light itself. No word is adequate to describe it. Union, marriage with the Universal, a supernatural alliance wherein all is endowed with equal importance, wherein the Eye set free from what is material does equal justice, as at the Creation, both to the Infinite and a blade of grass. A visionary is a poet— *vates*—of the highest powers, who makes real the immense, dimly seen dream of infirm humanity. What else is there to be said, finally, than this: *the visionary sees.*

To see is to be in heaven. Paradise is the contemplation of the Face of God. All who are in bondage here below can possess but a

10 *De Dieu Vivant* (Paris: Laffont, 1947).

commonplace, poor idea of it, one formed on a human level, a simple intuition.

"After the first steps in the path of virtue when the Lord desires to make them enter on the Dark Night to lead them to divine union, there are some who go no further." St. John of the Cross holds us back on the easy slopes of the Ascent, and Rolland de Rénéville rightly makes the following comment: ". . . attachment to moral values, discursive knowledge, interior harmony are . . . unrelated to that sacrifice of self to which the relentless reality of the Night demands consent. The soul has not to raise up its powers but to undergo, on the contrary, the terrible purification of darkness. The Night of the Spirit should accompany the Night of the Senses and these two Nights then lead to the Night of God. This last is defined as a white, a shining Night, because it effects the integration of contraries." [11] A passage of such distinction, supported by a quotation from the Mystical Doctor, seems a strange —or should it perhaps be a natural—comment on the humble attitude of one like Bernadette. We can perceive that *terrible purification* recorded on the saintly shepherdess' face. She, too, did not raise up her powers, but underwent purification. She gave herself, delivered herself bound hand and foot to the shining Night. How far are we from human powers, and from those commonplace arguments put forward even by certain priests who were unable to take their minds from the earthly condition of the visionary of Lourdes. "But she's only a child," they said, "just like all the others," and found it difficult to comprehend how God could be so humbled as to make choice of the most lowly of creatures. The priest at Bartrès evinced a finer intuition; meeting the little shepherdess by chance at a crossroads he trembled at the sight of her: on the features of the future saint, he read the fleeting reflection of the Divine Will and discerned in her the chosen one of God; his intuition did not mislead him. There again the blade of grass bore witness to Creation. Earthly values are of no account.

The mind of man rebels against itself, denies itself. Every man expresses himself in his own way, every man plays his own game under the cover of words. *The Mystic Bride Transformed into the*

[11] *Op. cit.*

Beloved [12] proclaims her annihilation [13] in the Light; the soul is engulfed in the Soul of all things. "And if Our Lady had found one more foolish than I, she would have chosen her," remarked Bernadette. The surest method to discern an authentic vision from a doubtful one is to apply the test whether the personality of the visionary remains discernible humanly speaking during the visions. For the visionary is one given to God. The fraudulent visionary does not escape from the trammels of his being, his own feeble ego holds him prisoner, *ego sum qui non video.*

[12] St. John of the Cross, *Mystical Poems.*

[13] Annihilation is a technical term of mystical theology meaning absorption without destruction—*Translator.*

R

6

Imitators and Fakers of Miracles:
Nicole Tavernier, Rose Tamisier,
the Ezkioga Case

How can a miracle be faked? And what strange mental process can lead to such a sacrilegious action which, after all, is easily detected by the combined indications of faith, reason, and common sense?

This question involves a further and more general one. Simulation of a miracle is in the first place a lie, and it is only to be understood when lying in all its aspects has been studied, just as knowledge of the human body is acquired by beginning with its skeleton. For this reason it appeared indispensable to devote a few pages at the beginning of this chapter to what might be called an analytical examination of sacrilegious plagiarism.

All men lie. But if lying is like a keyboard with infinite variations, men's fingers seem, nevertheless, always to strike the same keys, and to produce three of four tunes at the most, no more—but quite enough to take us far, terribly far from the Truth, that is, to hollow out that gulf which separates us from God. Roughly speaking it can be said there are two kinds of lies, the utilitarian lie and the gratuitous lie. The former is more usually employed; in certain cases there is almost a tendency to understand and excuse it. For example, a man accused of a crime before a court of law is not required to take the oath because the law deems him in an equivocal position with, in some sort, the right to lie. On a rather lower level, everyone expects a child to lie almost of instinct to hide a fault. And we might remember the Spartan code; there lying figured in the constitution and was only punished if it was unskillful.

On the other hand, the liar whose deception succeeded was admired.

This form of lie, therefore, surprises no one. Individuals and society merely take steps to protect themselves against it. It is looked on as a normal occurrence, a hazard to be encountered at every street corner, at every hour of the day, an inevitable factor of life in a human society. Far more astonishing, more questionable, frequently almost terrifying, is the lie which is not utilitarian but is told for its own sake, and serves no purpose at all. There are several points which could be taken up in this connection, but nine times out of ten it will be seen that the liar has not acted without cause. The principal reason in this case is generally prestige. Children, for example, are often liars for prestige, and this kind of lie is even a characteristic of childhood, so much so in fact that when it is detected in an adult it is very likely that he is but a grown-up child with retarded mental development. Arnold Mandel has written some striking pages on the "child-man." [1] The real adult avoids gratuitous lying. He has understood that his personality, even if imperfect, is something far better than any more or less attractive picture of it that he could provide. He has accepted himself as he is with his good and bad qualities. He has an undistorted view of himself for he does not inspect himself through a prism. He plays at being neither the hero nor the saint and is content with the honor of being an ordinary man.

How can the first form, the utilitarian lie, be used in simulating a miracle? It is popularly supposed that it is. If a fake miracle is reported in the newspapers, it is at once commonly asserted that its author contrived it because "he could make a good thing out of it." It is a common misconception to imagine, and to exaggerate grossly, the gains and profits of others; in its most popular form it becomes practically a hard and fast rule and is pushed to absurd lengths. In this way one columnist claimed that Hitler and Mussolini seized power and played the tyrant over Europe solely in order to "provide themselves with a profitable situation." Though the comparison must not be pushed to ridiculous lengths, the faker of miracles is quite shamelessly accused of being activated by simi-

[1] A. Mandel, *L'Homme-enfant* (Paris: Julliard, 1946).

lar intentions. He, too, we are told, is trying to make a good job for himself, and earn large sums of money and so on.

The "good job" that the Church offers to visionaries is not the kind to tempt the majority of men. It comprises a monastic cell, a hair shirt, a whole lifetime of meditation and prayer; it may lead to being eaten up with scruples as Bernadette was during the last days of her life, terrified that she was unworthy of the great grace she had received. At its very best it will mean continual supervision, the obligation of undergoing interrogation and of appearing before ecclesiastical commissions; not to mention the attacks from the outside world, the laity, and even religious, as well as the snubs and insults and the constant daily practice of humility. In reading the daily record of the "mysterious events of Beauraing" it is impossible not to admire the patience, the kindness, and the very great gentleness of the priests who interrogated the Voisin and Degeimbre children; although they were suspected of lying no one spoke to them harshly, no one had the right to do so. No doubt if Fernande had been acknowledged a visionary as a result of a series of extraordinary miracles like those of Fatima, she would have become a nun; but in that case she would have been treated like Bernadette and Lucia, forbidden to speak of her past life, obliged to undertake all sorts of humble tasks, and would have undergone severe corporal and spiritual mortification. Her sanctity led Bernadette to the flagstone floor of a convent, which she scrubbed with her own hands. Judged from a worldly standpoint, her success could hardly have brought her lower. Contact with the supernatural does not lead to earthly advancement.

To such arguments holders of the theory that miracle fakers perpetrate their frauds for personal advantage will reply with the standard reference to the offerings, the gifts in money and kind, the commercial profits of pilgrimage centers, and the "support of the priests." We can see the sort of examples they adduce and what these are worth.

The first condition required by the Church of an alleged visionary is complete disinterestedness. Later on in this section we shall discover Rose Tamisier discomfited for having accepted a five franc piece. Every day during the Lourdes apparitions an increasingly close and relentless watch was kept on the Soubirous. At Aljustrel the Marto and Dos Santos families not only gained nothing from the miracles, but were ruined by them; they were obliged to sell their cattle to make good the loss on their harvest caused by the pilgrims trampling down their crops. Nor does this apply only to the relatives of the visionaries, for even if they were covered in gold the visionary could touch not a penny of it for fear of exposure and suffering the penalties of the law for fraud. The fake visionary knows what to expect. The enemies he has automatically created would lie in wait for him, lay traps for him, only too glad to catch him red-handed. One day in Lourdes a stranger drove up in a coach, inquired for the Soubirous home and asked for Bernadette. Kneeling down in front of her he prayed fervently with her for a whole hour, then bade her farewell. It was noticed then that he slipped a twenty franc piece on the window sill; they ran after him and gave him back his money. He was an *agent provocateur*. One of Lucia's first requests to Our Lady was about the golden coins laid on the rustic altar at the Cova; the child was clearly worried about them, did not know what to do with them and asked what use to put them to; the money was burning her fingers. Let the faker accept but one cent and his whole structure crumbles to the ground.

It is obvious that the inauguration of a pilgrimage affords some advantages to the place in which a miracle has occurred: not only a chapel but, unfortunately, hotels of various degrees of luxury are put up, "overlooking the Gave" as at Lourdes, with all modern conveniences, and displaying signs indicating their approval by the touring clubs, restaurant guides, and the rest. The devout pilgrim may be observed giving these palaces a wide berth, for he is generally rather poor and has brought his food with him, and even the rich man who visits the place does so for other reasons than a gastronomic tour. Nevertheless the commercialization of holy places is a fact. But who, precisely, draws the profit? Certainly not the visionary nor his family. No matter how signal the miracle, years must go by before it is recognized by the Church, during which, despite the general belief, the place derives no profit. Why, then, should the visionary—always a person of humble condition

—be so eager to benefit his village and swell the bank roll of the proprietor of the local hotel? It can hardly be supposed that the Soubirous family were particularly keen to show their gratitude to their fellow villagers who had banished them to the jail. Moreover, the proprietor of the hypothetical hotel would not necessarily welcome such a manifestation. Not all villages would evince equal pleasure at harboring a saint who had seen Our Lady. The cry wrung from Mayor Lacade is there to prove it: "You'll see, that little nuisance has lost us the railroad!" Of this prediction it can be said that it was not entirely accurate; seeing what happened at Lourdes the mayor of a neighboring village would have given his eyes for a miracle which would have furnished his district with such sensational expansion. Quite often, in fact, distrust prevails. It is not necessarily the local inhabitants who profit by the miracle but often capitalists from outside and company promoters. When, as at Beauraing, all the indications were that the "miracle" would prove the foundation of a good business venture, and everyone vaguely hoped that a solution had been found to the economic crisis, it need hardly be emphasized that this side of the matter had not, at the outset, occurred to the children.

History is there to prove for us that in the case of fraudulent miracles there has never been a previous conspiracy on the part of the various interests likely to benefit from it. No secret society has been formed to organize a miracle from scratch, choose a visionary and corrupt the witnesses. Such a supposition would pass the bounds of the ridiculous. Every conspiracy—and it would be absurd to deny that there have been some—has occurred afterward. That a miracle is afterward profitable to some people is obvious. Bernadette's biographers do not hide the fact that from her convent at Nevers she wrote a pointed letter to her young brother who, impelled less by the solidity of his vocation than by the great consideration and other numerous advantages he expected to receive on his sister's account, intended to enter the priesthood. Moreover it is extremely rare that the parents of visionaries can make a career for themselves out of their children's sanctity. There is nothing very blameworthy in a great nephew of Bernadette's displaying his family tree just outside the grotto. The objects of devotion that are his stock in trade do not for that reason sell better than in the other stores.

History also relates the truth about the presents and the favors that the miracle fakers receive. In reality it is a pitiable story to tell. A few pennies here, some small change there, more frequently blessed medals, devotional pictures, untransferable relics—for the "visionary" is given what, it is imagined, will provide the greatest pleasure—the game indeed is hardly worth the candle. Much is made, of course, of the notorious support of the clergy mentioned above. But in fact the clergy do not uphold a visionary at all. On the contrary, they are the first opponents in the lists. Under the bishops their attitude to him (or her) is one of prudent reserve, bordering sometimes on hostility. They show not the slightest disposition to lavish gold on the visionary; what gold should they lavish? Country priests are poor. It may be urged that the local lady of the manor is on friendly terms with the parish priest; there are also devout folk of the village. Instead of gifts in money or kind, which would effectually destroy belief in the miracle, could they not provide hospitality on a more or less sumptuous scale, some well-paid post perhaps or a pleasant sinecure? They could, of course.

But generally speaking the miracle faker's lying is not purely utilitarian—practically speaking it never is. The advantages he derives from his imposture are only occasional, exceptional, and subordinate to the principal end. The lie of the miracle faker is always a lie of prestige.

When the devout Nicolazic, on his return from the field that he had been ploughing all day, informed the parishioners of Auray that St. Anne had appeared to him, some told him he was mad, others fell on their knees and proclaimed a miracle; but no one accused him of deception for a very simple and convincing reason; he was a peasant of mature age with both feet firmly on the ground, a man who feared God and perhaps the police a little as well, and was by no means given to nebulous daydreams. A man—that is the essential word; miracle fakers are nearly always women.

In cases, that is, when it is not a child; the Beauraing affair provided sufficient illustration of the reasons behind instances of that kind, and the point will not be dealt with again. Women, far more than men, suffer from a belated childhood. Sometimes it occurs in one who suffers disappointment that action has never accompanied her dreams of it, for whom by reason of her very state there has never been activity in the proper sense of the word. The world is full of these misunderstood women who pass their days sighing for the impossible realization of their dreams: if only they belonged to the stronger sex, they imagine, what adventures, what conquerors they would have been. It is unnecessary to go to Freud for reconsideration of these primary truths dear to more than one novelist.

The lie is feminine. Those ancients were right whose first requirement of a hero was that he should not lie; if he did, in certain countries, his sword was taken from him. The Gaelic epics go a step further: they tell us that every man convicted of lying was rigged out in a skirt, a symbolic castration of the liar who had chosen a feminine arm with which to defend himself. But every element, every principle may be considered at two levels. If woman is the personification of the lie, she is, too, of the legend. She is the pagan muse, the inspirer from on high; in later days, in Christianity, she is the Mediatrix.

When a man lies he is easily detected, because a man does not know how to lie. But a child knows and so does a woman. Both are instinctively aware of the rule which runs: the greater the lie, the better chance it has of being believed.

One of my schoolfellows had the annoying habit of lying. At table one evening his parents' conversation turned to a rescue carried out by a sailor on board a boat in the Ouessant channel. The next day the boy came home wet to the skin, the water running off him, and declared that he had just rescued one of his friends from drowning in the river. Every care was lavished upon him, dry clothes were brought and he was rubbed down. Finally he was asked to give an account of his adventure.

"But you can't swim," his parents objected.

"Oh, yes I can," came the unhesitating reply, "I learned in secret."

In spite of all this there was just a little skepticism about the whole affair; but the boy asserted that his name would appear in next morning's paper, was able to describe the policeman who had taken note of his courageous act and the journalist who, happening to be there, interviewed him on the spot. He added that the boy he had rescued would come next day to his home to thank him for what he had done. There was no report in the newspaper next morning. But two days later the "rescued" boy arrived at the house; the "rescuer" took him into the garden, beneath his parents' window, where the two of them shook hands; when the parents came down the visitor had left. The newspaper published nothing about the accident because, the boy asserted, the headmaster of the *lycée* objected. For a whole week this crude lie passed for the truth, although there was no accomplice, not even the "rescued" boy, who had been summoned to the house on some other pretext. Such a lie surpassed belief—"Where on earth," it was asked, "did he get hold of a tale like that?" And more especially, "Why, for the mere pleasure of lying, go to the trouble of inventing proofs like the sodden clothes?"

"It's devilish," sighed his father, when finally he was obliged to bow to facts. In dealing with Nicole Tavernier we shall see just how far a liar can go in providing proof for his lies.

This boy has now grown into a man and is at the present moment a staid industrialist in the west of France; he would be embarrassed and upset if he had to invent some lie to explain his lateness in getting home. Because he has become a man realities have a meaning for him; he is well aware, or imagines, rather, that if ever the fancy took him to invent such a story as that he told in his school days, everyone would laugh in his face. And that is where he would be wrong: for the simple reason that it was on so extensive a scale there would be a widespread tendency to give credence to his fabrication. But now he feels no need at all for lying; he may even have forgotten the lies of his youth for he no longer lives in his imagination.

The predominating impression produced by women miracle fakers is of the continuance of the imaginative life of their childhood. It is entirely and diametrically opposed to all reality, and, it may be added, hopeless from the start. It is the old tale of the iron and the earthenware pot all over again; sooner or later the lie will break in pieces against the wall of reality. And the liar—male or female—is well aware of it. But that by no means prevents their plunging deeper and deeper into their lie, inventing all sorts of imaginary proofs which are nothing of the sort, when just one real proof would carry conviction.

An example is furnished by a certain Annonciade prioress. Because she was a nun she was a woman whose life was largely passed in a cell where she was at the mercy of the first medical examination to be suggested. If, like Ramona of Ezkioga, she had made gashes in her hands, her trick would have been more likely to succeed; on the contrary, a mere coat of paint seemed to her enough for the purpose. Yet if anyone came near to examine her hands she cried out that she could see Jesus Christ and fell into a swoon; she appeared to be inspired, a prophetess; she foretold miracles for particular dates in the near future, rather in the way a murderer under interrogation by the police might say, "The proof that I did not kill him is that in an hour my supposed victim will come here to deliver me out of your hands." She was aware, too, that her lie could not endure longer than a fortnight. And her power of conviction was so strong that everyone believed her at once, right up to the fatal hour that she had known awaited her (perhaps she even longed for it) when one of her nuns brought soap and water and in a couple of minutes exposed the fraud.

The hour that she had longed for—the event seemed to show that this miracle faker was suffering a self-imposed torture. Who will take this burden from me, deliver me from this lie that I have allowed to govern me? A man lying for reasons of utility, to save his head or his honor, bears his lie so to say with outstretched arms, fearful lest he drop it, for if he does, it will fall like a thunderbolt; having decided to tell it, he is careful of every detail for fear of contradicting himself; only temporarily, for the needs of the moment, does he lodge in the temple of chance. But the miracle faker wears her lie like the tunic of Nessus. The Annonciade prioress had nothing to gain by giving herself faked stigmata, save possibly a reputation for holiness, and for that indeed more than these divine marks was required. Yet she played out the comedy to the end, dominated by her part in it, and even when comedy was gradually turning to tragedy, when her vision of adulation and bliss changed to punishment, torture, perhaps even the stake, she still refused to commit herself to a voluntary confession which would have caused merely removal from office and her becoming an ordinary member of the community again. After that, it is hardly surprising that persons of importance like the bishop of Lisbon, were taken in. In a remarkable little book [2] Vladimir Jankelevitch has provided what is possibly a valid explanation of this inveterate lying which might well apply to all lies of prestige.

He distinguished between irony, which deceives no one, and lying, which of set purpose is meant to deceive. He notes, with evident truth, that though men are not of equal intelligence, everyone, from the peasant to the intellectual, is naturally able to detect irony. For example, some broad allusion will cause laughter in the roughest soldier and the most fastidious man of letters. Irony moreover is not intended to cause a misunderstanding (*misintelligence*, as he names it) but is uttered playfully, whereas lying is a duel fought with cold steel. It results in demonstrating the superiority of one individual over another, indeed it creates this superiority. "I tell you a story that is untrue and you believe it, therefore I am clever and you are stupid."

Granting the truth of this idea—that the lie, like laughter, is an assertion of superiority—it remains to discover which is the weak and which the strong; or rather which one will be chosen to play the part of the weak by him who desires to be strong. It is obvious at once; he will choose not some poor dull-witted man but, in most cases, someone who is held in high esteem, whom he himself esteems, someone that is superior to himself. The Annonciade prioress concluded it was the right moment to lie when a meeting of learned ecclesiastics took place at Lisbon; her chosen victims were to be cardinals and bishops—it was possible, she thought, that even the pope might be deceived. If the deceiver is some peasant woman, she will select for her victims the important and distinguished people of her village, neighbors of hers who know her well for what she is—almost invariably a person of no

2 *Le Mensonge* (Paris: Confluences).

consequence. Her joy may be imagined at deceiving these people who are superior to her in the social scale, as they run to her bedside, asking, imploring her favors, kissing her garments and requesting relics. It matters little to her that the lie will necessarily be discovered in the end. She has experienced her moment, for a longer or shorter period she has known success, and is willing to accept her final defeat; she considers herself satisfied.

The question requires deeper examination still, to the point, in fact, which leads to the conclusion that it is the victims of a lie who are partly responsible for it. He who is deceived creates the deception.

Only superficially is that statement a paradox; in its real sense it contains profound truth. Most lies of prestige are aimed at those persons who really possess some prestige. An honest man encounters by chance some habitual criminal just out of prison. He talks to the criminal, and may ask him about his past; there are two courses open to the latter: he can reveal his record or turn on his heel and make off without more ado; yet in nine cases out of ten he will lie, giving himself every appearance of complete moral integrity; he will play a part. It is not with the hope of extracting some trifling sum of money from his questioner that he does this, or even to obtain a good meal (he would have a better chance of that if he told the truth); nor does he do so to effect some fraud. In fact the truth of it is this: the criminal wishes he were in the honest man's shoes, he would like to change places with him.

The miracle faker acts no differently. At the outset she is never an enemy of religion—there have never been alleged miracles for the benefit of well-known freethinkers. On the contrary, almost invariably she is a woman or girl whose childhood was passed in a religious atmosphere. Convents and convent schools and orphanages contain a very large number of persons all subjected to the same routine of prayer and mortification; together they frequent the chapel, receive Holy Communion, and see to the decoration of the altars. It is quite obvious that the morality and mentality of such persons—who at first sight are indistinguishable from each other—make a screen behind which may be hidden not only a sincere piety but also a piety that is feigned, and even unbelief. Similarly in a village, among the few hundred Catholics who frequent the church services, as likely as not there will be found some peasant girl for whom these services are just a formality; she received a religious upbringing but her whole temperament is entirely out of tune with it. Now this peasant—or convent schoolgirl —is an unbeliever and considers herself more intelligent than her devout companions. In her heart of hearts she jeers at them just as the thief, seated at table opposite an honest man, will sneer at him and think him a fool. It is true none the less that centuries of civilization have made of the honest man a type of superior being; centuries of religion, the example of the saints, catechism lessons, the contemplation of holy pictures, Sunday sermons have all combined to make the devout Catholic a respected figure, one on whom men are encouraged to model their lives. Whatever the tacit understanding with herself, the black sheep of the flock feels vaguely that she will be accepted only if all eyes see her, mistakenly, as white. And the whiter the better, she reasons, and she goes on to hanker for some supernatural light to transform her appearance. And so the mental process is complete: the convent girl no longer dreams of being equal with her devout companions, but of excelling them; the peasant girl will not rest until with her own weapons she has outdone not only the other sheep but also the shepherd of the flock. The favors granted to a devout soul after years of recollection, meditation, and prayer the black sheep desires for herself, publicly and immediately.

The thought of a miracle faker might well provoke a shudder, not indeed when she is perpetrating her trickery with a varying degree of cunning, but when the spectators have gone, when she is alone once more in her room going over the day's events. What thoughts, what visions then pass through her mind? No one knows. No fraudulent miracle faker has ever publicly confessed her thoughts at this moment. But one may perhaps imagine something of what then takes place in her mind. The "visionary," the "saint," whose lie has so far eluded detection, once again alone must feel more than human joy welling up in her heart, tremendous satisfaction at having deceived believing and upright people, the rapture of an actor on the stage who receives an ovation. At that moment she is overwhelmed by an uncontrollable desire to laugh. She bursts out laughing. I will now reveal the meaning of this laughter and whence it comes, and who it is in the shadows who laughs with the visionary.

For lying is not merely a fearful union, the possessing of the victim by the liar. It is more than that; it is a very counterfeit of creation itself, or rather a new creation, imitation in its most typical form. God created the world and right in the center of all things placed man with his freedom, his good, and his evil—good which is strength and evil which is weakness. But weak or strong, good or bad, man exists. He bears witness to himself; he is an affirmation of Creation. Now a lie is the mixture of good and evil, a distorting mirror which reflects a false image; it is a structure which at all points copies and reproduces remarkably the divine structure. In the Introduction it was pointed out that the Church takes good care not only to distinguish the true miracle from the spurious but also to detect whether in the spurious miracle there is a supernatural influence; in short, whether it is produced not by a human being but by the arch-counterfeiter, arch-imitator of God. There is none cleverer, none more artful than he who schemes successively to make the faithful ridiculous and to afford a visionary a momentary triumph; the "miracle" which has every mark of authenticity is in this respect more formidable than one which deceives no one. The evil one enjoys immense freedom of action. He has all sorts of power and may even deceive the just. At will he can assume a cloak of innocence. And in fact he deceives everyone, even the liar. For such a one never acts alone. His accomplice is always in the wings or the prompt box. He knows the whole part by heart, has always known it. He whispers the answers. The "visionary" may delight in possessing a secret and playing a part superbly; yet each word and gesture is primarily the ringleader's. He it is who laughs, who laughs until he is out of breath, filling the silence with his laughter when the farce seems to be a success. Even he will be unmasked eventually— meanwhile he has managed to stage his play. Now it remains but to name him side by side with his puppet without whom he is powerless to act. His puppet, his weapon, his double, his very essence, for the lie is the Devil himself.

I

The story of Nicole Tavernier does not require a long chapter. It has practically all been told when the reader is informed that Nicole was a mythomaniac, a woman of the consciously fantasy-ridden type, whose morals were more than suspect as the end of her life conclusively demonstrated. At another time she would have been nothing more than a common or garden-variety adventuress; but she lived at a period (in the reigns of Henri III and Henri IV of France) when civil war was devastating the land, and it is an accepted fact that wars bring in their train all sorts of charlatans, false soothsayers, and other exploiters of a credulous public. Men were afraid, the times were heavy with foreboding, and all who were at all simple-minded were glad to seek refuge in an easily obtained message from the other world.

It so happened that Nicole Tavernier's earthly career coincided with that of another woman who followed a very different path; Nicole's adventures are bound up with the life of Madame Acarie (Blessed Mary of the Incarnation). The two women, the saint and the faker, were so much together that it is difficult not to see the fact as an illustration of the point explained in the preceding pages; the lie is based on, the liar chooses, a truthful model. Nicole Tavernier was born in Reims. Very little is known of her origins except that they were obscure and unassuming. No historian, so far as I know, can tell us anything about her childhood. At a certain moment a young woman suddenly appeared of whom almost nothing was known, asserting that she was inspired by God, instructed by Him to bring back those souls who had been led astray, and was endowed with a mission of repentance and mercy. Nicole Tavernier, like a new Jeanne d'Arc, set off along the high-roads brandishing a cross.

These roads were infested by ruffian bands and robbers; crowds of wounded, starving men, and many sick were daily to be encountered on them; the times were apocalyptic and the end of the world was expected at any moment. Nicole started off, of course, by promising what everyone was hoping for, that is the end of all these troubles and the coming of peace—"Confess your sins, pray, throw yourself on the mercy of the Lord and He will take pity on you."

Nicole's message was really no more than what was being preached by the priests and monks. Nevertheless she would stop for a while in the towns, give open-air sermons and hold what amounted to religious meetings; before long she was going to private houses, though there is every reason to believe that she did so at first only by invitation. In these houses, in the presence of a quickly gathered audience, Nicole spoke of her visions and called for penance. She was given lodging and food. Right from the beginning the custom was formed of taking her to visit the dying. There, usurping the priest's place, Nicole heard the dying person's confession and did not scruple even to administer "holy communion." Witnesses assert that on several occasions she foretold the exact time of death. Very soon too she seemed to know in advance the confessions that were to be made to her; going into a sick man's room, at once, before even his relatives withdrew, she would mention the sins he had committed. There is nothing very surprising in that. Nicole's disclosures were quite vague and in that not unlike the utterances of any clairvoyant at a country fair. "Remember how you blasphemed! You swore in the name of the Lord lightly or rashly! Remember too that theft on your conscience. However small, even if you committed it as a child, it will weigh heavily on you when you come before the judgment seat." Having thus edified some of the townsfolk, Nicole, growing still bolder, demanded to be taken to the town hall and there, confronting the councilors, standing up to them, requested that her departure should be characterized by public processions, and special services at the church and a general Communion.

It was sufficient, obviously, for her to succeed in one town; others followed quickly enough. From town to town, cheered by the crowds, organizing a religious demonstration in every little hamlet, Nicole gradually made her way to Paris. On arrival there she knew that she must try to make a hit right away, for in Paris you are accepted or rejected at the outset. Nicole took no heed of the townsfolk but went straight to the archbishop. She told him that death was hanging over him and that he would die before three months were out if he did not hear her and do as she told him. He listened to the conditions she laid down: a general public procession round Notre Dame by the clergy and following them in order, members of Parliament, of the law courts, the army, merchants, craftsmen, laborers. The prelate complied with her request, and on his recommendation a public holiday was proclaimed for the procession to take place.

It must be admitted that to arrive in Paris without friends, support, or protection of any kind, preceded only by a somewhat doubtful reputation for sanctity and without more ado to bring ordinary life in the capital to a standstill, to make the clergy, the nobility, the commonalty carry out her behests, demands even at a time of crisis very much more than ordinary effrontery. Nicole Tavernier had brought off a masterly stroke. She decided, very wisely, that Paris which had given her so warm a welcome was worthy not only to receive her but to keep her. There, then, she remained; she could not have chosen a better center of operations.

From that moment "miracles" occurred with greater frequency. Paris, it appeared, had earned some reward. Day after day Nicole, now a public figure and welcomed by the people with open arms, presented her chosen city with prophecies, visions, all sorts of *charismata* and supra-normal cures. The smallest of the "miracles" was an "inspired" commentary on the Book of Wisdom, which Nicole delivered in the presence of the religious authorities; distinguished priests were to be heard proclaiming their admiration and claiming that "the divine wisdom spoke through the mouth of this young woman." Next she fell into ecstasy, declaimed passages from the Old and New Testaments that no one, of course, suspected for a moment to be learned by heart. Then she heard the confessions of the sick in her own special way. In the last place, to convince the skeptics, Nicole did not shrink from more obvious supernatural manifestations such as "communion" received at the hands of angels. One Sunday morning at Mass she fell into

s

ecstasy, opened her mouth, and the amazed congregation saw a host on her tongue. Everyone believed that of a certainty Jesus Himself had brought her Holy Communion. And the parish priest noticed that a host was missing from those he had consecrated. On that day Nicole had to be protected from the adulation of the crowd. A short time afterward some devout folk praying in a chapel were quite certain that they had seen her raised above the ground; the "visionary" asserted that she was so absorbed in prayer that she had noticed nothing.

Nicole was now at the height of her glory. Provincial townsfolk requested her presence in their towns "for the solace of the good and to drive out the wicked." Members of the nobility sent messengers to her. She was "booked" for their houses like an honored guest. Petitions were sent in to her, and also jewels and gold. Her portrait was printed and sold in the streets.

It was at this time that Madame Acarie made Nicole's acquaintance; the future Blessed Mary of the Incarnation could not fail to take an interest in this extraordinary young woman who seemed so obviously favored by heaven. On her side Nicole was well aware how advantageous it was for her to be intimate with this devout woman who enjoyed so great a reputation and who was better able than anyone else to render her position unassailable in Paris. The two women became companions and fast friends. They spent long days together, went to church and performed their devotions together. Nicole brought all her cunning to play in order to convince Madame Acarie of the authenticity of her miracles; she believed that she achieved her purpose definitively when in answer to a question Madame Acarie one day said to her: "I quite believe that these things are supernatural." A suspicion of a smile hovered on the "visionary's" lips. But it soon turned to a wry look as Madame Acarie went on to add, "I quite believe you, but have you asked yourself whether these things really come from God? For my part, I find it a very worrying matter. I have thought it over carefully and I very much fear now that the devil somehow is mixed up in it. We must pray, sister. Probably our prayers will drive out the devil and you will be freed from these strange powers of yours."

Nicole was not at all keen to be freed from her powers. Nevertheless she was sagacious enough to show no opposition; on the contrary, she pretended to agree with her friend, even to the extent of requesting her to lend her a relic. "In this way," she remarked, "if some miracle occurs, with this relic in my possession it will be proof that Satan has nothing to do with it." As a matter of fact, Nicole had not foreseen the objection that her "miracles" might be ascribed to the devil, but she did not treat it very seriously; sooner or later, she imagined, people would be convinced that they were from God. She was greatly surprised, then, the next day when Madame Acarie told her that on further reflection she was more than ever convinced that they were diabolic manifestations. The conviction was extremely distasteful to her, she went on, but henceforth they must keep careful watch; perhaps these "supernatural manifestations" ought to be repulsed. In any case she had taken steps. She had mentioned her suspicions to certain priests who also were worried. They too required time to reflect about the whole matter.

"But what about all those visions," stammered Nicole, "those ecstasies and the many graces sent me by heaven?"

"They may just as well be given you by hell, sister," came the reply. "These visions, graces, and ecstasies prove nothing as far as I am concerned. The Evil One certainly has the power to work these marvels."

"But would the devil go so far as to deprive himself of souls?" objected Nicole. "For don't forget, sister, many great sinners have been converted in my presence. And in yours too. You have seen unhappy souls, lost to the Lord, repent of their sins before me, beseech God to pardon them, and die at peace with heaven. And all that owing to me. And had it not been for me I fancy it would not have occurred."

"Who can tell?" answered Madame Acarie. "Satan is a gambler. He is willing sometimes to lose a little in order to win much . . ."

Nicole realized her danger. She was frightened by her companion's good sense. She who with little difficulty had won to her cause important and highly placed ecclesiastics was tripped up for the first time by the straightforward simple reasoning of a woman who, though not a luminary of the Church, understood its teaching far better than most others. It instinctively occurred to Nicole that elementary prudence required her to flee at once. But then, she further considered, that would mean the loss of her position in Paris, and in a few days Madame Acarie would have both clergy and laity on her side. The country was small enough for it to be common knowledge in a short time that Nicole had been forced to take to her heels. And after all she wanted to remain in Paris and continue to play her part. All she had to do was to convince just one woman who had given her her friendship and who, all said and done, did not distrust her. A certain vanity, the desire to vanquish all obstacles, was possibly an additional motive for her determination to remain. She decided to attempt a bold stroke. Lying had brought her to her present position, lying would help her round this difficult corner.

One morning, Nicole asked Madame Acarie to go to Mass with her at the Capuchin chapel at Meudon. The two women set out, praying as they went along, to their mutual edification. They traveled on foot and Nicole, knowing Madame Acarie's faculty for intense meditation, felt sure she would soon be so completely absorbed in her prayers as to forget her companion's presence. And so it turned out; Madame Acarie in interior converse with God did not raise her head until she arrived at the chapel; there she became aware that her companion had disappeared. She had vanished as if she had been carried away in some marvelous manner. Madame Acarie wondered in vain where she could possibly be. Then at last she saw her reappear, coming towards her, showing every sign of extreme stupefaction. Her face bore an ecstatic look as she joined her hands and fell on her knees. And this was the tale she told: she had indeed been carried off, and by angels; they had taken her to Tours and she found herself in one of the rooms of the palace in the presence of an important personage of the kingdom with whom she had a long conversation. Religion, she went on, was mysteriously threatened; sore trials awaited the faithful and the evil one was certainly connected with them, for these terrible trials would appear in the guise of benefits. But God had warned his faithful servant and these misfortunes might be avoided.

The two women went into the chapel and heard Mass; as they came out again Madame Acarie seemed wrapped in thought. She arranged to meet Nicole the next day, and the "visionary," believing the time had come to go over to the offensive, declared that now she was sure of the divine origin of her miracles. In fact she had noticed Madame Acarie's anxiety and was now congratulating herself on having convinced her.

On bidding her farewell, Madame Acarie gave her a letter. Outside it was written the name of some mutual acquaintance who was to fetch the letter from Nicole in three or four hours' time. Having undertaken this small kindness for Madame Acarie, no sooner was her back turned than Nicole made haste to open the letter, certain that it would give her definite information of Madame Acarie's good opinion of her. To her great astonishment a cloud of little scraps of paper fell out of it; Nicole tried in vain to catch them, but the wind carried them off. She had to seal up the letter with nothing inside. Three hours later Madame Acarie came back and asked for the return of her letter which no one had called for. She opened it at once; a glance was sufficient to show her what had occurred.

"So it seems," she remarked, "that you are given to prying and tell lies. But those are both sins for which contrition can earn forgiveness. But that experience is enough to show me that you are no servant of God. Either you are lying or else Satan has you in his clutches!"

Nicole had lost all. This time she was obliged to take refuge in flight. In vain she endeavored to save herself by further lies; Madame Acarie's sincerity, piety, and austerity spoke louder than anything that Nicole could say. In a few days Paris, then the provinces, learned what to think of the "visionary." Nicole Tavernier was soon forgotten. What finally became of her is unknown. Certain historians assert that she turned into a very coarse, unmannerly, loose woman, others that she gave herself up to scandalous conduct and sinful habits. There is every reason to believe that she came to a bad end, for those who would pose as angels act like fools. And Nicole was probably better qualified to act like a fool than to play the part of an angel though, in that field, she showed clearly enough what was the sum total and extent of her capabilities.

II

Although the story of Rose Tamisier is nearer to us by two and a half centuries than that of Nicole Tavernier, it would be no better known were it not for the witty and carefully documented hundred and thirty pages devoted to it by Maître Maurice Garçon, the brilliant lawyer and Academician; the essential information for this chapter has been taken from his book [3] and the reader especially interested in the visionary of Saint-Saturnin is referred to it; he will find there many details that the more restricted scope of this study precludes our mentioning.

It is to be noted that in a letter to the Minister of Public Worship about Bernadette Soubirous, the Lourdes Imperial Procurator mentioned the name of Rose Tamisier in comparison with the little visionary of his district. The comparison—or the contrast —was obvious. The apparitions of Lourdes occurred in 1858, the Rose Tamisier case dates from 1850. When the miracle of Massabielle took place, the "miracle" of Saint-Saturnin was still fresh in men's minds. It caused much ink to flow. It aroused controversy all over France. Opinion about it was divided. But it is enough for a miracle to be counterfeited for the stir it has caused to die down fairly quickly and in our days the "Tamisier Case" lies practically unknown, gathering dust in the provincial archives. *Fugit tempus.* . . .

Rose—or more familiarly Rosette—Tamisier was born in 1818 in the village of Saignon in the department of Vaucluse; she was the daughter of a small farmer and the eldest of five children. As early as her ninth year she attracted attention by reason of her piety at catechism lessons and in church. It was claimed—or rather *she* claimed—that at this time the Blessed Virgin appeared to her one evening and healed a small and by no means serious wound in her chest, the result of a childish accident. Ten years later

[3] *Trois histoires diaboliques* (Paris: Gallimard).

Rose's religious outlook had not changed and she gave evidence of it by entering the community of Sisters of the Presentation of Our Lady as an oblate. At this time occurred certain incidents and events which were not publicly known at first; they are referred to later when they are clearly relevant to this study.

The following facts, essential to the story, should however be mentioned. From 1837 onward, Rose Tamisier began to experience strange disorders varying from a simple headache to progressive numbness of the body. She was frequently confined to her room. In 1845, François, one of her brothers, married a certain Delphine Jean whose sister kept an inn in the village of Saint-Saturnin-les-Apt. From the first year of the marriage a friendship grew up between Rose and Delphine's sister; the two women visited each other frequently and at the inn Rose soon came to enjoy board and lodging whenever she desired it. In the end she stayed there as part guest, part servant for long periods at a time. Her life henceforward, so far, of course, as her illness allowed her, was passed between Saignon and Saint-Saturnin. In these two villages she continued to attract attention by her devotion and her fervor in church and at Saint-Saturnin, especially, the parish priest, Father Grand, held her up as a model; Father Caire, his curate, was more cautious; candidly he questioned the virtues of this young woman whose conduct appeared to him to be suspect. He was the first to assert that she was possessed of the devil. In any case the village was practically unanimous in praising Rose's moral virtues. She was known to have no suitors; it was the common opinion that she would never marry and even the boldest youths in the village hesitated to pay her their attentions or to joke in her presence.

In addition to the Jean family, Father Grand, and a few devout country folk with whom she conversed, Rose had at Saint-Saturnin a faithful and devoted friend, Josephine Imbert, a somewhat uncultured, not very intelligent young woman of her own age whom she had taught to read and write. Both displayed the same religious turn of mind; their outings together were exclusively centered on the chapels and wayside crosses of the district. One of these chapels, founded apparently in the eleventh century, drew them particularly and they were frequently to be seen kneeling before its altar. It was one of those historic buildings of the countryside which have been periodically restored, and somewhat disfigured, by successive tinkering; its only claim to artistic distinction was the possession of a Gothic pulpit which had contrived somehow or other to withstand the march of time and revolutions. Fifty years earlier the priest in charge of this chapel had "embellished" it with a picture, a Descent from the Cross, from the brush of a local painter. Saint-Saturnin, the patron of the village, is depicted on the left, the center is taken up with a moving but rather crude *Pietà;* curiously enough the wound in the side of Christ is painted on the left side of the body and not on the right. But it is only a small detail, due probably to some inadvertence on the part of the artist, and can cause no distraction to the prayers of the faithful.

We have now come to the point of the story. On November 10, 1850—a Sunday—at about 4 P.M., Josephine Imbert and Rose Tamisier, who had carried out their usual pilgrimage to the calvary overlooking the village, entered this chapel and knelt down in front of the altar, opposite the picture. After saying the rosary Rose was moved by a deep feeling of love for the sufferings of Christ; the two young women were alone so that their actions could astonish no one; instinctively she rose to her feet, went up to the picture, and placing her lips on it left a kiss on the painted wound. As she walked back to her place she noticed a strange taste on her lips. This would not have caused her any great astonishment had she not at the same moment experienced considerable amazement at the sight which met her gaze. For just at the exact spot in the picture where a brown smear crudely represented the wound drops of blood began to ooze, and then to flow. In her bewilderment Rose undid the handkerchief which she had knotted over her head as some protection against the heat, and applied it to the wound. There could be no further doubt; the handkerchief was soaked in blood.

Rose and her companion hurried out of the chapel, rushed down to the village and called on Father Grand to whom they narrated the incident. Father Grand, dumbfounded, examined the handkerchief. His first care was to have the matter "authenticated" by a specialist, namely the local doctor, Dr. Bernard, whom he summoned from Apt. Dr. Bernard confronted with the handkerchief had no difficulty in recognizing that it was indeed stained with blood. The priest, the doctor, and the two young women went at once to the chapel; all trace of the blood had disappeared from the picture or rather, all trace of damp blood, for there was a film of dried, congealed blood still remaining over the representation of the wound. With an emotion that may well be imagined, the country doctor—a practicing Catholic well known for his fervor—verified the fact carefully. Then the four of them looked at each other in silence until Father Grand, the first to recover the use of his tongue, fell on his knees and thanked heaven for having allowed this miracle, adding a prayer that it might be repeated for the edification of the village.

An hour later the news had spread in Saint-Saturnin; its reception was about equally divided between credulity and skepticism. But the next day credulity prevailed. From all parts came supporting testimony with no other tendency than to prove the authenticity of the miracle by Rose's conduct and the incidents of her former life; in short, this *miracle of the bleeding picture* was not the first in her career; her infancy, her adolescence, and her youth were as impregnated with the supernatural as was her handkerchief with blood.

The first evidence was provided by the Sisters of the Presentation who revealed the following incident. In 1837, when Rose was an oblate in their establishment, the community, which was by no means rich, besought Providence to send them food. Directly after the prayer Rose was "inspired"; in the convent garden she planted "a cabbage, its leaves in the earth and its roots pointing to the sky." Just one night was all that was required for this cabbage to grow to an incredible size; when it was discovered at the time for Matins it was so large that there was considerable difficulty in pulling it up. It was cooked at once and served at the midday meal at which it provided food for the whole community.

That was the nuns' story. At the same time, Father Lucas, parish priest of Saignon, described to his colleague of Saint-Saturnin the wonders displayed by Rose Tamisier in his parish. They had begun with the pains of the Passion suffered by the invalid during Holy Week; very soon the stigmata appeared, to be followed by the phenomenon of the angelic communion; lying in bed, unable to go out, or even to move, Rose received the host at the shining hands of an apparition. When Rose managed to get up and go to church the sacred host came supernaturally to her lips. She had communicated in this way on upward of eighty occasions and always with hosts belonging to the church which had "flown" from the ciborium. The parish priest on returning to his church found a host missing and was thus able to count Rose's mystical communions. For in this connection the following detail should be borne in mind: these mystical communions only took place when Rose was "in solitary converse with Our Lord," that is, when she was alone in the church, with no spectators and in the absence of the priest. Father Lucas had been quick to notice this and had entertained some doubt about the girl's sincerity. He mentioned it to Rose who implored him to put her to the test, declaring that God himself desired it. Father Lucas agreed, locked up the tabernacle and kept the key on his person; the next day Rose communicated "supernaturally" with the large Benediction host. Father Lucas thereupon carried out an investigation of these communions as well as of the stigmata, and although this investigation brought to light some few suspicious circumstances—the fact, for example, that Rose, who undertook the care of the altar and the arrangement of flowers upon it, had in her possession a second tabernacle key—nevertheless he came to the conclusion that the phenomena were supernatural, being convinced that the girl could not have constructed so complicated a series of lies.

At Saignon, too, ever since her childhood she had passed for a saint, and to those in the village who bewailed the progress of irreligion, the cause of all France's misfortunes, it was usual to answer, "The wicked indeed flourish. But here we have a girl singularly privileged by grace, and very soon she will accomplish great things."

Next it was Josephine Imbert's turn to speak and narrate the marvels which she, too, had witnessed. No doubt there was some tendency to distrust her evidence because she was Rose's companion and therefore potential accomplice; but after all, as Josephine was able easily to retort, friendship is bestowed on those who deserve it and Rose had deserved hers by a whole series of kind actions which, too, were not without their supernatural side. Thus Rose had taught her to read without giving her one lesson, and from a distance, by means of a single prayer to the Holy Spirit; one day Josephine had suddenly opened a book and understood the characters, she had taken a pen and begun to write. She did better than that: shortly afterward she had sent to a nun of her acquaintance a "sublime letter." Something like one hundred educated presons had found it wonderful until one day someone produced the model from which it was taken: a passage copied from *The Way of the Cross*. There was talk then of plagiarism and imposture; but it was at once admitted that the unlettered Josephine could not have known the book and that in consequence she must have been in touch with a Higher Intelligence which had prompted her word by word.

Every period of Rose's life, therefore, was accompanied by extraordinary phenomena of a kind to stagger a village mentality which was eager for supernatural prodigies. With "the miracle of the bleeding picture" the climax appeared to have been reached. Right at the beginning those who believed in the "miracle"— and they were in the majority—received considerable and important backing. First and foremost was Dr. Bernard, "convinced by what he had seen," to quote his own words; then there were most of the important people of the village and the great majority of the devout (among whom, however, figured also the keenest of the opponents); finally, unexpected support was given by the sub-prefect of Apt in person, Monsieur Grave, whose interest, aroused in the first place by a report on the subject, was quickly turned to conviction. All classes of the population had been affected by the miracle, including an ordinary policeman, one Briol.

Of course, everyone looked to the ecclesiastical authorities, anxious to know their reaction. But the archbishop of Avignon preserved a prudent silence, confining himself to setting on foot an ecclesiastical inquiry which should discover the truth. But in Saint-Saturnin ecclesiastical authority meant Father Grand, the shepherd of the flock. And Father Grand made no mystery of his conviction. He declared to all who would listen that Rose Tamisier had been specially favored by heaven. He even went further. He looked into the immediate future and foresaw a new sanctuary, a pilgrimage, fervent crowds, riches for the whole district, the floor of the unassuming little church paved with gold. To a villager who confessed himself skeptical of the whole affair Father Grand replied in a voice of fury, "You fool! Within a year this whole district will be another California!"

That heartfelt exclamation requires no comment. In spite of the serious circumstantial evidence against him it has never been definitely proved that the parish priest of Saint-Saturnin-les-Apt was Rose's accomplice; the mind recoils at the idea of a servant of God mocking Him even in His own service. But the fact remains that Father Grand was not a good priest. We shall observe him successively selfish, cunning, ingratiating, and then so extremely prudent as to appear cowardly. He has been dead so long and the "miraculous adventure" which occurred in his parish lasted so short a time that he need not be judged too hardly. We can leave him with all his failings; perhaps he was aware of them; certainly none of us can tell what interior struggle he went through or whether he asked the mercy of God for his sins.

Questioned on the day after the occurrence, Rose Tamisier showed no surprise whatever at being thus favored by heaven, nor yet at the choice of place. She claimed to have received a spiritual message giving the reasons for this choice. Saint-Saturnin, she asserted, had four years previously been the scene of a terrible and blasphemous action regarding which she desired to keep silent; but God, in His goodness, not only pardoned the village but wished to offer it as an example to the rest of Christianity. Consequently, there was every reason to believe that the "miracle of blood" would be renewed very shortly. Asked whether she had been given light on this point she replied that she was not quite sure but thought that the picture would begin to bleed again on Friday, December 20th, between eight and nine in the morning.

From dawn on that day Saint-Saturnin was the scene of extraordinary activity. There were present: the Archbishop of Avignon, Monsieur Grave (the sub-prefect of Apt), the examining magistrate and his deputy, Dr. Bernard, Father Grand, the mayor, and, lastly, the police. At half-past seven, Maître Garçon informs us, Madame Jean, wife of the village innkeeper, appeared in the crowd stationed in front of the chapel and announced that during the night Rose had been visited by her guardian angel who informed her that the miracle would in fact occur again but that God wished that first the "visionary" should pass some time in prayer before the altar, alone, and she—Madame Jean—had come now for the key of the chapel so that Rose could obtain entrance. It was thus revealed that the archbishop—and the examining magistrate—had insisted that the door of the chapel should remain locked all night to avoid any possibility of fraud. It was a very necessary precaution, which was now nullified by Rose's friend's request. There was some discussion whether it should be allowed and in the last resort it was decided to abide by whatever decision the archbishop might reach. Although he was, as he put it, "very disappointed," none the less he gave orders for the key to be given. Very probably he considered that if fraud there were, other proofs of it would not be wanting.

The key, then, was delivered over to Madame Jean. A quarter of an hour later the crowd drew back to let Rose through; she came walking slowly and ponderously, with eyes closed and radiant face, leaning on Josephine Imbert's arm. She entered the chapel. About a quarter of an hour went by. Suddenly a thrill passed through the crowd as the bells began to peal out. They were rung by Father Grand's orders to announce that the miracle had just taken place. At once the crowd poured into the holy place. At their head, unable to restrain himself, burning with curiosity, rushed the sub-prefect, infringing every precautionary measure, and entirely regardless of the dignity of his position; he ran in, almost flew up the chapel and was first at the picture; he looked at the blood flowing out drop by drop; hastily he tugged his handkerchief from his pocket and pressed it against the canvas. Next came the archbishop (he had paused at the threshold to say a prayer). But it was too late; all the blood was now on the sub-prefect's handkerchief. The picture was intact. The archbishop desired to say a few words to the crowd. Monsieur Grave again forestalled him. "The wonder has been renewed," he shouted, turning to the crowd. "It has been renewed, that is the right word to describe it." All present fell to their knees.

The whole thing was dreadfully confused and it is not surprising that some of the more important persons present exchanged a few acid remarks at the rectory later on. In short, one spectator alone, the archbishop, had in all the uproar kept his head. Indeed, once the first enthusiasm had passed, a sneaking feeling of disappointment was the prevailing sentiment. The whole affair of the key did great harm to Rose's reputation. However, the archbishop took the second precaution that had been decided upon. The "miraculous" picture was freed from the wall and, after he had ascertained that no mechanism was concealed behind, a policeman was ordered to stand guard over it. Quite by chance, this duty fell to Briol.

It was midday when the second sensation of the day abruptly occurred. Briol, the policeman, shouted that the picture was bleeding again. Everyone rushed to the chapel. It would have been more accurate to say that the picture had bled again, for Briol, like the sub-prefect, soaked his handkerchief in the miraculous blood. And the picture was again quite dry. Briol showed the handkerchief but refused to give it in charge to anyone, even to the archbishop. "It's mine," he said, "and I shall keep it for my poor old mother." A new fit of enthusiasm seized the crowd; the first handkerchief was torn to tiny pieces which were taken away as relics.

So concluded this day of all fools. The following weeks brought partisans of the "miracle" and their opponents to grips with each other until finally the truth prevailed.

The first sign of a certain decline in Rose, of her inability to maintain the role that had fallen to her, was revealed quite by chance one day when a devout woman of the district arrived in Saint-Saturnin to see her whom some called the "visionary," others the "wonder-worker" and others still the "saint." Father

Grand's prediction had in part come true. The Vaucluse was not yet California and the paving stones of the chapel were still rough granite, but at least one inhabitant of Saint-Saturnin was progressing rapidly along the road to fortune: Jean, the wily owner of the only inn.[4] At all hours of the day a crowd, packed in front of the door, was demanding Rose. The visitor observed this, and, like the sensible and decided woman that she was, made for the back of the house in order to avoid having to wait. She came to a yard and then a staircase which she climbed. On the upstair floor she was pulled up short. From behind a closed door—without any doubt the door of Rose's room—she could hear the young woman in what seemed a fit of uncontrollable laughter while a man's voice—her brother-in-law's—made joking remarks of this sort, "If they want to see the saint, they'll see one, and no mistake." Those remarks were innocent enough, perhaps, but a minute later Jean changed his tune and his words were such that the woman who heard them from the other side of the door never dared to repeat them. She merely went back downstairs without disclosing her presence. But once in the crowd again she made no bones about expressing her opinion; the ears of the saints are, as a rule, chaster than Rose's seemed to be.

The second incident was caused by two priests who did not scruple to lay a trap for Rose; a trap into which she fell without any difficulty. One of these priests wrote her a letter describing supernatural phenomena that he was supposed to have experienced; he made haste to add that he felt sure that he owed these graces to the intercession of our "dear sister." To which Rose answered that God had in fact revealed these things to her. So was she caught in a bare-faced lie.

In the last place the visionary herself was not entirely without a certain greed for the things of this earth. It was noticed that she found herself unable to say what she had done with a five franc piece, the gift of a visitor. It was only five francs, and even at par, in 1850, five francs was not a very considerable amount;

[4] A few months before the "miracle" a peasant asked Jean why he kept in his house the sickly girl who did nothing for him. Jean answered, more or less as follows, "Just a little patience and she'll pay me a hundred times over for all my food that she's eating now!"

all the same, Rose had kept the coin and faced with the scandal that the incident aroused gave herself away by pretending that she had given it to some charity. But she had forgotten that among the people of Saint-Saturnin there were some of discriminating mind who, though they were drawn to belief in her, required proofs and if necessary were prepared to make a thorough investigation. Up to this time Dr. Bernard had shown himself one of her most ardent defenders, but all the same he retained his critical sense. He had merely to write to the charity to obtain a negative answer. He informed Rose of this, but she persisted in her lie. A few days later the doctor received a further letter from the charity relating this time that the five francs had indeed arrived accompanied by an embarrassed little note asking the treasurer to antedate the receipt. A trick not difficult of detection. Once more Dr. Bernard called on Rose and very coldly expressed to her his extreme disappointment and displeasure. Her only answer was to point to a cupboard in which she kept her linen. Some of this was stained with blood, and there were even stains in the form of a cross. "Look," said Rose, "Our Lord's wounds have appeared on my body. His blood has flowed down my sides." It was just one more miracle, and, if the truth were told, Dr. Bernard himself could not have compiled a complete list of them. There were too many of them and they were all much too easy.

The reader who has borne in mind the introduction to this part of the book will experience little difficulty in guessing the subsequent course of events, in foretelling, that is, how Rose Tamisier would react and how she would endeavor to continue to mislead the faithful. She was caught up in an adventure which had proved beyond her powers, and she was now constrained to confess, or take refuge in flight, or else to devise still more colossal and desperate lies. She decided, of course, on this last solution. To all intents and purposes she had been convicted of fraud and now had her back to the wall; already people did not scruple to name with certainty two of her accomplices: Jean the innkeeper and Josephine Imbert. There was more than a lurking suspicion, unfortunately, that Father Grand made a third. The trickery with the key, that quarter of an hour alone which had been absolutely essential to fake the miracle, was by this time the common talk of the district; Rose's letter to the two priests who had laid a trap for her was also an element in effectually destroying any lingering notion in the public mind that she had received special graces and favors from the Holy Spirit; if indeed from a distance Rose taught her friends to read and write, it was curious, to say the least, that by the same power of the Holy Spirit she had not herself learned spelling and punctuation. But all that was of little real importance. Rose, like Nicole Tavernier, had only to bring off a bold stroke, to be freed from all her troubles. She considered what she could do. Probably the innkeeper and his wife lent their aid in concocting a plan. Together they reached the conclusion that the miracle of the bleeding picture would never be taken really seriously unless it occurred in Rose's absence. On the other hand, if the whole village were to witness this . . . hemorrhage, and it was at the same time quite obvious to all that Rose could have had no part in it, her position would be definitively recovered and the "miracle" of Saint-Saturnin re-established on a firm basis.

The matter was extremely urgent. Those who believed in the miracle were growing progressively fewer. The parish priest of Saint-Saturnin and his curate were squabbling every day, the former positively maintaining the miracle, the latter claiming that the whole thing was a scandal. There were witnesses who asserted that they had seen Father Grand pass the key of the chapel to Josephine Imbert. Rose's own father shrugged his shoulders at the mention of the marvels wrought by his daughter; he dubbed them a "carnival." The opinion of the experts was brought to prove that the "supernatural" blood was merely blood disgorged from leeches. This was shown by its composition and its possession of the same property of slow coagulation. This analysis was unanswerable.

On February 5, 1851, at six in the morning Jean ran out of his inn and knocked on the mayor's door. "Come quickly," he shouted, "Rose wants you, she has something important to tell you." The mayor dressed hurriedly and set out at once. It was still dark, and the weather was cold. As they went along Jean told his companion what had happened during the night. In a broken voice he related how Rose felt very ill, she sweated profusely and cried out with pain; it had been necessary to change her sheets though she was unable to leave the bed which she shared with Madame Jean. When the mayor entered the room he judged that the innkeeper had told the truth: Rose was very pale, obviously extremely weak and appeared almost on the point of death. Seeing the mayor she struggled to a half-sitting half-lying position, and gathering what strength remained to her managed to speak to him.

"Go quickly to the chapel," she gasped, "I suffered so much during the night that something extraordinary must have happened there."

"Go, go quickly," she repeated.

The mayor, greatly impressed, obeyed at once. He went to the chapel, stopping twice on the way to pick up the policeman and the parish priest. Both hastened along with him, the priest carrying the notorious key. The door was flung open and they hurried to the picture; by the light of a lamp it could be seen to be bleeding. This time there was no question of just traces of blood: blood was flowing over the whole width of the picture, coming from the heart, the wound in the side, and the head. We are not told whether this time Father Grand had the bells rung, but in any case within the half hour there were hundreds of people crowding into the chapel, pointing out the miracle to each other —praise for Rose was unanimous: on this occasion an accusation of fraud was no longer possible.

At the same time the visionary on her sickbed found a little strength to ask Madame Jean for news; the latter had only to look out of the window to inform her that the village had taken her back into favor. Even Dr. Bernard had come from Apt again. Although for some time past he had determined to have nothing more to do with the case he was bound to admit that he had been somewhat disturbed by the unforeseen occurrence that morning. It was his business as a doctor to examine the patient and to decide whether her disabilities were feigned or not. He sat about it at once. His examination was decisive: Rose Tamisier was very ill: her skin was mottled, her knee was seriously swollen and showed considerable hyperaemia; her pulse was rapid. The long and the short of it was that Rose could not possibly have risen during the night and walked to the chapel. After putting one or two further questions to the patient Dr. Bernard went home and noted down immediately in his diary the details of all he had just observed.

Jean was openly triumphant; Father Grand, too, and—as we shall see—in opposition to the Church. The supporters of the miracle, including those who had revised their opinion, celebrated by illuminating their houses. Father Caire alone shook his head and continued to assert that, since the occurrence must now certainly be acknowledged as supernatural, it could only be the work of the devil. Hourly, pilgrims crowded into Saint-Saturnin. Soon, it was thought, they would be coming from all over France. Few of the villagers did their usual work on that or the following days. The miracle was all they could think about. Rose was given official protection from the fervor of the crowd; everyone wanted to see and speak to her and obtain a relic. The inn was coining money.

Finally, four days later Beauchamp, a retired stonemason, requested his neighbor, one Bourgues, to make up his mind to divulge what he had communicated to him in secret. Simultaneously the mayor's own nephew and a peddler who was staying at the inn decided to tell what they knew. They had all been up before dawn and two hours before the miracle had seen Jean leave the inn. He was carrying Rose on his back; his wife went with them. The three of them hastened to the chapel. "I was the nearest to them," added the mayor's nephew, "and I noticed a fourth in the party, Father Grand."

One man to whom these revelations came as no surprise was the Archbishop of Avignon who for a long time past was convinced that he had the rights of the matter. The findings at the ecclesiastical commission of inquiry were in his possession: they rejected purely and simply any supernatural intervention in the case. "Hell is raging round us," cried Father Grand. The events of the immediate future constrained him to sing more softly.

For now the law began to take an interest in the case. Not a few were convinced that Rose Tamisier, by perpetuating a sacrilegious fake, bordering on fraud, deserved punishment. And this last chapter of her story brings us to her punishment.

Rose Tamisier was arrested on February 13, 1851, on an accusation of fraud, offenses against religion, and theft. What had she stolen? The hosts which she abstracted for her "mystical communions" at Saignon should not be forgotten. She alone appeared in dock; no accomplice was accused. Directly he was informed of the arrest, Father Grand wrote hurriedly to Dr. Bernard that as an ecclesiastic he was "obliged to maintain an attitude of extreme reserve" and that it was important that his "name should not be mixed up in this very sad case."

The case was first heard at Carpentras, but the court of summary jurisdiction decided that it was not qualified to try it, and on appeal by the Procurator Rose was remitted for trial to the court at Nîmes where she received the maximum sentence of six months in prison and a fine of sixteen francs. She remained in prison for twenty-one months since she was unable to meet the costs of the trial. She proclaimed her innocence to the end and to such effect that a few of the villagers of Saint-Saturnin continued to believe in her as an authentic visionary. The ecclesiastical commission had the benefit of giving its verdict before that of the civil court. The Pope sent his personal congratulations to the archbishop. The picture in the chapel never bled again.

As was to be expected Rose Tamisier never confessed to her frauds. Her biographer informs us, on the contrary, that she bombarded the clergy with letters demanding the Communion which she was refused on account of her perseverance in error. During the last period of her life she was just a poor woman hanging round the churches, stoutly refusing to confess, abandoned by all, a poor solitary wretch endlessly mumbling over the tale of her fantastic fabrication. She was her own victim and her own executioner. The fearful part, the sacred role of God's chosen one, cannot be played with impunity.

III

Was Rose Tamisier a hysteric? In spite of her illnesses and disorders which no doctor could diagnose with certainty, she does not seem to have been one. Nevertheless the fundamental characteristic of hysteria requires to be here recalled: the patient at first tells lies consciously but comes in the end to believe in her own lie. And Charcot's well-known dictum can be added: "This patient (suffering from hysteria) is perhaps simulating madness: in any case, she will certainly become mad." Fantasy does not long remain man's servant: sooner or later man will become its slave. Hamlet belongs to every age and to every walk of life.

In the light of this clinical truth one may wonder how quite serious-minded people could find any problem in "extraordinary events" which, in reality, were so ordinary as those connected with that group of young women known as the "possessed women" of Ezkioga. The "miracles" of Ezkioga have this advantage to them: they occurred in 1931, at a time, that is to say, not very far removed from our own. They were not, though, the latest in date (Beauraing has already been dealt with), very far from it indeed. Fraudulent miracles are almost a permanent news item. Canon Ribet and Monsieur de Bonniot have filled huge volumes that even summarized, or, in the modern expression, "condensed," would attain the considerable dimensions of *Gone with the Wind*. At the very time that this book is published there is every probability that in some part of the world one more fake miracle will be firing the enthusiasm of credulous crowds; that level-headed, serious-minded worthies, realists in business and morality, will be bowing in reverence before the vulgar exhibition of a twopenny "miracle"; that on their own, without the usual process, an over-eager populace will be canonizing some peasant girl and some community of good Sisters—it is by no means impossible—will be found to claim that this "saint" made cabbage grow as large as cathedrals. And all these people will wax indignant at the severity and decided views of the Church. Yet manifestations such as these are by no means surprising. The fake miracle is a kind of serialized adventure story on the borders of the history of Christianity.

In 1931 in Spain, then, in the province of Vittoria, a group of girls claimed to be favored with supernatural visions under conditions that led most people to expect an exact reproduction of the miracle of Fatima. The village of Ezkioga was not unlike another Aljustrel; the same mountains, the same moors, the same scorching sky, and in addition the passionate mystic temperament of the Spaniards who, it should not be forgotten, were experiencing political conditions similar to those in Portugal in 1917. The "miracle" encountered there, as elsewhere, an equally divided number of supporters and opponents; but whether for it or against it everyone seems to have lost very largely every critical sense. Some made up their minds to deny the miracle on principle; others were enthusiastic at the idea that God was "mindful of the misfortunes of Spain and was righting her wrongs." It is a common and crude view that Our Lady and the saints may appear at the right moment, veritable *dei ex machina,* to manage the elections or to support the approved diocesan candidate: miracles occur for loftier reasons. No precise figures have ever been given of the number of the "visionaries" of Ezkioga, for while the "miracles" were occurring their number was continually increasing. There seemed almost to be a competition between them as to who should see the most. Many of these visionaries were consciously insincere, others of them, no doubt, were victims of their own imagination. Two among them, Ramona and Evarista, were more prominent than the others. Ramona was fifteen, Evarista seventeen. Our Lady, they asserted, appeared and enjoined on them "prayer for sinners."

Ramona was the most eloquent and the cleverest in obtaining acceptance for her fantasies and dreams as the truth. The account of her "visions" very closely resembled that of the Beauraing children. As at Beauraing, the message had no dogmatic content, and consisted merely of vague, apparently edifying and rather childish expressions. But there is this important factor to be mentioned: in addition to the "visions" occurred the stigmata and, also and more especially, ecstasy, a state which is much harder to imitate and consequently forms a particularly disturbing factor in this case. In the presence of the so-called apparition Ramona went pale and fainted. Sometimes she remained unconscious for upward of half an hour in full view of the crowd, her body rigid, her pulse weak and irregular. Doctors kept her under observation without being able to diagnose her complaint. When she had recovered consciousness for a considerable time Ramona remained deep in a para-hypnotic state (Bernadette's complete "return" should be recalled: ecstasy is not a disease but "ravishment"). The spectators dared not question her and her incontestable physical weakness seemed to them—quite wrongly—a further proof of her sincerity. Exactly as at Beauraing no precaution had been taken to prevent the "visionaries'" communicating with each other; these girls, all belonging to the same village, met every day and talked together without witnesses. A barrier of respect protected them from the public.

In September, Ramona, coming out of one of her ecstasies, informed the crowd that the Blessed Virgin had at last granted her request, and that "very shortly" she would perform a wonder to convince even the most skeptical. A marvel, a miracle was all the Spaniards desired. So far this manifestation of the supernatural had consisted of only rather questionable miracles. At once all kinds of conjectures were rife. Would there be cures, or some solar phenomenon as at Fatima? October was drawing near, and with it, of course, the anniversary of the miracle of the Cova. Three days later Ramona fell into a trance once more and announced the date: October 15th. It was to be Fatima all over again. Everyone looked at the sun; in anticipation some of the spectators even brought dark glasses.

But solar phenomena are by no means easy to fake. Faced with the colossal desires she had aroused, Ramona was frightened. For a whole week she was noticed to be upset and anxious, as if meditating flight. Then she spoke again. She had not revealed all, she said. Our Lady had not confined herself to promising a miracle, she had let her into the secret of her plans. The sun would not dance, the blind and the paralyzed would not be cured;

the Queen of Heaven would merely—all the same the "merely" denoted a supranormal phenomenon—bestow a heavenly rosary on her faithful servant. Rather in the way, it might be said, that a medium "produces" an object at a seance. This promised rosary was at least something tangible and real; everyone could see it and touch it before it was placed, as no doubt it would be, in some reliquary. Ramona went on to say that perhaps Our Lady would allow the most faithful adorers of her divine Son to share the beads of the rosary between them.

At the same time Evarista was favored with another "vision" which also promised a miracle. Our Lady appeared to her "dressed in blue and white" as at Lourdes, but with an additional and novel emblem: she held a sword. What did this "shining sword" portend? Was there to be a fearful conflict between the forces of faith and doubt, and was the Mother of God to take up arms on behalf of Christianity? By no means. The sword was to strike one of the visionaries, "the one nearest to heaven," and impress on her flesh ineffaceable wounds. Evarista was asked if she was the visionary nearest to heaven. She appeared to recollect herself and then replied humbly in the negative. "There is one whom the Saviour loves more." There could be no mistake: she meant Ramona. On the day before the miracle Evarista finally named her companion.

On October 15, 1931, some fifteen thousand pilgrims gathered on the Ezkioga mountain. About 8 A.M. Ramona appeared. Some elementary precautions had at last been decided upon. The girl had been isolated from the others and had been kept under continuous observation; women from the village and the district had been present while she dressed. A very careful examination of her body had been made and, within the limits of decency, parts of it had been photographed; her hands and face were free from scars and all signs of a wound, whether old or recent. As an added precaution it was agreed that the visionary should wear no devotional objects, and lastly she was required to walk through the crowd with her hands raised and held open so that the "supernatural rosary" could not be passed to her. As she came out of the house an order was sent round that no one was to go near or touch her. Ramona made her way to the mountain repeating continually, "Don't touch me." She drew back as if in terror whenever one of the spectators stepped towards her.

On arrival at the site of the apparitions, Ramona fell at once into ecstasy, by which is meant that, following her normal practice, she rolled over on the ground in a faint. The pilgrims held their breath in expectation or fell to their knees in prayer. A quarter of an hour went by and then Ramona opened her eyes again and the spasmodic twitching of her body informed the spectators that the "ecstasy" was over. Then occurred what can only be called a headlong rush by the crowd: the voluntary guards surrounding Ramona were obliged to push back the spectators, all eager to know what had happened. An examination of the girl's body in its trance-like state revealed a rosary wound round her waist so tightly that it could not be undone; in addition her hands were covered in blood. Spectators literally fell upon her, kissed her hands and with handkerchief on handkerchief staunched the flow of blood. As at Saint-Saturnin the handkerchiefs were divided up among the spectators, people quarreled over them and carried pieces off with them in feverish excitement. Her hands, when they were finally washed clean, showed thin gashes in the palms and on the fingers. They were at once photographed and the doctors present took Ramona aside to examine these supernatural wounds.

They did not require a long examination. A few yards from the exact spot of the "apparitions" some pilgrims picked up a razor, and an hour later it was discovered that before setting out for the mountain Ramona had asked to be left alone for a few moments while she relieved herself. By forbidding anyone to go near her or touch her, an order which she herself had also requested, the investigators had helped her to keep the rosary hidden. The wounds, of course, had been self-inflicted in the obvious way and the razor thrown clear, during one of the bodily spasms, without even one of the fifteen thousand spectators noticing anything at all.

The reader will not be surprised to learn that, of those fifteen thousand spectators, several thousand, in spite of what had occurred, continued none the less to believe and to proclaim that at Ezkioga the Blessed Virgin had struck a girl with a "shining sword." In time these people realized their mistake, they were helped to do so, no doubt, by the bishop of Vittoria's pastoral letter which rejected completely this "Spanish miracle." Once again the Church in her great prudence unmasked a miracle faker by basing her conclusions on the reports of experts and of those actually present. It only remained now for the "visionary nearest to heaven" to confess her sin and obtain pardon by penance and sincere contrition. The last word belongs to the silence of the confessional.

· 7 ·

The Miracle Within Us

EVEN accepted, authentic miracles leave some of the faithful cold. Bernadette's moving experience teaches them nothing that they did not know before, right from the days of their catechism. One told me that the chief impression made on him by Lourdes was the evidence of the earthly passage of a saint. "I learn more from the life and virtues of Bernadette than from the favors she was granted. I go to Nevers to see her in her shrine as a friend and an example; at the hour of death I shall be particularly happy at the thought that in an instant this face will appear before me living, smiling and kindly to welcome me perhaps to heaven. Of course, God works miracles; it is the least of His powers. Why, miracles occur at every hour, every day. Do you really believe that God who created us with such great love would consent to forsake us utterly?"

One more observation may be made. The more the world advances in time and the greater the progress of what is called civilization, the less does the soul act as a window overlooking creation. From those far-off times when life was natural, when a pastoral people led their flocks over the vast grassy expanses, down to our modern days when the machine is interposed like a screen between our eyes and the natural elements of the cosmos, a revolution has occurred; the senses have become specialized, sealed off in compartments; it seems agreed that men shall see only with their eyes, think only with their brains, touch only with their hands. We have departed from that primitive wisdom according to which man formed one whole, thinking and seeing with his entire body. In this connection the poet Lanza del Vasto reminds us that this power is now to be found in the East, which is nearer than we are to primitive times. Thus some of us require the visible signs of God's presence on earth to strike us forcibly, almost roughly. We do not go out to meet them; we demand that they come to us. We want them to swoop down like a thunderbolt through the superficial structure of our dwellings. The heavens must open, the sun must leap from its zenith to the horizon, from one horizon to another, the paralyzed must rise and walk. And prodigies as striking as these are still not enough to convince us.

Throughout this book it has been constantly repeated that miracles do not always convince. Each one reacts in accordance with his temperament. The uncultivated mind will adapt itself to any wonder, cry miracle at the sight of any hysterical, vanity-obsessed woman, whereas the skeptical mind will refuse to admit even the instantaneous ossification of an aperture in the skull; some superior or honest-minded men recognize that the universe is not entirely a laboratory specimen, holding no secrets, to be observed or dissected at will, that Nature, treacherous to her own self, mocks at Nature. But in either case neither those who peacefully await another life nor those who believe in final extinction in an everlasting nothingness will change their position, for neither will make the necessary effort.

And yet Bernadette was right: to contemplate infinity there is no need to look at an exceedingly high point. To the fleshly eyes of man the heavens appear unchanging and limited, a grey, an azure vault wherein move the clouds which he has tamed to his own uses. The Christian God is no Jupiter seated on a mountain, flinging down his childish thunderbolts and, by way of recreation, busying himself inciting martial men to battle. God breathes in the smallest particle of the universe and His presence absorbs every one of our thoughts, every act of our life. How should we not be His intimates since not only did He create us but He became one of us. In one of his novels Graham Greene wrote that for him (or rather for one of his characters who was obviously expressing the author's view) the Crucifixion and the sufferings of the Passion were only additional sufferings to that inconceivable torture by which God took on our poor human frame with its difficulties and infirmities. Before making the journey up to Calvary, jeered at, scourged, crowned with thorns, and a reed thrust mockingly into His hand, God was that child in swaddling clothes described by Catherine Emmerich, wailing, crying, and undergoing all the hardships of earthly life. He shared the very lowest state of bondage with us. And He continues to share our life, at its good times and its bad, with us mortals. He has said so, He has proclaimed it, and He has even instituted a Sacrament to confirm it. Now ordinary reason—it has nothing to do with mysticism, it is just common sense—should be sufficient to prove to us that a God so closely bound to us, dwelling in our flesh, does not require to be contemplated from afar. In His manifestations He emphasizes His own Word, when He desires to do so; and then He chooses a witness to the miracle and this chosen one—pledged inexorably to be humbled on this earth—will surely possess virtues that we most certainly have not. But each one of us, day by day, is steeped in some particle of grace—and even in the entirety of grace. When we break bread, when we plane wood or plough land or write books, when after our work we fall asleep at night, God is there. The conscious Christian relates all things to God. His own unworthy life is adorned, illuminated with the infinite perfection of Heaven.

A blind man goes to Lourdes and asks God to restore his eyes. Near him one suffering from incurable Pott's disease promises, if he is healed, to offer his orthopedic jacket as an ex-voto to Our Lady; that is a natural and a moving gesture. It is normal for a man to ask God to end his sufferings. But if the blind man or the sufferer from Pott's disease should be cured, will it be considered the first and most wonderful miracle granted them by God? The grotto at Lourdes is full of these ex-voto offerings proclaiming men's and women's gratitude for deliverance from their ills—and now they are dead and reduced to an intangible dust. For some years they lived with less discomfort; their last days were less clouded with suffering; the blind were given the time to glance about them, the paralyzed to try a few steps. Then they died, and now it may be believed they contemplate the Creator of all things. But in contemplating Him they contemplate themselves as well. Their whole life is spread out before their profound spiritual gaze like a marvelous film of which human memory is but a wretched caricature; in a flash they see all, the important moments of their life—the landmarks—as well as the forgotten and supposedly insignificant minutes. They see again that moment when the miracle occurred which they remembered until their death and which their descendants will continue to remember, that moment which in some sort was historic. But it is hardly that moment which they now dwell on or hold important, although it was important, important for themselves and for those who witnessed it as a proof of the mercy of God in their regard. Yet that mercy itself was conditional, and they showed themselves in the years to come perhaps unworthy or unmindful of it. And so, the provisional cure of their bodies in itself, the reprieve from suffering, with the necessity of dying ever awaiting them at the end, counts only a little more than the preservation from other hazards—some germ, some bullet, perhaps. But what counts most for them now is the thread of their life, the texture of their destiny: some intuition which turned them away from evil, some supposedly chance encounter with an earthly companion which revealed them to themselves, some bestowal of grace which brought them nearer to God; a joy occurring at the right moment, some salutary suffering. For it may well be for a pain, an infirmity that cries of thanksgiving go up in Heaven: "I thank you, my God, for not having heard my prayer."

In this sense the miracle is a daily phenomenon. It can be achieved within each of us. At the end of this book it is appropriate to make that statement.